DANIEL DAY-LEWIS
THE BIOGRAPHY

Laura Jackson

Published by John Blake Publishing Ltd,
3 Bramber Court, 2 Bramber Road,
London W14 9PB, England

www.johnblakepublishing.co.uk

www.facebook.com/Johnblakepub facebook
twitter.com/johnblakepub twitter

First published in hardback in 1999
This edition published in paperback in 2013

ISBN: 978 1 85782 605 0

British Library Cataloguing-in-Publication Data:

A catalogue record for this book is available from the British Library.

Design by www.envydesign.co.uk

Printed and bound in Great Britain by CPI Group (UK) Ltd

1 3 5 7 9 10 8 6 4 2

Papers used by John Blake Publishing are natural, recyclable products
made from wood grown in sustainable forests. The manufacturing processes
conform to the environmental regulations of the country of origin.

Every attempt has been made to contact the relevant copyright-holders,
but some were unobtainable. We would be grateful if the
appropriate people could contact us.

To my husband David – Simply the Best

ACKNOWLEDGEMENTS

Grateful appreciation for their time and trouble to all those people whom I interviewed. My thanks for all contributions to: Sally Baxter; Ann Broadbent; Philip Martin Brown; Simon Callow; Patrick Connor; Dame Judi Dench, DBE, OBE; Julian Fellowes; Barry Foster; Arthur Ibbetson, BSc; Philip Jackson; Saeed Jaffrey, OBE; Tony Jordan; Arthur Lappin; Elizabeth Lloyd; Alan MacNaughtan; Richard Mayne; Kevin Moore; Barry Norman; Daniel O'Herlihy; Jenny Passmore; Elizabeth Pursey; Sir David Puttnam; Bruce Robinson; Roshan Seth; Nabil Shaban; Jack Shepherd; John Southworth; Neil Stacy; Janet Stone; Ronald Wilson.

Also thanks for their help to: Arts Council, Belfast; Arts Council, Dublin; *Asheville Citizen-Times*; Belfast Central Library; *Belfast Telegraph*; British Academy of Film and Television Arts (Doreen Dean); BBC Libraries & Archives (Trevor White); British Film Institute (Ian O'Sullivan); Bristol Old Vic Company; Directors' Guild of Great Britain; Elgin

Library staff; Ewan Marshall; Will Muir; *New York Times*; Queens Theatre, London (Malcolm); Patricia Ramsey, United Nations Department of the Foreign and Commonwealth Office, London; Royal National Theatre (Nicola Scadding); Royal Shakespeare Company; *Spotlight*; *The Irish Times*; The Shakespeare Birthplace Trust (James Shaw); Tilleys, Chesterfield; Gay Wilson; Working Title Films Ltd. (Juliette Dow). And very special thanks to David for all his outstanding research and invaluable help.

Thanks to John Blake and all at John Blake Publishing.

CONTENTS

'Daniel Day-Lewis's performance as Johnny in
My Beautiful Laundrette was a lovely piece of acting,
a triumph. The best performance by an English
actor since the war.'

SIMON CALLOW

CHAPTER ONE

GROWING PAINS

'Life is ladders, that's all.'

GUY BENNETT, *ANOTHER COUNTRY*

Slanting shafts of early morning light pierce the dense woodland, glinting off the deadly blade of the curved hunting knife gripped in Nathaniel's right hand. He is stripped to the waist, his long unruly black hair bouncing off his muscular shoulders. His breath comes in faint rhythmic pants as he runs swift and sure, crashing through the undergrowth in unison with his blood-brother Uncas.

Nearby, another kind of crashing tells him what he needs to know He sheathes the knife. Smoothly, purposefully, he slides the wooden-handled, long-barrelled rifle from his back and slots it under his arm as the powerful deer breaks cover.

Arrestingly intense eyes set in a strong, unlined face concentrate with deadly intent as he takes aim. Slowly, inexorably, the sleek blue-grey steel barrel moves round in a sweeping arc to stare the viewer straight in the eye. Seconds later he fires. As the fierce flame flashes across the screen, Daniel Day-Lewis blasts his way to Hollywood heart-throb status. The part is frontiersman Hawk-eye; the film is Michael Mann's lavish 1992 adaptation of James Fenimore Cooper's classic novel *The Last of the Mohicans.*

The description, heart-throb, does not sit easily on Daniel Day-Lewis who often questions the validity of being an actor at all. Yet, the following two decades would see him inhabit with raw intensity a string of diverse roles, turning out vivid portrayals of, among others, a tortured soul, a wronged Irishman, a hideously unhinged New York gang leader and a chilling oil prospector before astonishing audiences the world over, in 2012, with a barnstorming performance as one of America's most revered Presidents, Abraham Lincoln. Daniel's immense talent for assuming another's identity on screen perpetuates the mystery of who this gifted chameleon is in real life.

What is hardly a mystery is why he should have opted for a career in film at all. His maternal grandfather was the legendary film producer Sir Michael Balcon, one of the pioneers of British cinema. He reputedly gave Alfred Hitchcock his first job and was head of Ealing Studios during its most fertile period from the 1930s to the 1960s. He was responsible for turning out such influential comedy classics as *Whisky Galore, Kind Hearts and Coronets* and *The Lavender Hill Mob.* Respected film critic and BBC television presenter Barry Norman defines his importance. 'Ealing Studios was the best ever,' he says, 'the jewel in the crown of the British film industry, particularly in the war and post-war years, and Michael Balcon was the head of all of that.'

Michael Balcon's family were Latvian refugees from Riga who had come to England around the turn of the century. The family of his wife, Aileen Leatherman, whom he married in 1924, came from Poland. Their daughter, Jill Angela Henriette Balcon, Daniel's mother, became a familiar voice on British radio as a continuity announcer and verse reader during World War II. Later she was famous as one of the country's star radio actresses.

Daniel's grandparents on his father's side were the Reverend Frank Cecil Day-Lewis, a curate in the Protestant Church of Ireland, and his wife Kathleen Blake Squires. Their only son Cecil became a writer, an Oxford professor and eventually Poet Laureate. Born in what is now County Laois, Cecil had strong roots in Ireland. During the 1930s, when he was briefly a member of the Communist Party, Cecil's name became inextricably linked with a clutch of left-wing, anti-fascist poets comprising W.H. Auden, Louis MacNiece and Stephen Spender. Collectively they were often satirically referred to as MacSpaunday.

At this time Cecil was married to Constance Mary King, and during their twenty-three-year marriage they produced two sons, Sean and Nicholas. The marriage ended in divorce early in 1951. By this time Cecil had struck up an association with Jill Balcon, twenty-one years his junior, whom he had met when they were co-readers for the BBC Home Service programme *Time for Verse*. They married in April 1951 and two years later had their first child, a daughter Lydia Tamasin. It was a further four years before their son was born on 29 April 1957.

Inheriting his mother's jet black hair and startling pale green eyes, Daniel arrived two days after his father's fifty-third birthday in the front room of the Day-Lewis family home at 96 Campden Hill Road, west London. Cecil immediately penned a poem in celebration of the birth called *The Newborn*. At the christening at the church of St Martin-in-the-Fields, the baby was baptised Daniel Michael Blake Day-Lewis – Daniel as an amalgam of the parents' Jewish and Irish associations, and Michael Blake to honour one grandparent from each family, thereby keeping the peace with both.

In keeping with Cecil's socialist sympathies, one of Daniel's four godparents was Julia Gaitskell, whose father Hugh was the leader of the British Labour Party, then languishing in opposition. Then, like his sister Tamasin before him, baby Daniel was promptly placed in the care of the live-in nanny, Minny Bowler, who became the centre of his day-to-day life.

With the addition of a second child to their family, Cecil and Jill decided to look for a roomier house and found one almost immediately. In its heyday, 6 Crooms Hill in Greenwich, south-east London would have been a fine example of Georgian architecture, nestling snugly at the foot of a sweeping hill, opposite an equally grand, and lively, music hall. By the end of 1957, when Daniel was eight months old, its elegance had faded and the four-storey end house, complete with imposing sash windows and fronted by black wrought-iron railings and gate, was in serious need of renovation. The adjacent music hall was nothing but a derelict eyesore. Nevertheless the family moved out of Campden Hill Road and into Crooms Hill, or rather Cecil and Jill did. Daniel and Tamasin were farmed out to the comfort of Jill's parents' family home until work on the house was completed.

When he was reunited with his mother and father, family life for the young Daniel in the exquisitely refurbished Greenwich dwelling seems, by today's standards, to have had a somewhat remote quality to it. For his first few years he lived mainly on the third floor, which had been set aside as the nursery wing. By the time he was three, and had lost his older sister to infant school during the day, he was normally alone with Minny Bowler. She, from the tips of her yellow streaked hair to her laced-up flatties, was every inch a formidable-looking nanny of the old school with very set ideas on the care of her charges. Only when they were ready for bed and turned out in faultless cherubic perfection could the children visit the sumptuous drawing room on the floor below where one of their parents would take pleasure in reading them a bedtime story.

The children would also make an appearance at weekend family meals but apart from these occasions it would appear that Cecil's interaction with them was, by choice, limited. By this time he was a director of the publishers Chatto & Windus. When he was not at his office at the publishing house, he would closet himself in his wood–panelled, book–lined study at home. This room was steadfastly out of bounds to Daniel and his sister, as a previous study in a previous house many years before had been out of bounds to his two elder sons by his first marriage. Cecil appears to have been a remote figure to his children, perhaps more comfortable encouraging sedate respect and affection from his offspring than with a display of anything deeper and demonstrative.

If this affected Daniel at this time, it did not show. Neighbour Ann Broadbent, who had been an Oxford student when Cecil was Professor of Poetry there, recalls, 'He was a sweet little boy, very fond of long words even at a young age. I remember being very surprised when he came out clearly with 'helicopter' – a big word for a little one, then hardly more than a tot.' She adds, 'He and my son Tom, who was a little younger than him, played together quite a bit.'

As a young child Daniel was unremarkable in appearance, but pleasant faced with a wide-mouthed cheerful smile. His coal black hair, neatly barbered and sprayed in a straight uncompromising fringe across his pale brow emphasised his resemblance to his darkly attractive mother. Through primary school that resemblance would deepen pronouncedly, carving out a well-defined nose and jawline, and developing the same willowy frame and long slender hands.

To outsiders he appeared to be a bright, certainly sensitive, but entirely normal young boy with impeccable manners. He was prey too to all the normal childhood ailments. Mumps struck when he was six, laying him low for most of the summer of 1963 and delaying the annual family holiday. That year the trip was to the west of Scotland and it proved to be a washout in more ways than one. As bad weather battered the rugged coastline, tensions and undercurrents bewildering to Daniel spilled out between the adults, resulting in a spate of arguments that ruined the entire break for everyone.

In addition to the strict formality of his highly organized life in the nursery, another significant aspect of Daniel's upbringing is that, rather than mainly mingling with children of his own age, he was surrounded by distinguished and eminent adults. This was the case both at Crooms Hill and when he accompanied his parents and sister on holidays to the home of Janet and Reynolds Stone at the village of Litton Cheney in Dorset. The Old Rectory was usually bursting at the seams with a cross section of the cream of the literati of the day, but Daniel looked forward to his visits and from the age of five spent many happy times here.

Janet Stone, a bishop's daughter and a descendant of the Quaker Elizabeth Fry, was born in Cromer in 1912. After training as a singer at the Royal College of Music, Janet married the painter and engraver Reynolds Stone. After her marriage, she became a professional photographer. Today her work forms part of the permanent collection of the National Portrait Gallery in London.

The Old Rectory, a large rambling house positioned halfway

down a hill, nestled snugly below the ivy-clad walls of Litton Cheney's ancient churchyard. Its nine acres of wild and wonderfully overgrown grounds were a profusion of leafy ferns, bubbling streams and concealed lakes which provided an adventure playground for the young Daniel. Bounding along the sandy lanes leading to and from the house and scattering the odd hen on his way, he would head for the many tangled tree tunnels, exploring as he went.

Friends of the Stones for many years, Cecil and Jill enjoyed rubbing shoulders here with a shifting galaxy of guests, including the celebrated composer Benjamin Britten, the writer J.B. Priestley, John Betjeman the poet and broadcaster and the actress Joyce Grenfell. While Janet played the ever-perfect hostess, Reynolds, a quiet gentle man, spent much of his time working at his engraving in the corner of the drawing room. This was a haven of spacious chairs covered in floral chintzes and exquisite period furniture, while floor-to-ceiling shelving crammed with a vast variety of books barely left room for the numerous paintings and framed photographs on the wall.

The gatherings in this charming drawing room, especially in the evenings, took on the aura of old-fashioned soirées. Cecil and Jill, already used to public reading, vied for floor space and much enjoyed reading aloud for the assembled guests. Altogether the atmosphere was one of intellectual stimulation and mutual appreciation.

Janet's most vivid memories of the small dark-haired child centre on what she refers to as his very formal upbringing, but it is the picturesque winter scenes he would wake up to on Christmas morning that Daniel recalls from those days. These and the comforting yearly ritual of sitting snugly by a roaring coal fire while Cecil read aloud the poem *The Christmas Tree*, or from Beatrix Potter's *The Tailor of Gloucester*. Although there were four Stone children, they were all considerably older than him, which left him more often than usual in the company of his father, who would occasionally take him boating on one of the hidden lakes.

Holidays played an important role in Daniel's growing up. When not spent at Litton Cheney, they mainly centred on trips to Ireland, his father's birthplace. Cecil adored Ireland and, as Ann Broadbent recalls, at Oxford he would often take delight in regaling his eager audiences with anecdotes about the wide variety of people he met there. She says, 'As Professor of Poetry, Cecil gave something like three lectures a year. He didn't teach there on a full-time basis. Well, I remember him, during one of his lectures, telling us a very funny story about a trip to Ireland where he'd gone to see someone on business. He got to the house and announced himself, whereupon the butler promptly took him straight to the barnyard as he thought Cecil had said he was the Professor of Poultry at Oxford!'

Misunderstandings aside, Cecil's love of the emerald isle was all-encompassing and he was determined to imbue this passion in all of his children. He certainly succeeded with Daniel, whose deep and lasting affinity with all things Irish took root. Perhaps one reason for this is that being there effected a welcome change in his father. For the duration of the trip he seemed to lose the need for any barriers and became carefree, even playful, and certainly far more emotionally accessible to his children.

Cecil was, of course, in his sixties by now. There were limits to how much he could physically lark about with them, but nevertheless Daniel lapped up his attention. His happiest childhood memories, without question, focus on trout fishing or cheering on the winners of many an unofficial horse race along the beaches around County Mayo. In troubled times ahead he would draw on memories of these halcyon days to help him through.

It is true, though, that moments of emotional confusion in his life began early on for Daniel. Cecil, a man described as having exuded considerable charm, elegance and style, as possessing a spirit of generosity and laughing easily in company, was not a faithful husband. Emotionally at least, if not also physically, he was untrue to Jill – as he had been to his first wife Mary – and this naturally led to distressing outbursts between the pair.

When Daniel was just eight years old, on holiday with the family in the west of Ireland, his mother happened upon a love letter which had fallen from her husband's coat pocket. As a result of the ensuing quarrel, Jill suddenly disappeared and stayed away for a couple of days. It must have seemed a very long time to the young boy, anxious and bemused as to what was going on. Worse still, there was no reassuring explanation to Daniel or his sister from their father, and no indication as to when their mother would return either.

Indeed, Daniel's pre-teen years had more than their fair share of shadows. In the rest of Britain during the swinging mid-sixties the seams of society had given way to a much happier and more progressive freedom of expression, but life within the walls of 6 Crooms Hill clung to the mores of a bygone era. For most youngsters at this time pop music was God, with a major battle for supremacy being slugged out between devotees of the Beatles and those of the Rolling Stones. However, even the squeaky-clean Fab Four were deemed unsuitable for Daniel's young ears, so the raunchier Stones stood no chance.

By now, in accordance with Cecil's socialist principles, Daniel was attending Sherington Junior Boys School on Sherington Road, one of the local state primaries. Initially he was picked on by the other children for living in the big house and for not being one of them. His cultured accent also marked him out, earning him the nickname of 'Poshie', and the fact that he was not encouraged to bring his working-class acquaintances home highlighted the division.

Daniel quickly realised that here the rule was survival of the fittest. He would only break down the barriers by taking whatever steps were necessary to becoming more like his classmates. Determinedly he set about integrating himself into the daily fabric of life at Sherington and succeeded well enough to eventually establish himself fairly happily there.

But it cannot have been an easy situation for the young boy, operating in two entirely different worlds. At school during the day he was pretending to be something he was not. In the evenings and at weekends he reverted back to the behaviour expected of him at home, demonstrating all the while that he was not falling prey to what he knew would be considered undesirable influences. Putting on this act, however, was something he refined to a fine art. Perhaps, unknown to him, here lay the rudiments of the tools he would employ so successfully in the future as an actor.

At home, meanwhile, there had been other minor troubles. Nanny Bowler had hung up her starched uniform after nine years, service and been replaced by Jenny Dormer, who had previously worked for the Broadbents, a few doors along in Crooms Hill. She was a much younger woman, whose ideas on child care were radically different from those of both her disciplinarian predecessor and her new employers. Clashes of opinions about raising children became fairly regular occurrences. The result seems to have been that moments of unscheduled fun for Daniel, Tamasin and their new nanny became clandestine ones.

GROWING PAINS

Jenny recalls, 'I had formally trained as a nanny but was breaking away from the way that things were done. This was the Sixties after all. Minny Bowler had been rather old-fashioned in her style of care and I had different, more modern ideas which often led me to rebel.' She continues, 'I worked every day from 9.00 a.m., when I used to take Daniel to school, to 6.00 p.m. or 7.00 p.m. with some occasional babysitting. The first thing that struck me when I joined the Day-Lewis household was how completely separate the nursery wing was from the rest of the house. It was literally like a different world altogether.'

Although on the whole Jenny has fond memories of her years at Crooms Hill, certain practices that were the norm under Minny Bowler's regime seemed distinctly outdated to her. She explains, 'For instance, every day I would have to take Daniel for his walk which was often along by the banks of the river Thames and for this he had to be at all times very formally dressed. I'm talking coat, gleaming shoes and pristine white gloves and all. At the time I thought it was such a shame, especially when you looked about at other children and saw what they were wearing. But it didn't matter what I felt or said, as most of my progressive ideas met with firm objections.'

She goes on, 'Daniel was a gifted child, that much was certain, but he was also quite a temperamental little boy. At the time I just got on with things and coped with it and it's only really as I've got older and looked back that some of the disruptive things he got up to have begun to make sense. Cecil was very socialist while Jill was extremely traditional in her views of upbringing and I honestly think that he was torn apart, poor kid. It certainly wasn't easy for him.'

Although Daniel was in the hands of nannies before being sent to boarding school until he was eighteen, it would be claimed in later years that Jill, often described as 'highly strung

11

and ultra-protective of Daniel', smothered him with maternal affection. Describing what she saw herself, Jenny Dormer adds, 'He was a bit of a mother's boy I thought, and in fact, it seemed to me that at times he didn't like his father very much.'

By now early signs had begun to emerge of a natural attraction towards acting. Like all children he had his toys, together with a vivid imagination. His own first recollection of performing for an audience was of dressing up in a rather fine soldier's uniform and doing his Fainting Guardsman act. His first real-life hero, however, was Russian cosmonaut Yuri Gagarin. Watching Yuri on television, Daniel was fascinated by him and would often pretend to be the Soviet hero, improvising as best he could by using a string shopping bag in place of the spaceman's helmet. He would while away the hours like this, happily locked in his make-believe world.

Despite the solid acting background on his mother's side, the predominant influences in the home were literary. From the 1940s onwards, Cecil's poetry had become progressively less political, taking on a more lyrical and traditional tone. During his five-year term as Professor of Poetry at Oxford University in the first half of the 1950s his main preoccupation had been with public poetry reading, often assisted by Jill. In the ensuing years the number of prestigious lectureships that he undertook mounted ceaselessly.

His tireless advocacy of English literature in general, and poetry in particular, was rewarded when in mid-December 1967 he was approached by the Labour Prime Minister Harold Wilson about succeeding John Masefield as Poet Laureate. The office of Poet Laureate had been instituted 300 years before and Cecil would be the sixteenth incumbent, following in such distinguished footsteps as those of William Wordsworth and Alfred Tennyson.

It was also over 250 years since there had been an Irish-born poet in office. Cecil indicated his acceptance and by Christmas that year his appointment was secured; the official public announcement was to be made early in January 1968. Before then, the family enjoyed a private, very happy festive season, during which Daniel took great delight in ribbing his father relentlessly over his illustrious new appointment.

However, 1968 was a year which would turn out to be anything but delightful for Daniel. Until now he had been attending the state primary school, where he had learned the non-academic but highly valuable lesson of how to be streetwise. His hard work at blending in had been mostly successful, but Cecil's august new appointment brought unforeseen problems.

Daniel has referred to his father as having seemed a lofty and imposing figure. Although he has no recollection of the two of them indulging in much companionable chitchat, he was proud of him without understanding exactly why Cecil attracted so much respect. The trouble began when Cecil, in his new post, began to feature a lot in the newspapers, often photographed surrounded by his family. This served as an unwelcome reminder to the other school kids of the distinction between them and Daniel. In turn, Daniel was forced to compensate for his background all over again.

By now he was hanging out with the school gangs and had added some distinctly unpoetic colour to his vocabulary. But, if he was happy with this latter state of affairs, his parents were less content. Once a professed believer in the communist doctrine and an advocate of a classless society, Cecil was now unhappy that 'Poshie' no longer deserved his nickname. He had, in fact, traded in his naturally well-bred accent for something distressingly downmarket. This state of affairs could not be allowed to continue. So the Day-Lewises whisked their son away from Sherington Junior and installed him that autumn, aged eleven, as a weekly boarder in a private school.

They chose Sevenoaks, an all-boys public school with a tradition stretching back over some 500 years, set in acres of rich woodland looking south over the picturesque Weald of Kent. Here Daniel was to be abjectly miserable. Years later he confessed to having suffered appalling pangs of homesickness which took him a long time to conquer. The kind of unsympathetic, cold shower, authoritarian regime that a school like this represented was anathema to Daniel. It would lead him, as an adult, to hold an ingrained scorn of this very English tradition.

Fear of the bullying that went on coupled with the ever-present homosexual threats which led to him spending hours in hiding, quietly crying behind a locked toilet door, were not all that he had to contend with. On top of everything, he laboured under a sense of all-round inadequacy because of his inability to cope with his studies. This must have been soul-destroying.

Although never a slow child academically, he had the burden, as he once confided to an actor friend, of being dyslexic. On top of that he had not studied Latin or French at the state school, so from the start he experienced serious difficulty in keeping up with the other students. This necessitated hours of intensive extra tuition, and so deep were Daniel's feelings of failure that he lost a great deal of self-confidence.

One incident which took his mind off his problems occurred in 1969, when he was twelve. He found himself in the right place at the right time and ended up with a tiny part in a new John Schlesinger film. As a weekly boarder he escaped home to Greenwich after classes ended on a Friday, returning to Sevenoaks and his spartan dormitory late Sunday afternoon. One weekend Daniel was playing in Greenwich Park, directly opposite his home, with some of the other local children, unaware that the British director was shooting in the area.

The film was *Sunday Bloody Sunday* and for one scene Schlesinger required three kids to play vandals. He enlisted the help of a nearby shopkeeper to round up what he called 'the local hooligans' so that he could make his selection. He was on the hunt for youngsters who could look particularly mean and nasty. Of the original hopeful hundred, Daniel made the final chosen three: a dubious distinction he found thrilling. For a couple of days he got to run amok, scratching cars with broken bottles, and be paid for it.

One of the other two children picked out was Daniel's friend Tom Broadbent. His mother, Ann, who it transpired had known John Schlesinger at school, recalls, 'I remember when they came dashing home to tell us. They were so excited to have been selected, but to be honest what delighted them the most was that they got paid extra money over and above the others, for being the ones who actually got to vandalise the cars.'

Sunday Bloody Sunday would be released two years later, in July 1971. Directed by Schlesinger and produced by Joseph Janni, its cast included Glenda Jackson, Peter Finch, Peggy Ashcroft and Tony Britton. In this stylish character-study drama, Penelope Gilliatt's screenplay delicately handles what was considered at the time to be a risky subject – a young bisexual designer's affairs with both a divorced female executive and a Jewish male doctor. Daniel's scene comes into the category of 'if you blink you miss it'. Still, it stands as his film debut.

Although Daniel had thoroughly enjoyed the experience, it was a shortlived pleasure. Soon he was back in the misery of Sevenoaks. Until now any rebelliousness he had shown had been brief and not very profound. Finally, though, the kind of existence he was leading during the interminably long week at school became too much for him to bear. After two years of misery, he could stand it no longer and ran away. He fled in the night, leaving his housemaster to discover an empty unslept-in bed the following morning.

Significantly he did not head for home. In contrast to his own unhappiness in Kent, all reports he received in his sister's regular letters about her mixed school in Hampshire led him to believe it to be almost paradise. When he ran away, therefore, while his parents and anxious school officials contacted the police, he made a beeline west for Tamasin and Bedales School at Petersfield.

Originally founded as a pioneer school, Bedales became co-educational at the turn of the century. With its broad-based curriculum encouraging the arts, it offered a much freer regime than most normal boarding schools. For a start there were no uniforms at Bedales. Pupils could indulge in whatever crazy, colourful fashions they chose. For a boy brought up to adhere to a strict dress code both in and out of school, it sounded like heaven. Daniel so desperately wanted to go there that, although only thirteen years old, he was determined to make a stand regardless of his parents' reactions.

As it happened, far from flying into a temper at his son's defection, Cecil handled the whole situation with calm and reason. He listened carefully to Daniel's tale of his deep-seated unhappiness at Sevenoaks and his fierce desire to attend Bedales. Then he set about looking into the necessary arrangements to organise the transfer. They were worked out easily enough and soon Daniel joined his sister in Petersfield in the autumn of 1970.

The new school was everything he had hoped it would be, but his time at Sevenoaks had left its mark. Two years of feeling persecuted had built up a brimming reservoir of deep resentment and frustration in Daniel, which was to spill over in aggressive fashion. To the teenager, hardened by his experiences, it seemed as if a vital choice had to be made in life – whether to allow yourself to be bullied or not. He was not about to choose the former.

He never crossed the line to becoming a bully himself, but he did discover an ability to cut deeply with his tongue. He took grim pleasure in wielding this incisive weapon to its best effect for quite some time at Bedales. It's not something he is now proud of, but it seems to have won him a form of wary respect. Former fellow pupils looking back remember a Daniel whose moods were at times so mercurial that, on certain days, it was wisest to give him a wide berth.

Time, however, mellowed this aggressive defensiveness. Instead, Daniel channelled his energies into a wide range of activities. He found that he was not only good with his hands at woodwork class, but that it had a very therapeutic effect on him. Under the auspices of craft teacher David Butcher, for a time he began to consider a career as a cabinet maker. He also started to take part in school plays, attracted by the sense of escapism – an extension of the happy hours he had whiled away dressing up as a youngster at home as well as his one and only film experience. Expressing the creative side of his personality helped to lighten his outlook in general and allowed a happier, more carefree young man to emerge.

By now his physical appeal was strengthening. Although his height had shot up and he was somewhat gangly, his thick dark hair and unusual catlike eyes already made him very attractive. Acting was teaching him how to make the most of his aquiline profile and natural grace, and he became, whether by accident or design, a magnet for impressionable young Bedales schoolgirls.

What Daniel himself was in love with was the sporting life. A staunch supporter of Millwall Football Club, he also played soccer himself – perhaps with more haste than grace, but no one could say he lacked enthusiasm. His other passion was cycling – a passion he pursues to this day – which he took very seriously. Every year the school staged its own bike race along a route mapped out around the grounds and every year Daniel would enter, training for it for weeks in advance with great, at times grim, dedication.

For all that, the most persistent attraction was still towards acting. At primary school he had appeared, like virtually every other child in the land, in the Christmas nativity play – in his case playing one of the Three Wise Men. The part of a little black boy in a Sevenoaks production of Alan Paton's novel *Cry, the Beloved Country* still features in his memory to this day, mostly because of the heavy make-up it required. This was followed by another couple of stage productions there. In themselves these were nothing particularly significant, yet, to his mother, early shoots of real talent were already beginning to show.

It was not so much his delivery of the lines, but the way in which he listened closely to the other actors, tuning in to every nuance around him. This heightened and sharpened his responses, which in turn breathed increased life into his own portrayal. Here were the first hints of his now renowned intensity, creating a vibrancy clearly evident even to those without a parent's natural bias.

Outside school life, summer holidays continued to be very much family affairs. They were still mainly spent in Ireland, but by now the atmosphere was more subdued. Being father to a second generation of children is never easy. The age gap usually means a drain on energy levels, as well as a strain on the tolerance threshold. At the same time it is often true that the second wave of children enjoy a far laxer attitude to discipline from their parents than their older brothers and sisters did at the same age.

The teenage Daniel and Tamasin of the psychedelic seventies were a new breed to Cecil. They were more self-assured, even bold, and a far cry from the sober and obedient adolescents Sean and Nicholas had been in the 1940s. Sadly, too, an extra element of difference crept in. In 1970, Cecil, now approaching his sixty-sixth birthday, fell ill and had to undergo an operation to remove bladder stones. His fragility while on holiday that August was plain to see.

The following April Cecil was sick again, but this time his illness was much more serious. He was diagnosed as having pancreatic cancer. The prognosis was not encouraging and doctors estimated his life expectancy to be perhaps a year. Faced with this devastating news, Jill agreed with the specialist's advice that it was best that her husband should remain in ignorance of his terminal condition. Bravely she bore this heavy burden almost entirely by herself, telling only a very few people close to her. To shield them, Daniel and Tamasin were for the moment left in the dark. All Daniel knew was that his father had been ill and had developed diabetes.

By the end of that year, Tamasin had secured a place at Cambridge University, much to her proud parents' delight. By contrast, Daniel had been getting himself into all the kinds of scrapes that moody fourteen-year-old boys frequently do – messing about with girls, despite suffering the dreaded acne, smoking and underage drinking, even a spot of shoplifting which had resulted in a run-in with the police. Needless to say this brief brush with the law made his mother and father very unhappy. Already sorely tried by his rebellious behaviour, they now felt thoroughly shamed into the bargain.

On the positive side, even if achieving academic excellence was not a top priority in his life, the desire to act had now become persistent enough to be taken seriously. Daniel's drama teacher at Bedales, keen to encourage this promising boy, cast him as the lead in Shakespeare's *The Winter's Tale*. Daniel played Florizel, the son of King Polixenes of Bohemia who falls in love with the heroine, Perdita.

Although extremely unwell, Cecil attended the play to watch his son perform. He himself had played Florizel many years before in his own school production of the play and no doubt he was Daniel's biggest critic in the audience that night. But what he saw filled him with unmitigated pride and delight. Sadly it proved to be the last time he would see his son on stage – he never lived to witness Daniel's professional acting career take off.

Although his mother had tried to shield him from the knowledge that his father was dying, by now Daniel must have begun to have his suspicions. He was not an insensitive boy and Jill was under an increasing strain in nursing Cecil, although she tried her best to hide her distress and the effects of too many sleepless nights. Fourteen is a difficult age at which to have to handle the serious illness of a parent – not so young as to be blissfully unaware of the tension, anxiety and other giveaway signs, and yet frequently not considered old enough to cope with the reality of impending bereavement. The result can often be a debilitating state of frightened foreboding, made all the worse for being unspoken. A sense of impending doom must have permeated Daniel's heart during this time and, indeed, looking back, he will admit to this period having been very bleak.

It was difficult for everyone in the family and worst of all for his mother. Although mostly associated with radio, Jill did undertake television work when the opportunity arose and in spring 1972 she was committed to a drama series, *The Strauss Family*. This was the independent television company ATV's story of the famous nineteenth-century Austrian family of composers, starring Eric Woofe, Stuart Wilson and Anne Stallybrass. Her scenes for co-directors David Giles and David Reid were to be recorded at Elstree Studios in Hertfordshire, and her primary concern was the care of her, by now, very sick husband while she carried out this work. She could not leave him unattended at Crooms Hill, but the idea of hospitalizing Cecil did not appeal to either of them. Then came a welcome compromise in the shape of an invitation from friends.

The writer Kingsley Amis and his then wife, novelist Elizabeth Jane Howard, owned Lemmons, a large house in Hadley Wood, close to Elstree. In this grand old house, with its extensive and well-manicured gardens, Jane had long been accustomed to playing hostess to a stream of guests. At this time she was also caring for her invalid mother with the help of a live-in nurse. On learning of Jill's dilemma, the Amises invited the Day-Lewises to come and stay with them for whatever length of time they needed. Cecil and Jill took them up on their kind offer in early April.

Daniel spent his fifteenth birthday at the end of April by his frail father's bedside at Lemmons. Cecil's health was clearly deteriorating. He was seriously weakened and by the third week of May it was obvious that he was on borrowed time. Daniel was back at school when one Sunday night he received an urgent telephone call from his mother, telling him to catch the first available train from Petersfield the following day and get himself to Lemmons as fast as possible. He arrived at mid-morning on Monday, 22 May, the last of the family to arrive. Cecil had slipped into unconsciousness the night before and had been fading so fast that anxiety that Daniel might not arrive in time had added to the family's grief. But he did, and in just enough time to join the others in the sickroom before his father peacefully passed away.

Expressing grief at any age is a very private and individual thing. In Daniel's case he immediately left the bedroom and sought solitude in a quiet corner of the stricken house. He would maintain later that he was not at all devastated at his father's actual passing. That, as he had sat holding Cecil's emaciated right hand as he finally gave up the fight, he had experienced a bizarre, almost emotionless detachment from what was happening. That, in fact, at the time, he had coped quite unnervingly well with it all.

As time went on, however, it would be an entirely different story. Yet, while Daniel's later reactions to his father's death would indeed prove traumatic, the sequence of events would – when he had become a star and his life was subject to public scrutiny – be neatly and quite wrongly telescoped together, resulting in widespread misrepresentation in the press.

Cecil was buried at Stinsford in Dorset, only feet from the grave of Thomas Hardy, whose work had been a great influence on him. There were the usual public tributes in recognition of his literary contribution over the years, and his one-time fellow guest at Janet and Reynolds Stone's home in Litton Cheney, now Sir John Betjeman, succeeded him as Poet Laureate. For the rest of the family, life had to go on.

Daniel returned to Bedales where he encountered a total, no doubt awkward, silence about his father's death. Not a soul mentioned it, which seemed very strange to him. Initially, he found himself in an emotional vacuum from which there was no easy outlet for his troubled thoughts.

When the feelings did begin to come to the surface, they

were an uneasy mixture of many things – none of them good. Reflecting on the adolescent lawlessness of his past few years, Daniel gradually began to feel a natural, and expected, sense of deep regret. He mourned too the fact that he had not, as far as he was concerned, achieved anything before Cecil's death of which he felt his father could be proud. This was a harsh self-criticism considering his youth, but one he would still be feeling twenty years later. Perhaps most worrying of all, he was aware of a deep sense of shock at the indifference he had felt at his father's actual passing. It was not until he found himself physically missing the presence of his father to ask questions of that the permanence of Cecil's loss finally began to take some shape in his mind.

This final realisation came at an inopportune moment. Daniel had been prescribed some migraine pills and gradually, entirely by accident, he had begun to discover that if he took more than the stated dosage it had what he has since described as 'a rather interesting effect' on him. Recklessly, but ignorantly, he had been dabbling with a little of this, a little of that and as the effect of the migraine pills was not at all unpleasant he took more and more of them. Whether he was subconsciously seeking to blot out the painful regrets which were now gathering is debatable, but he certainly had no idea of the dangers he was courting. He is adamant that it was not a deliberate overdose. He was simply ignorant of what he was messing with.

When the effect of his actions hit, the physical and mental fallout was frightening and Daniel went through an extremely rough patch as a result. Taken as prescribed, migraine pills, which are designed to relieve pressure on the brain, can result in a euphoric feeling of being detached from reality. Taken to excess, their cumulative effect was to have Daniel hallucinating wildly and dangerously. Those around him, presumably ignorant of what he had done, could only see his outward behaviour and came to the conclusion that he was severely disturbed. As a result, he was immediately admitted to a psychiatric hospital for examination and treatment.

That treatment initially consisted of locking him in a room with a nurse, to ensure that he did not injure himself, and simply letting him hallucinate. The doctors' primary concern was that they might be dealing with a teenage heroin addict. It was a terrifying experience for the boy, made worse when he had returned to his normal self and realised where he was. He misinterpreted what someone said to him and some-how gained the impression that he was going to be a hospital inmate for the rest of his life. Somehow, he was led to believe that by his actions he had caused irreparable damage to his system and he was convinced that he was never going to get out.

His fear of being buried there forever made him temporarily lose all sense of time. His two-week ordeal only came to an end when he managed to prove to the medical board dealing with his case that he was perfectly recovered, that he had not made a deliberate attempt on his life and that he was now fit for release. In his own words, he had to give his 'greatest performance of sanity' to get out of the mental hospital.

When he was discharged, with his family adopting a determinedly low-key attitude to the matter, he returned to Bedales. There, true to form, not a word was said to him about what had happened but, now back on his feet, Daniel was doing a lot of thinking. That crucial performance for the medical board's benefit aside, his leanings towards a career in acting were born out of a healthy enthusiasm which had been steadily strengthening. The tantalising aura of escapism that the theatre offered continued to appeal to him very much — even more so in the light of the bleakness which had shrouded his recent past.

Although, compared to Sevenoaks, his sojourn at Bedales had been far better than bearable, it was still an English boarding school, confining and, in its own way, even conventional. Looking to the future he was also very aware that he could not see himself fitting into any regular way of life. The anarchic opportunities that he imagined were available to be explored in acting, therefore, drew him like a lodestar. But he knew it was a notoriously difficult field in which to succeed. There were no easy shortcuts, even for someone with his solid family connections in the business. And anyway his first step towards this possible career proved to be less than inspiring.

In the summer of 1973 he signed up for a season at the National Youth Theatre in London. The experience was hardly a memorable one. He later damned it as having been seedy and distasteful, and, by the time he returned to Bedales when the new term began that autumn, his desire to be an actor had, if anything, diminished.

For the remaining two years at school Daniel's attentions seemed centred on non-academic pursuits. His athletic endeavours on the football pitch and the cycling track certainly gave him a lot of pleasure. A by-product of this was that his already strong appeal to the opposite sex was strengthening. He also continued to act in various school productions, often in Shakespearean roles. By now his long, angular face and refined, unconventional good looks lent him, at least in period dress, a style not unlike that of the haughty young Laurence Olivier.

By the time he was seventeen there was a noticeable coiled, restless energy about him which seemed only just contained, giving him a vibrant aura of riskiness. One direct consequence of this was a heartbreaker reputation among the ladies which others attribute to him at that time. Personally, though, Daniel steadfastly refused – as he still refuses – to discuss the women in his life. When he left Bedales in 1975 with just two A Levels to his name, he had been dating a fellow student, Sarah Campbell, for some time. She remained his steady girlfriend for several more years to come.

CHAPTER TWO

STAGECRAFT

'Smiling at things beyond our ken.'

CECIL VYSE, *A ROOM WITH A VIEW*

By Daniel's own admission, when he left Bedales he still
carried a lot of emotional baggage with him. There had
already been so much turbulence in his world, some of which
had scrambled his emotions to the point where he hardly
knew what he wanted out of life. A part of him continued to
indulge the dream of an idyllic existence as a solitary
carpenter, dedicated to his craft, untrammelled and, he
imagined, unchallenged by other people. While he had made
some good friends at school, he had, at the deepest level,
created and zealously maintained an impregnable state of inner
isolation. He was a loner who, although only eighteen, had
already spent years keeping people at bay, preventing them
from getting too close and masking his real feelings from the
outside world. He firmly believed that working with your
hands was good for the soul. In search of the serenity that he

hoped it would bring, during the following few months he began applying for jobs as an apprentice in the carpentry trade. In late spring 1976 he landed an interview with John Makepeace, a respected furniture maker based in the south of England whose pupils have also included Viscount Linley.

Around the same time, however, Daniel also received news that his application for a place at drama school had been accepted. The two worlds were so opposite. As a carpenter his life would be as invisible as he wanted. As an actor he set himself up for public scrutiny, at least while he was on stage. Of course he already knew all about pretending to be something he was not. While it is perhaps overstating the case to say that he longed for the chance to regularly submerge himself in someone else's personality, acting held the paradoxical promise that, should he become successful, even in the most famous of roles he could somehow remain unknown. There was little doubt as to which avenue he would pursue.

The Bristol Old Vic Drama School had an excellent reputation and was the only acting school to which Daniel applied. Indeed, becoming a member of this renowned establishment would later be cited as the first of only two personal ambitions he has held in his acting career to date. He rented himself a flat in Clifton and enrolled on a three-year course in the autumn of 1976.

Among his tutors at Bristol was to be Rudi Shelley. Despite suffering a stroke in 1994, from which he fully recovered, Rudi was still coaching there in 1995, at the age of eighty-six. In his forty years of teaching drama, thousands of students have passed through his care. Some of the careers he has nurtured have blossomed to great things. His most notable successes, besides Daniel, have included Anthony Hopkins, Stephanie Cole, Greta Scacchi and Jeremy Irons. Rudi had known Daniel's mother during her own years in training at the Central School of Speech Training and Dramatic Art and was delighted to welcome her son into the fold. There would be no preferential treatment, however. Joining the new influx of students, Daniel was just another young hopeful. But, once installed at the school, Daniel did discover a mentor in the shape of the respected British actor Pete Postlethwaite. Here, too, he finally realised the need to fully interact with other people.

In this respect he found himself, at first, ill-prepared for what was expected of him. Initially it was a daunting experience, for one of the first hurdles he had to get over – a prerequisite of being at theatre school at all – was that you had to be prepared to learn very quickly how to make a complete and utter fool of yourself in front of others. This was not an easy thing for such a private person. He had overcome worse, however, and the discipline proved to have its rewards. For the first time Daniel felt he was really investing his time and energy in something worthwhile, even if he became frustrated that it was over a year before he was allowed on a stage. By which time he felt himself to be overtrained and straining at the leash to get on with things.

A fellow drama school student at that time who recalls Daniel's early days is actress Sally Baxter. 'Daniel was in his first year when I was in my final year,' she explains. 'We would come together again later in a play at the Little Theatre, but at that time at drama school we found that we got on really well together. Almost at once he struck me as being highly interesting to talk to and to listen to. He had a calm air about him that was noticeable but difficult to explain, and yet at the same time was a very physical person. For one thing, he seemed to be forever training, whether it was running or cycling or whatever. I have a vivid memory too of him quietly playing what I think I'm right in saying was the flute.' She adds, 'In your first year you don't get to do anything but training and classes. It's in your second year that the stage work comes, which is when you can start to get your teeth into things. It's much more fun all round then.'

As it happened, early in Daniel's second year at drama school any fun to be had was temporarily suspended when, five years after he had lost his father, his grandfather Michael Balcon died. Over the years he and Daniel had grown close. Seeing in which direction his daughter's boy was headed, Michael had also been able to impart some of his breadth of experience to him. It is thanks to Michael Balcon that, in later years, some directors have openly envied Daniel's acute understanding of the practicalities of the film world. At any rate Michael's passing that October 1977 was a great personal loss to Daniel.

It was also a major loss to the film world. A film producer since 1920, as well as heading up Ealing Studios, Michael's other posts had included being Governor of the British Film Institute and founding film company Gainsborough Pictures. He had long been considered one of the leading lights in the British film industry, and the tributes to him were warm and widespread. All extolled his invaluable contribution to the world of cinema, for which he had received a knighthood in 1948.

When Daniel completed his stint at drama school in the summer of 1979, he was one of three students transferred straight to the Bristol Old Vic Repertory Company on a one-year contract. At the same time he was given his Equity card. Let loose on the famous Old Vic stage, he would now have his work cut out, appearing in no less than eight productions which were scheduled to run back to back over the next twelve months.

He got his feet wet straight away that September at the Theatre Royal with a small part as a soldier in George Farquhar's *The Recruiting Officer*, directed by Adrian Noble and starring James Cairncross, Neil Stacy, Lindsay Duncan and Pete Postlethwaite. Pete would join Daniel again the following month at the same theatre, this time in Shakespeare's tale of star-crossed Trojan War lovers, *Troilus and Cressida*, in which Daniel played the character Deiphobus. In fact, he and Daniel worked alongside each other in one capacity or another in Daniel's first three plays with the Bristol Old Vic Company. The third was Mike Stott's *Funny Peculiar* at the Little Theatre in which he was cast as the halfwit Stanley Baldry: a role he played to good effect, with Pete this time as his director.

After all his impatience to start accumulating hands-on experience in the theatre, it must be safe to assume that Daniel now felt a sense of purpose and direction in his life. He was funnelling all his energies into hopes of carving a prosperous career in a world which excited him. The way in which he was developing as an actor in these early days, however, draws two distinctly varying opinions. His mother's friend and neighbour, Ann Broadbent, made a point of catching a couple of Daniel's Bristol stage performances and is completely partisan about them. 'He was always striking,' she insists, 'even in these earliest days.' But not everyone was instantly impressed.

Experienced actor Patrick Connor was rehearsing for his role in *Troilus and Cressida* at the same time as Daniel was completing his last term at the theatre school. During his days working in radio with the BBC he had sometimes had occasion to team up with Jill Balcon. At the same time he had what he terms a 'nodding acquaintance' with Cecil, and so he had been disposed to take a particular interest in this son of theirs who 'had just stepped off the bus' – a favourite expression in acting to describe a newcomer on the scene.

Patrick's first impression of Daniel was, he says, that he had clearly inherited his mother's intensity. He recalls, 'During rehearsals I saw an end-of-term student performance of *Camino Real* in which Daniel played Lord Byron. He looked suitably Byronic and had some stage presence, but his voice tended towards the inflexible and his movements were stiff. Overall, I rated his performance as no more than competent.' He adds, 'I've since followed his career with interest and it was *The Last of the Mohicans* that convinced me that he had major film-star potential which, of course, is something different from being a good actor.'

Stardom, Hollywood-style or otherwise, could be no more than a faint elusive flicker right then, though. The role of The Amazing Faz in Ken Campbell's *Old King Cole* at the New Vic Theatre saw in Daniel's new year, followed in quick succession by Iron in *Class Enemy* and Leicester in *Edward II*. Returning to the Theatre Royal, he appeared in *Oh, What a Lovely War!* and finally *A Midsummer Night's Dream*, which ended in September 1980 and in which he played Philostrate, Master of the Revels.

Revelling was the last thing he felt like doing when the curtain fell on his final performance. The previous twelve months had been valuable experience learning his craft, but with his year's contract up at the Bristol Old Vic, Daniel found himself back in London. Suddenly he was adrift and rudderless, with no idea of where, professionally, he was going next. At twenty-three he chose not to return to live at his mother's home. Instead, he moved into a spartan, but rent-free, flat in West Hampstead with Sarah Campbell, with whom he was still involved, and another young man, Simon Dunstan, who later became an accomplished animator working in television. Sarah's long blonde hair was the perfect foil to Daniel's dark colouring and together they made a striking couple. Their relationship had survived intact while Daniel was in Bristol – a fact which led to speculation among their friends that in due course they might marry. Right now, though, Daniel had other, more pressing, matters on his mind.

For the first time in his adult life he found himself without a job and he didn't like it. After signing on at a north London dole office in Neasden, he drew his unemployment benefit, scoured the pages of the weekly trade newspaper *The Stage* for job adverts, as every out of-work actor does, and wondered where his next part was coming from. He was desperate to work, but the immediate future looked bleak. There were only odds and ends on offer, such as the small spot he picked up in an episode of the BBC1 television series *Shoestring*.

The series starred Trevor Eve as Eddie Shoestring, a reporter with a West Country radio station. Daniel's appearance was as a disc jockey in one episode – not exactly a showcase performance, but it is credited as marking his British network television debut. Today, strangely, the BBC Archives Centre in Reading have no record of a contract for an appearance by Day-Lewis in *Shoestring*, but Daniel jokingly insists that he occasionally receives a minuscule royalty from the BBC when the episode in which he appeared is screened anywhere in the world.

The acting profession is notoriously one of the most overcrowded and insecure. Throughout any actor's career, especially early on, there are frequent and sometimes lengthy periods of 'resting', when there is no work to be had. Equity has in excess of 40,000 members and on average, around eighty per cent of those are unemployed at any given time. For Daniel, this stretch of being on the dole looked set to last indefinitely. It was such a demoralising prospect that, for a while, he let himself go.

With no particular anchor in his life, no daily routine to follow, the disciplines he had had drummed into him all his life deserted him. His days began blurring one into another as he loafed around experimenting with what he has called one 'intoxicating substance' after another. As a result he turned himself into a tired and lethargic wreck who had lost a great deal of pride in his appearance. This state of affairs went on for months until one morning he looked in the mirror and recoiled.

His facial bone structure had by now matured into the naturally triangular shape which tends to give him a lean, hungry look at the best of times. His thick black mane, especially when grown long, adds a degree of wolfishness to his appearance. But even so the gaunt, almost demonic, appearance that was the result of his lifestyle then gave him a considerable shock.

It is undoubtedly easier to fall into bad habits than it is to shake them off, but realising he was in danger of sliding ever downwards in a hopeless spiral, Daniel made determined efforts to pull himself together. Stringent exercise had worked before, so the running shoes came out and he began pounding the pavements. Physically as well as mentally he needed to get himself into shape and he drove himself hard.

Finding a productive purpose to the day was important to him. Having discovered that it was impossible to find any paid employment, he fixed himself up with some voluntary work as a despatch rider making deliveries to London's St Stephen's Hospital. His passion for cycling progressed beyond racers as he happily bombed back and forth to the hospital on his precious, newly acquired motorbike. Despite all this determined activity, however, there were still times when depression crept in. By his own admission this occasionally translated into physical aggression, when he was quite capable of smashing up the flat's furniture as he tried to vent his very deep frustration at life.

But then Fate smiled on him when he unexpectedly landed the role of the rebel Jimmy Porter in *Look Back in Anger*, John Osborne's groundbreaking 1956 play. When it had opened at the Royal Court on 8 May that year it had caused a major stir. Its uncompromising hero, Jimmy Porter, was the original Angry Young Man – a rebellious working-class hero, railing against the British establishment of the mid-1950s.

Three years later Tony Richardson, who had originally staged the play, directed a hard-hitting film version which starred Richard Burton. As Porter, Burton glowered and snarled with supreme arrogance throughout as only Burton could, but at thirty-four he was considered by some to have been just a bit too mature for the role. Although a rebel, Osborne's Porter is a mixed-up young man and something of a weakling too, confronting social issues and the myriad frustrations of youth. It is undoubtedly a star part but one most suited to the younger actor.

The stage production for which Daniel had been invited to take the lead was to be performed at the Little Theatre in Bristol, directed and produced by George Costigan and scheduled to open in January 1981. The cast included Nigel Cooke, Rosalind March and Sally Baxter. Daniel had not been first choice for the part, as actor Philip Jackson, a familiar face in film and British television, recalls, 'What happened was the chap who was supposed to be playing Jimmy Porter dropped out unexpectedly the night before rehearsals were due to start and they were suddenly frantically searching for a replacement.'

Philip, himself appearing in a play in Bristol at the time, was approached about taking on the role. 'I was asked to play Porter one night in a pub about 11.00 p.m. but I couldn't do it of course.' He goes on, 'Anyway at the last moment they got Daniel in. My wife-to-be then, Sally Baxter, was playing Alison Porter and so sometimes I'd go along during the day to the rehearsals to see how it was all coming along.'

Speaking of those rehearsals, Sally, who as Alison plays Jimmy's downtrodden and degraded wife, says, 'As is often the case, they were the most fun. Perhaps it was because of the short notice, but Daniel came to the play quite unsure of himself. It was a difficult role to play in the first place and of course he didn't play it working class. He gave it a rather middle class touch which certainly meant that we had a lot of things to have to get around, shall we say.'

Sally was still conscious of those hurdles when rehearsals were over and the real thing began, but she had faith in her former drama school friend. She explains, 'Because we had known each other for some time by then, it meant there was an enormous support and trust there for both of us, and that helped a great deal. Personally speaking, he was a joy to work with and, even though the story is all very moody and bleak, we actually had enormous fun doing it. As far as the play itself was concerned, although I think Daniel's intensity worked extremely well in it, it wasn't the greatest of productions, to be honest.'

In Philip's opinion, part of the reason for that lies in the fact that Daniel was not ideal for the title role. He explains, 'Well, I know he'd do it very differently now, but then, try as hard as he might, Daniel came across just too much like a public-school boy, which of course was all wrong for Porter. I think it was actually having to pretend to be genuinely working class which gave him a few problems. He was young too, of course, but, whatever, it didn't quite come off, I felt.'

The theatre critics felt the same way as Philip Jackson and

proceeded to give Daniel a fair pasting in their reviews of the opening night performance. Some of their criticism was savage and, unprepared, he took it deeply to heart. But, Sally Baxter is adamant: 'All the complaints were to do with him not getting to grips with the accent, and nothing else.'

If he *was* miscast, however, Daniel tried hard with the role and, recovering from his first critical onslaught, attacked it with heart, vigour and his own brand of moody intensity – familiar hallmarks which would surface frequently in the future. All this helped the play to make up for its disappointing beginning by gathering strength and, with it, popularity.

So popular did it become that, when the Little Theatre decided to follow *Look Back in Anger*, in February, with a production of *Dracula* adapted by Christopher Bond, Daniel was invited to stay and take on the role of the Count himself. Created by Abraham (Bram) Stoker, the character of Dracula was first brought to the screen in 1931 by Bela Lugosi. Innumerable film versions followed, most notably those made by the legendary Hammer Film Company with Christopher Lee taking over the mantle of the Count and making it very much his own. For this West Country stage production, Albie Woodington was among those joining Daniel and again the director was George Costigan, this time assisted by Colin Butler.

Bond's version of one of the fiction world's most horrific figures was certainly different. A degree of mystery had been whipped up in the hype before the play's opening night, designed to intrigue and attract the widest possible audience. The secret was revealed then when it transpired that the master vampire sported a very unconventional peroxide-blond crew cut. Albino or not, though, he was still fearsome.

Dracula ran for two successful months, with little free time for Daniel in between. Midway through the run, however, he did manage to snatch a day off for another small television spot – a one-off appearance in another BBC production, David Rudkin's science-fiction story *Artemis 81*. This weekly serial starred Hywel Bennett, Dinah Stabb, the pop star Sting and Daniel O'Herlihy. Recorded on 8 March, Daniel's role is listed as being that of the 'Exhibitioner' and once again his appearance was scarcely noticeable.

But breaking into the world of television was not easy. The theatre still held out the most opportunities of work on a regular basis and so it was straight back to Bristol that night for Daniel. His six-foot two-inches height, coupled with his ability to project an extremely saturnine image, helped him to create an effectively sinister Prince of Darkness – effective enough to make an impact, not only with audiences, but also on a director who made a special trip to the theatre to weigh him up, with a view to casting his leading man in an upcoming project.

The man responsible for bringing Daniel to the director's attention was actor Neil Stacy, with whom Daniel had appeared in his very first Old Vic production, *The Recruiting Officer*, eighteen months earlier. He had caught another of Daniel's Bristol theatre performances and was one of the first to recognise his star potential. Says Neil, 'I can't for the life of me remember the name of the play Daniel was doing, but I do clearly recall he was playing a right thug in it. Technically he was superb but the attraction lay in the fact that he was so frighteningly realistic in his pretence at being such a demented hoodlum. He performed the role with such complete understanding that had to have come out of his imagination entirely.' He goes on, 'I guess I was so struck by it because it seemed strange to me that he could be so utterly convincing in such a role, when in reality I knew him to be the very gentle, slender son of a highly academic family, but I was very impressed.'

So impressed was he that he lost no time in talking enthusiastically about Daniel to a friend of his, director Ronald Wilson. Ronald recalls, 'As it happens, I had actually seen Daniel myself on stage at the Bristol Old Vic some time before that. Like Neil, I can't remember which play it was, but Daniel was playing an old man in it and this was just when he was virtually newly out of drama school. It wouldn't have been an easy part to play and it's possibly that fact that first made me take an interest in him that night. Whatever it was, though, I came away thinking he had been outstanding.' He goes on, 'Then, some time later, Stacy had newly come back from Bristol where he had just seen Daniel in a play. He told me he thought he was superb and that he was going to recommend that his own agent, Michael Whitehall, put Daniel up for a part in a production I was in the process of putting together for the BBC.'

As far as Ronald was concerned, the timing could not have been better. He says, 'This was just as we were at the point of casting for a four-part serial, *Frost in May*, and so Neil, Michael Whitehall and I went to the Little Theatre in Bristol to see Daniel in *Dracula*. His performance was nothing short of extraordinary. I was glued all the way through. That was it as far as I was concerned. I knew I didn't have to go through with auditions because I'd found the person I wanted to play Archie and we cast him literally there and then.' Michael Whitehall was then in partnership with Julian Betfrage, who would later become Daniel's agent, breaking away from Michael and setting up his own agency.

With his Bristol stage run coming to an end, Daniel considered himself very fortunate to have landed the BBC role. He was to be cast as Archie Hughes-Follett, a rather gauche young Englishman, and this time it was very far from a bit part. 'It was an excellent part and a big part,' confirms Wilson, 'and an important one too.' It was also a demanding role for someone only twenty-four years old with relatively little experience behind him, but Ronald had complete confidence in Daniel.

For Daniel, who features heavily in episodes two and three, with a brief appearance in the fourth, filming for his scenes in the drama *Frost in May* began in May 1981 and would carry on until mid-September. Based on Antonia White's novels of the 1930s, its cast included John Carson, Elizabeth Shepherd and Charles Dance. The story centres on the life of a young girl in pre-World War I Britain. Fernanda Batchelor, played by a sweet-faced Patsy Kensit, enters a strict Catholic boarding school, but is later expelled in disgrace for writing a racy sex and drugs novel.

Archie Hughes-Follett comes into her life some years afterwards when, now played by actress Janet Maw, she has a post as tutor to the headstrong young son of a wealthy family. Archie is a neighbour and, although about to be commissioned as a lieutenant in the army, is the child's only friend. In Peter Pan fashion, Archie doesn't seem to want to grow up. He is happiest when playing childlike games, or loping around like an overgrown schoolboy. Deeply uncomfortable with girls, he nevertheless falls in love with the complex Clara (Fernanda has changed her name) and proposes to her. Much to his astonishment, she accepts, only to jilt him close to their wedding day. Archie, who has been considered a dud all his life, is left lurching, always luckless and usually drunk, from one disaster to another. Then he meets Clara, who has by now become a stage actress, again and this time they marry. But his inability to relate to women on any physical level means the marriage is never consummated and ends in an annulment.

All the main players in the drama have their own particular

torments to bear, but no one's torment seems quite as raw as that of Archie Hughes-Follett. Daniel's portrayal of a young man, well meaning but riddled with low self-esteem, was solid and very convincing, creating real sympathy for one of life's inadequates. According to the director, it could have been a very difficult role to get to grips with, but his faith in Daniel was entirely justified.

He recalls, 'Daniel was extremely inventive. He had an astonishingly deep understanding of Archie. An impotent character is not always an easy one to play, but he was very committed. The truthfulness of his performance, I suppose, is what stands out the most for me. I found what he did with the character very moving. He really enjoyed the role and it was a pleasure to work with him.'

This respect was also echoed by one of the cast's older actors, John Southworth, who played the character part of Merton Mordish. Says John, 'What struck me straight away about Daniel was that he rehearsed and acted with rare conviction and a certain passion which seemed absolutely right for the play and the period, and that's not something one often gets from young actors playing romantic leads in television. Not then, and certainly not now!' He adds, 'Off set, although always perfectly pleasant, he was serious minded and committed in a wholly professional way to the job in hand.'

In later years Daniel would become famous for inhabiting his roles to a sometimes excessive degree. In these early days, were the signs already starting to show? 'Yes and no,' says Frost's director, 'I mean, not exclusively. His intensity was certainly clear to see. He went deep into the character and made a thorough study of his subject. He pored over the novels and script, getting under its skin so much so that he actually became Archie and lived his role all the time, although not quite as

41

much as he is reported to do these days. For instance, he didn't go around off screen practising at being impotent, that's for sure. He went about with his girlfriend at the time like any other young man.'

There was a good rapport between director and actor which extended to beyond the set and, when they were not filming, they got to know each other well. 'He would come to our house to play tennis with myself and my son,' explains Ronald. 'I remember he used to wear the most extraordinary costume! His father's shorts, he said they were. They were certainly weird looking, that's all I can say, and he'd borrow other bits and pieces and end up looking a strange sight indeed. Played a mean game of tennis though.'

Frost in May would be screened on BBC2 during May and June of the following year. 'It was critically well received and popular,' says the director, 'but amazingly the BBC have done nothing with it since, not sold it or repeated it. It's something I must confess I find myself being somewhat bitter about, I suppose because I regard it as one of the best things I've done.' He adds, 'As Archie, Daniel had to sing quite a bit and it has always amused me how, since he's become famous, so many people have now taken to saying what a wonderful singer he is. I'm afraid he isn't but, never mind, we can't have everything.'

For the first time since leaving Bristol, Daniel's diary was beginning to look healthy. Only a week after he finished filming *Frost,* he joined the cast of another BBC2 production, about to start filming under director Moira Armstrong and producer Innes Lloyd. This was a film for the BBC Playhouse season entitled *How Many Miles to Babylon?,* based on the novel of the same name by Jennifer Johnston and adapted for television by Derek Mahon.

Again set before and during World War I, it revolved around

the friendship between Alexander Moore, the son of a landed Irish family, and Jeremiah Crowe, a peasant boy from the village. It begins with Alexander, played by Daniel, sitting in a bare cell writing to his parents, having been condemned to death by a court martial. It is accompanied by a narrative spoken by Alexander in his clipped English accent, using flashback to return the story to the turn of the century and his childhood in Ireland.

As in *Frost in May*, Daniel's role as Alexander Moore is once again of an unhappy young man, only this time – unlike Archie who often displayed excruciatingly naked insecurity – one who because of his coldly formal upbringing, masks his feelings behind unstintingly polite manners. He has a gentle nature, but it is his inability to mix, to develop the warmth and openness clearly untapped inside him, which is in *Babylon* one of the most touching aspects of the character. The victim of his vain and domineering mother, played by Siân Phillips, who is almost unhealthily obsessed with her son, Alexander is close to his father, portrayed by Alan MacNaughtan.

Alexander is a character of many facets. There is quiet strength, shown in his stubbornness in maintaining his friendship with Jerry – a loyalty which will later lead him into trouble. And there is also weakness, when, despite the fact that there are no conscription laws in Ireland, Alexander enlists because his mother desperately wants him to.

Daniel's job was to embody a young man constantly at odds with the various rules of society or class, both at home and within the army. Belonging by birthright above stairs, but finding his only real friendship with someone considered to be of lower orders adds to the confusion he has always felt while growing up. Every inch the typically stiff-upper-lipped English officer, Alexander's curb on his emotions is complete. His vulnerability is conveyed solely and to poignant effect through his eyes alone.

Alexander's restraint, coming hard on the heels of Archie's frequently awkward exuberance, enabled Daniel to explore techniques of portraying what were, in essence, similar traits but displayed in very different ways. In terms of experience, this would have been both productive and rewarding. For Daniel there was also an extra pleasure in undertaking this role, because it took him on location to his beloved Ireland and in particular to County Wicklow.

Daniel was brought up to consider Ireland as much home as anywhere and he revelled at the chance to combine business with pleasure, working for a month amid the beauty of granite mountains, peat and heather-filled valleys and long stretches of sandy beach. English landlords have left their mark on the east coast in the shape of the many stately homes set in well-kept estates. It was at one such estate, Ballinacor in Rathdrum, that *How Many Miles to Babylon?* was filmed.

Another pleasure was the opportunity of making new friends, among them actor Alan MacNaughtan, who played his father Frederick Moore with great class and dignity. Says Alan, 'It was the first time we'd met, the first time we acted together and for me it was a wonderful experience.' The emotional on-screen communication between their two characters is among the most effective aspects of the film. A lot of this success was owed to that warmth being reflected in off-set reality. Alan confirms, 'I played his father, yes, but we truly did have that feeling of father and son and I think it couldn't help but get through.'

They certainly spent a lot of time together when filming was over for the day. Indeed it seems Daniel preferred Alan's company to that of anyone else. 'Well, the big house we were using was beautiful and a wonderful place to be around,' explains Alan, 'but Wicklow has some lovely beaches and Daniel and I would disappear often to the coast to walk along the sand just talking. Sometimes he'd go in swimming. I didn't. The water was much too cold for me.' He adds, 'I'm older than him, obviously, but he would strip right off and not in the least bit concerned, no inhibitions at all, off he'd be, into the water completely nude.'

When Daniel wasn't sea dipping, during their many long walks and talks along the sand Alan discovered a young man, full of warmth and friendliness and, as the time went on, more and more outgoing. But, as well as a growing affection for Daniel, Alan came away from *Babylon* with a deep respect for his acting skills. Unwittingly mirroring director Ronald Wilson's opinion, Alan maintains that what struck him the most about Daniel was what he too called his 'absolute truth'.

'Playing opposite him, it is the first thing I was clearly, vividly aware of. Look in his eyes,' he urges, 'that's where you'll find it. His actual technique, of course, was so meticulous and intense, even then, exactly right. And he is endlessly particular to get the most minute detail right. During this filming he went to great pains with his part.' He goes on to point out, 'Of course, he has a reputation nowadays for this kind of preparation but he's a star today, he wasn't then and you couldn't possibly have the opportunity to go into the kind of detail he's famed for now. For a start, at that stage you're very much in the hands of your director who, with the best will in the world, just can't indulge everyone. Still, if you really believe in the role, then you should let it go as long as you can and that's what Daniel did, even then.'

The second half of *Babylon* sees the action switch to fighting in the front line in Flanders. In the Royal Irish Rifles regiment, Alexander holds a captain's rank, while Jerry is a private under his command. County Wicklow continued to provide the location, doubling now for France. Kevin Moore played Daniel's batman, Corporal O'Keefe, and, while Daniel's intense concentration during the scenes they played together struck him forcibly, his most vivid memory of this film centres on how hectic the schedule had suddenly become. He says, 'By halfway through we were working literally every day from the crack of dawn and there was a lot of night filming too. The production itself was such a big thing – I mean the scale of it with all those trench scenes. Moira Armstrong did a wonderful job creating all those realistic explosions, which were extremely effective.'

The actor who now had the most scenes with Daniel was Barry Foster. Although he had appeared in many films, Foster was at the time best known for his role as Van der Valk, a Dutch police inspector in the popular 1977 Thames Television series of the same name. As Major Glendinning in *Babylon*, Foster portrays the CO from hell, a complete bastard who displays unadulterated arrogance, snobbery and a cruel, very English, contempt for all Irish troops. His biting wrath invariably targets the quiet, kind Captain Moore, whom he keeps threatening to make a man of. Barry's performance is powerful and so believable that, when Daniel, as Moore, finally defies the Major, the enmity between the actors during their on-screen clash looked all too genuine. The reality was very different and behind the scenes they got on like a house on fire. Says Barry, '*Babylon* was hard but enjoyable work and to me Daniel showed great presence and skill in one so young.'

How Many Miles to Babylon? went out on BBC2 in February 1982. Alexander was, for Daniel, another character cursed with an inner unhappiness – one of life's loners, struggling to identify just where he belonged. Whether or not Daniel heard any echoes in his own head which injected such acute authenticity into his performances, he was already proving to directors, fellow actors and audiences alike that he was very adept at convincingly portraying the misfit. For some time to come this would more or less dictate the types of roles he would be offered.

CHAPTER THREE

PARADISE PUNCH-UP

'Charming people have something to hide.'

HENDERSON DORES, *STARS AND BARS*

By 1982 Daniel had graduated from insecure no-hoper to no-account lout when he appeared in a small walk-on but speaking part in the Columbia Pictures epic *Gandhi*, based on the life story of the remarkable man who led India's campaign for independence and directed by Sir Richard Attenborough. Ben Kingsley, whose portrayal of Mahatma Gandhi deservedly won him an Oscar, was supported by a host of other star names including John Gielgud, Trevor Howard, Saeed Jaffrey and Roshan Seth.

Daniel's only previous experience in feature films had been that bit part as a child vandal in *Sunday Bloody Sunday*. Now, thirteen years later, he found himself elevated from hooligan to racist as Colin, a loud-mouthed South African youth, who suddenly confronts the mild-mannered Gandhi in the street and arrogantly orders him off the pavement, cursing him as a 'bloody coon'. It is a brief blink in a movie over three hours long, but it is a part he did not think he would get.

Auditioning for any role is a nerve-racking affair for any young actor keen to land the work, but Daniel seems to have run up against a couple of extra obstacles – his appearance, for a start. His normal style – laid-back, unshaven, even scruffy – was one he was reluctant to change even when going up before a casting director. This often backfired on him, not only losing him the role, but sometimes also resulting in complaints to his agent, which Daniel found extremely humiliating. Secondly, he would encounter a kind of prejudice because he was the son of the late Poet Laureate.

There was little he could do about the latter, but his appearance was easier to rectify. When he turned up punctually to meet the casting director for *Gandhi* he was perfectly groomed and wore a second-hand suit and bow tie. But he couldn't win. The lady took one glance at him, promptly informed him that he looked too much like the son of a poet and sent him away. She did it kindly, unlike some previous directors he had faced, but it still stung. It also left him back at square one.

His wrong choice of gear was down to the fact that he had not known which part he had been recommended for; somehow he had assumed it would be for a stuffy British officer. Now he knew different and was determined to get a second bite at the cherry. This time though he opted to circumvent the casting director and instead targeted Attenborough himself. He allowed the dark stubble about his jaw to grow, donned his oldest clothes and bearded the film's director in person.

If Daniel had thought he would come up against a serious grilling from the bluff and bearded Attenborough, though, he was wrong. Except for asking the young actor his height and telling him somewhat unhelpfully that he was a 'good boy', Richard did not say another word. When Daniel left he had no idea whether he had got the role or not.

Much to his delight, he did secure his first speaking part in a major motion picture. His small scene was shot on location in India in the spring of 1981, after his Bristol run in *Dracula* ended and before he began work with Ronald Wilson on *Frost in May*. Ben Kingsley's portrayal of this extraordinary man of peace was a startling and masterly piece of work – a model performance for any aspiring Method actor. And it is said that Daniel was thoroughly captivated by Kingsley's approach to the role, in particular by Ben's total concentration and the strange other-worldly quality he exuded even when not in costume and on set. Film work itself excited Daniel as nothing else in the acting business had done. It had an entirely different feel to either stage or television, and also offered more scope for rehearsal. This eased the pressure on the actors a little, especially for someone like him, who already took preparation so deadly seriously. Since October 1981, however, it was not the pressure of too much work from which he suffered, but rather the strain of its lack. His first taste of unemployment had lasted four months. This time, by spring 1982, he had reached his sixth month of idleness and there seemed to be no end in sight. By summer the situation left him extremely downhearted and life in his west London flat was often very gloomy. Prone to pessimism anyway, Daniel probably felt as if the rug had been snatched out from under his feet just as he had believed himself to be on a roll.

The uncertainty of the business weighed him down, and networking – doing the rounds of showbiz parties, being trailed through the shark pond to see who bites – held no appeal for him either. But as autumn approached, just in time to save him from sinking even further, a break came his way. He learned that he had secured work – back on stage, but this time he would be making his London West End debut.

Another Country had begun life on 5 November 1981 at London's Greenwich Theatre, which had been built on the site of the derelict music hall opposite 6 Crooms Hill. Early reviews of the play, produced by Robert Fox, the younger brother of actors James and Edward Fox, directed by Stuart Surge and starring Rupert Everett, had been so warm that word had quickly begun to circulate that it was destined for the West End. Speculation proved correct when after four months, with the same number of cast changes, it transferred to the Queen's Theatre in Shaftesbury Avenue.

Here the dark and brooding Everett, who had already made an impact upon the theatre-going public's consciousness, continued to play the character of Guy Bennett. One of the new faces was that of the young Irish-born actor Kenneth Branagh, who had taken over the role of Tommy Judd, the other main character in the cast of twelve. At the time Branagh had just been awarded RADA's top prize, the Bancroft Gold Medal, and he has described landing the role of Judd as having been an unbelievable break. The play's creator was Julian Mitchell, a prolific writer of several novels and innumerable stage and television plays, as well as many episodes of the acclaimed ITV detective series *Inspector Morse. Another Country* itself won the BAFTA Best Play Award for 1982.

Its popularity had not waned at all after a further six months when, yet again, there were some changes in key personnel. This time Rupert Everett decided to move on, which meant that the casting director, Celestia Fox, was left looking for someone with enough experience to handle a now high-profile part. At the same time Everett's replacement had to look convincing as a seventeen-year-old and preferably have some understanding of the public-school life depicted in the play. It was a tall order but there would be no shortage of actors queuing up for the chance to take on the challenge.

Daniel was quick to hear of this golden opportunity. It had been a year and a half since he had acted in a theatre and that was in Bristol, while this would be in the heart of Britain's theatre land. But, undaunted, he determinedly pursued the part and finally won through. He may have been terrified at the prospect of making his West End debut by filling such celebrated shoes, but it was to prove a significant milestone in his acting career.

Kenneth Branagh had also decided to broaden his horizons at this time and so the role of Judd fell to John Dougall. As the languorous Bennett, Daniel took the stage in September 1982 and for the following nine months would proceed to pull clear of Rupert Everett's considerably long shadow. He was to carry off the part with a great deal of panache and wit, stamping his own identity strongly on it, growing in confidence and expanding his range with every performance.

The story is set in the claustrophobic uppercrust atmosphere of an English public school in the 1930s. The two main characters, Bennett and Judd, are said to be based on the teenage Guy Burgess and Donald MacLean – the men who, after World War II, spied for the USSR while working for the British Government and subsequently defected to Moscow before they could be arrested and put on trial.

Bennett is a scruffy young individual, who loathes boarding school and resents his parents for sending him there. A closet gay, he resents the system which is one rife with bullying and a disturbing preoccupation with corporal punishment, in particular with caning. His best friend is the heterosexual Judd, a committed communist who avidly studies *Das Kapital*.

The play depicts events which shaped the lives of the men who later turned traitor to their country. Mitchell parallels Bennett's (Burgess's) homosexuality with Judd's (MacLean's) Marxism and suggests that both were made to feel outsiders within the boarding-school system and that this became the root of their later rebellion.

Bennett's soul searching as he strives to conceal his sexual proclivities, along with his deep dislike and fear of the bullying, are coupled with the misery of boarding school life in general. Daniel had no difficulty in tuning in to the not so-distant memories of his own desperate unhappiness at Sevenoaks in Kent to help him with his performance.

It was an absorbing and riveting play which worked effectively on many levels. In the ruthless world of commercial theatre, its backers had taken their share of risk in mounting a new production with no established stars in it. For Daniel, too, taking over the lead was a huge responsibility. Rupert Everett had been blindingly successful as Bennett and was undoubtedly a hard act to follow. However, Daniel studied and prepared with his usual thoroughness. And, as one of the first rules of stagecraft is to relate your character to something you can associate with in your own life, then as far as portraying deep personal unhappiness was concerned, Daniel had no difficulty whatsoever in finding the right buttons to push.

But his performance extended much further than that. Writer and broadcaster Richard Mayne, a Day-Lewis family friend of long standing, was struck most by what he calls Daniel's 'whiplash sexuality'. He credited him with having woven a dangerously ambiguous, other-worldly aura around the character – perhaps a throwback to days spent studying Ben Kingsley at work the previous spring. While actor Alan MacNaughtan, who had starred the year before with Daniel in *How Many Miles to Babylon?*, concludes, 'He was remarkable in *Another Country*, quite splendid. He has a terrific presence and charisma on stage which reaches clean out into the heart of the audience. He was entirely immersed in his role of Bennett and gave an uninhibited performance.'

Director Ronald Wilson goes further, 'I thought Daniel brought new layers of depth to the character, layers that were, I think, missing before. Rupert Everett was obviously very good and was certainly highly acclaimed in the role but his was a showy performance. The difference with Daniel's Bennett was that you cared so much about the character and that's a quality he brings to his acting time and again – even to the most absolutely unsympathetic of characters. He still finds something he can bring to it which softens your attitude towards him.'

But *Another Country* did more than prove that Daniel could take over a role synonymous with one particular actor and successfully make it his own. It marked the beginning of his rise to acting prominence. By the early eighties a new breed of actor had begun to emerge. Coming up behind the likes of Robert Duvall, Marlon Brando and Robert De Niro, the new generation, which embraced Tim Roth, Gary Oldman and Daniel, chose to focus mainly on disaffected, aggressive types of roles, on the mixed-up loners. Although Daniel's range was to greatly expand in time, these were the parts to which he was most attracted and at which he seemed to excel.

His showcase performance at the Queen's Theatre was what secured Daniel his first decent movie role – a part in the third film version of one of history's best-known seafaring adventures, the famous mutiny on the *Bounty*. In May 1983 he brought a memorable nine-month run to an end, handing the part of Bennett over to Colin Firth, then fresh out of drama school.

In fact, the role would also pitch Colin Firth into film work for he went on to star as Judd, alongside Rupert Everett returning as Bennett, in the 1984 movie version of the play, directed by Marek Kanievska. Daniel had to travel to Tahiti to start filming the day after his last performance in *Another Country*. Even so, he proceeded to celebrate both its completion and the dawn of a new challenge by getting blindingly drunk. His hangover the next day was so bad that someone else had to do his packing for him to get him on his way.

The film, to be called *The Bounty*, had been plagued with problems from the start. The screenplay had been written by Robert Bolt, an English dramatist well known for his ability to popularise history, most notably with his 1966 Academy Award-winning *A Man for All Seasons*. It had originally been the pet project of Sir David Lean, with whom Bolt had successfully worked twice before, on *Lawrence of Arabia* and *Doctor Zhivago*. This promising start, however, soon gave way to trouble when Lean quit the project after Italian producer Dino de Laurentiis objected to a budget of $80 million for a single film. Eventually co-producer Bernard Williams scaled this down considerably by enlisting the services of New Zealand director Roger Donaldson instead.

The next problem revolved around the casting. The vital role of Lieutenant William Bligh had been battened down by securing the services of Anthony Hopkins. He was destined to be joined by, among others, Edward Fox and Laurence Olivier in a cameo role as Admiral Hood. But the role of Fletcher Christian had proved difficult to fill. Among those approached to play the part were the American actor Christopher Reeve (of *Superman* fame) and the singers-turned-actors David Essex

(David Lean's choice) and Sting. The four-month shooting schedule, however, proved to be a sticking point until eventually the producers found their man – Mel Gibson, the dark-haired Australian heart throb who had been catapulted to fame at the end of the 1970s as the star of George Miller's cult movie *Mad Max*.

For *The Bounty* Daniel was cast as John Fryer, Lieutenant Bligh's officious second-in-command. Major headache or not, he was soon on his way to Moorea, a small island off Tahiti, to report for duty with co-stars Bernard Hill, Liam Neeson, Philip Davis and Philip Martin Brown, who were among those making up the ship's officers and crew.

In 1787 Bligh was put in charge of an expedition to transport bread-fruit plants from Tahiti to Jamaica. When assembling his crew, he sought out his friend Fletcher Christian with whom he had sailed before, but the Admiralty assigned him John Fryer as Master of the ship. As in *How Many Miles to Babylon?*, Daniel again played the typically well-spoken, upright English officer, but this time one who was much disliked by the men under his command. Straight from playing a seventeen-year-old schoolboy on the London stage, Daniel had acquired a sudden maturity for the role. His hair, with a single faint streak of grey, was swept aggressively back from his forehead and he was decidedly imposing looking.

At the start of the film Fryer is superior to Mel Gibson's character Fletcher Christian, and so for some time the action revolves around Hopkins, Gibson and Daniel. The crunch for Fryer comes when, to serve Bligh's personal ambition, the ship attempts to circumnavigate the globe by rounding Cape Horn – a dangerous endeavour Fryer had been against from the first. Ultimately he confronts Bligh in a blazing row to demand that they turn back – a snarling, furious exchange, which results in

Bligh demoting Fryer for cowardice and replacing him with Christian as Master of the ship.

The mutiny occurs after a spell of several months on a paradise island, during which the crew and most of the officers live the good life and want nothing to do with Bligh's brand of strict discipline. Only Daniel's character remains as unbending as his captain's. Neither the presence of the beautiful island girls nor the free-flowing liquor proves a temptation to him. Indeed, very little seems to please him. By now Daniel plays only a semi-significant role in the film, and is distinguishable mainly by his height and a natty line in headgear.

Featuring third on the cast, behind the two high-profile actors, the pressure was not on Daniel. He was not the 'money', which he would later learn was the on-set nickname attached to the star from whom the studio is expecting to earn its profit. What the four months ought to have provided him with was yet more experience, and the surroundings themselves were certainly a far cry from muddy trenches in rainy Ireland. The charms of the idyllic blue waters, sand and interminable sunshine, though, quickly wore off. Following the problems getting the project off the ground in the first place, more troubles began setting in with the actual shoot. They obviously left their mark, for five years on Daniel described Moorea as having been 'a desperately sad place to be'.

According to the film's director of photography, respected cinematographer Arthur Ibbetson, whose previous credits include *Where Eagles Dare*, the problems stemmed from a variety of things. 'It was just not the usual run-of-the-mill film,' he explains. 'Moorea was a very small island, no skyscrapers, no bus service, and, once you were in your accommodation for the night, that was you until the car came to take you to the location the next day. On top of that the accommodation was all very spread out. There was no communal meeting place, like a bar for instance, and so consequently no one really got much of a chance to get to know anyone else.'

Even the style of accommodation created a sense of isolation, in that it consisted mostly of individual straw-thatched bungalows set well apart. Daniel stayed in the same area as Arthur, but a good distance away along the beach. Arthur describes Daniel as: 'Always very professional but at the same time there was what I call no acting profession side to him, none of the Charles Laughton "big time" attitude for instance.' Anthony Hopkins was another who preferred to keep his distance. 'Tony is a great friend of mine,' says Ibbetson, 'but he had his wife with him and so when the shoot was finished for the day she was waiting for him and he'd have a tonic water or ginger beer and be off.' He adds, 'The director also had his wife and even his children with him and so he'd vanish as well.'

The daily schedule was long and often frustrating. 'Every morning at 6.00 a.m. there'd be a bang on the door to wake you up for breakfast before assembling at 7.30 sharp to be driven to the boats which would ferry everyone out to the ship,' says Arthur. 'Once out at sea, there we'd stay until it began to get dark. Then it was a boat ride back, a car ride to your bungalow, a beer, sandwich and bed before starting all over again; and this kept up for sixteen weeks with only the Sundays off.'

Even the shoot itself had its complications. Arthur goes on, 'It was supposed to be an eighteenth-century Royal Navy ship but it wasn't even a full-size ship we were using and the space was very limited. There was a professional crew handling her on top of the acting crew who were *looking* like they were handling her. There was so little room, in fact, that there was practically no space to manoeuvre and anyone who wasn't absolutely essential on film for that particular shot was bundled unceremoniously below deck and out of the way.'

The tensions on set have been said for the most part to have focused on alleged problems with the director Roger Donaldson. Directing a feature film on this scale appears to have been new to him and perhaps this was responsible for the apparent stream of problems. It has been claimed since that arguments, or at least misunderstandings, hampered any form of rapport between Anthony Hopkins and the director, and certainly a lack of communication lay at the root of Arthur Ibbetson's concern.

'Well, I certainly blame lack of communication for causing big problems with the technical crew,' he states. 'We'd start work just after dawn; my crew would spend ages laying track and suddenly for no reason the director would come along and say, "Pick up the tracking, we're using hand held cameras now," or something like that. And so after all our preparation the shot would end up being done by some guy with a camera virtually glued to his forehead. OK, so if there was some reason for the change then that can't be helped and everyone at least knows why all their work has been for nothing, but with Donaldson there would be no explanation. Take after take he'd do this and never a word why. It built up a great deal of frustration in everyone.'

He goes on, 'I mean, to be fair, it wasn't just that. There were the usual delays which lie outside anyone's control. For instance, we'd just be getting the filming right and into shot would come a plane's vapour trail or a yacht would sail into view about three miles out. There's no point in sending a speedboat out to ask them to get off the horizon line because they can't go any faster anyway and so, with your shot completely ruined, you'd have to sit back for hours waiting for the yacht to clear off. As the weeks went by everyone had had enough.'

Arthur adds, 'You know at the drive which led to my bungalow there was a sign which said "Welcome to Paradise". One Sunday I saw Gene Kelly arrive from Los Angeles for a break. Three days later I saw him leave. He was standing on his verandah surrounded by all his luggage looking harassed and I shouted across to him, "Going already?" He swung round and barked, "Yeah! I've had enough of Paradise!" I knew how he felt!'

The hours, indeed days, of sitting around with nothing to do began getting to Daniel too. He called it four months of waiting for the sun to shine, and during this time the tensions and frustrations grew deeper, eventually erupting into physical fights. Philip Martin Brown, who played the mutineer John Adams, remembers, 'There wasn't a lot to do on the island. Once you'd visited their four or five restaurants and one disco, in no time at all it got very boring. The first fortnight was OK and after that we all felt like tearing our hair out.'

He goes on, 'The producer was the one who had come up with the shrewd move of allowing actors to take their girlfriends or wives along, which is unusual in film work. But for those of us who didn't have someone with us we found it hard to let off steam, shall I say, and there was quite a head of steam building which ended up in some punch-ups with a few of the islanders. Nothing too serious and no one actually got hurt, but there was some amount of hellraising went on.'

Years later, Daniel, perhaps referring to these brawls, also blamed the sheer boredom for bringing out everyone's primitive streak which resulted, he recalled, in a deal of punches flying about.

When he was not filming, Daniel at times kept himself very much to himself and would often prefer to go back to his bungalow to read the script or study the original story and his character in it. But when he was not shutting himself away he hung out mainly with Philip Davis, one of the other officers who all invariably stuck together. According to Philip Martin Brown this never fails to happen. 'It's a peculiar phenomenon, but it's always the same,' he states. 'Whether it's some TV cop series or a film like this or whatever, as soon as actors put on the costumes designating their rank, then that's it. Officers eat, drink and hang out with other officers and the rest of the plebs stick with their own – totally polarised.'

The first film version of the famous revolt had been the Frank Lloyd 1935 black and white *Mutiny on the Bounty* starring Charles Laughton and Clark Gable. Twenty-seven years later Marlon Brando and Trevor Howard revamped the tale in a stunning remake under the stewardship of the veteran director Lewis Milestone of *All Quiet on the Western Front* fame.

Robert Bolt's treatment in *The Bounty* painted a far more accurate picture of the relationship between Captain Bligh and Fletcher Christian than the two earlier versions. It also expanded on the complexity of Bligh's character and on the chain of events which resulted in the infamous mutiny itself. But, for all that, it turned out to be the least successful of the three films.

Says Philip Martin Brown, 'It was critically a success, but unfortunately it bombed in that it just didn't put enough bums on seats. Personally I think it stuck more faithfully to the story than either of the other two versions and it wasn't as glamorised either. Although, having said that, in the actual log Mr Christian is stated as being "short and much marked by the pox". So what did they do? They cast Mel Gibson in the role. There you go – that's the movies for you.'

It was with great relief that Daniel returned to London

after the Moorea shoot was over. It had not been the best of experiences but it was, nevertheless, the first time he had played a bigger role in a feature film. Little time, however, could be spent reflecting on this for he had signed up to join a Royal Shakespeare Company tour which was to start in a few weeks' time. Still sporting the beard he wore in the latter stages of the film, he was plunged headlong into rehearsals at Alford House, Kennington, an old school in south London.

It had been three years since the RSC had put a show on the road and a great deal of work and enthusiasm had already been invested in the preparation of this tour, which was to be sponsored by the National Westminster Bank and subsidised by the Arts Council. It would last from 10 October 1983 to 28 January 1984 and its intention was to take professional theatre to parts of the country otherwise starved of such entertainment.

Appearing in twenty-two towns and villages spread across the UK, it was one of the most taxing tours ever mounted. The plays to be performed were the ever-popular standards *Romeo and Juliet* and *A Midsummer Night's Dream*, directed respectively by John Caird, in his first year as Associate Director with the RSC, and actress Sheila Hancock, the Company's Artistic Director appointed for this regional tour. There would also be morning performances of a play called *Derek* by playwright and director Edward Bond. For the thirty-strong troupe of actors, musicians, stage management and technicians it promised to be an arduous undertaking. The actors included Robert Eddison, Penny Downie, Polly James and Philip Jackson. Daniel was to take the lead role in *Romeo and Juliet*, partnered by twenty-one-year-old Amanda Root, who had only newly completed her training at the Webber-Douglas Drama School. In *Dream* he played the part of Flute.

The pairing of Amanda with Daniel proved to be inspired.

With her innocent round face and trusting eyes and his darkly predatory flair, they looked extremely well together and from the beginning established a strong working affinity. *Romeo and Juliet* was to be a traditional production with Daniel – although now twenty-six, having no trouble in looking the requisite seventeen again – epitomising all the adolescent anguish and mercurial passions of the tragic hero. The swashbuckling, moody romantic seemed to present him with little real difficulty and the weeks of intensive rehearsing flew by. They had one dress rehearsal in the Round House in London and then were off on the road, heading to the Yarborough Leisure Centre in Lincoln for their opening night.

From the very first night, the tour proved eventful. Philip Jackson, a fine actor with many strong stage, television and film appearances already to his credit, played the weaver Nick Bottom in *Dream*. He recalls the tour's inauspicious start.

'We'd all arrived to rehearse in the auditorium that afternoon and were going through our paces with *Dream*. Well, at the end of the play there's a moment when Daniel, as Flute, has to jump on top of me. I don't know why, but at the last moment I suddenly sat up and he hadn't been expecting that. We got into some mess! It all went completely wrong and I ended up getting his elbow full force smack in my mouth. It was a pure accident, of course, but there was blood spurting everywhere and I was rushed off to hospital. Thinking of that night's performance just a few hours away, panic set in as you can imagine and poor Daniel was going around hardly knowing what to do with himself – he was so apologetic!'

Although Philip's injury had looked bad, the hospital managed to fix him up easily enough and they returned to the Leisure Centre only to discover that something else had gone wrong. Neither Daniel nor Philip were taking part in the morning play to be staged and so in their absence *Derek* had been getting a last minute run-through. 'The problem was,' explains Philip, 'that its writer, Edward Bond, had unexpectedly come along to see it. It's only a short play, about forty minutes long, and Jimmy Yuill and the others were about quarter of an hour under way when Bond suddenly shot to his feet announcing angrily, "I don't really think there's any point in going on with this," and then he proceeded to give all concerned a right dressing down and stern lecture on where exactly they were going wrong – not exactly a confidence builder! A great start this was to the beginning of the tour!'

Sheila Hancock's style of directing owed much to her avid, if newfound, enthusiasm for Shakespeare's works right then. 'She was very passionate about *Dream,*' confirms Philip, 'very excited about every aspect of it which made it an absolute pleasure working with her.' Daniel's Flute appears to have been, however, less a product of Hancock's, or anyone else's, skilful direction than a creation entirely of his own. 'He really relished this role,' reveals Philip, 'really enjoyed this play as a whole and I think it had a lot to do with the fact that, even by then, Daniel was used to playing the oh-so-serious characters and this was pure fun.' He goes on, 'It's a play within a play, of course, and for the entire tour he played it as if Flute was a chap who wasn't taking it very seriously at all, which meant he went about with a damned silly grin permanently plastered over his face. It worked though, and very well too. It certainly caught the audiences' attention night after night.'

Opening night is always a big thing for actors, normally relieved to get through it without either forgetting their lines or bumping into the stage props. Despite the potentially demoralising mishaps earlier in the day, although nerves were somewhat stretched, this particular opening night went well.

Philip recalls, 'I had some friends who'd come to see it and afterwards they told me it was good. Not quite as good as it should be, they had to go and add, of course, but that it would get better and it did.'

The other play, *Romeo and Juliet*, saw Daniel back into the kind of intense dramatic role with which he was better acquainted. Set in Verona, the two star-crossed lovers snared in a feud between their families, it lasted three and a half hours. Strikingly encased in sleek black leather, he captivated his audience with his passion for the hoydenish yet dewy-eyed Juliet. And while fighting two duels a night, for which he was coached by fight arranger Malcolm Ranson in the tricky art of realistic swordplay, he managed to display everything from adolescent impetuosity to growling maturity.

Almost exactly three years before, Philip Jackson had had reservations about Daniel in the role of Jimmy Porter. Now his opinion was very different. 'He made a very romantic, very dark and brooding Romeo,' he explains, 'a lot of actors do, but I thought Daniel was also distinguished in the role.' Night after night he fell in love, fought his duels and, mistakenly believing his beloved dead, took his own life, to the pleasure of audience after audience.

When the auditorium had emptied, however, a problem behind the scenes refused to go away. It concerned the relationship between Daniel and *Romeo and Juliet*'s director, John Caird. As Philip explains, 'The chemistry wasn't there. I guess the easiest way to describe it is that there was a personality clash between John Caird and Daniel. John had a very academic approach to directing this play which was, shall I say, less warm than Sheila's was with *Dream* and it just didn't work for Daniel at all. Sometimes it happens that way.'

In addition to the effect of this on Daniel's enjoyment of the tour, the schedule itself was also hard going. Philip continues, 'You'd be in a town for three nights, doing two venues a week then you'd move on. I had a car with me that time but most of the others, including Daniel, all piled into a bus, which can get pretty claustrophobic. Having said that, this kind of whistlestop touring has its good points too because you don't get fed up with any particular town.'

As the troupe criss-crossed their way around the country they felt that the tour, although tough at times, was worthwhile. It was certainly critically well received in virtually every area they touched upon, with universal praise heaped upon them in many regional reviews. However, the spectre of the RSC would from time to time appear in their midst to spoil the party.

Says Philip, 'We got the distinct feeling that, precisely because this was a regional tour and not a Stratford-based production, it was being looked on by the directors as second class and to be honest we didn't appreciate that. To us it was very important. Also, as we went about we used to get these "visitations" from RSC directors, who would appear unannounced and, certainly for me, conveyed a totally elitist attitude to all and sundry. All I know is, it always cast a right shadow over proceedings when they were there.' He goes on, 'They certainly didn't endear themselves to Daniel, that's for sure.'

To add to a growing list of sour notes, when the tour crossed the water to Ireland and hit the Whitla Hall in Belfast in mid-November, something else happened to upset Daniel. Philip recalls, 'Ian McKellen came to see us and afterwards made – how shall I put it – certain remarks. He didn't like Daniel's performances at all.' Hyper-sensitive on occasions to all forms of criticism anyway, Daniel could have done without McKellen's opinions on top of everything else.

Ireland itself holds other vivid memories for Philip Jackson, who, as the run progressed, was spending more and more time in Daniel's company. He reveals, 'By this time, we had started hiring cars during the day of the performance and going out and about, looking around the countryside. Well, I remember one afternoon Daniel was in my car with some other folk and we'd been driving for some time before we all converged on this particular spot, totally out of the blue. I can't recall where it was except that I thought we must be pretty close to the border. Anyway we all filed into this little pub and I clearly remember thinking how all of a sudden we all sounded so terribly English.'

He goes on, 'Danny is very well spoken, of course, and so were some of the others, and quite quickly I felt a horrible sensation come over me and I was thinking, God, we don't know where we are. We could be in Republican territory for all I know. I tried to ignore my unease, but it kept getting stronger in my head. Then I began to notice this old geezer perched on a stool at the bar and all he kept doing was slowly shaking his head at us and muttering in a low, very thick Irish voice, "Ah you're brave boys, *brave* boys." That was enough for me. I hurriedly cut in to the chatter round the table and said to the lads, "Hey, I think we ought to get the hell out of here and fast!"' Philip adds, 'Danny, I think, was the only one of us who wasn't in the least bit concerned. But then he was used to Ireland, I guess.'

For these reasons, and a few more besides, Daniel's experience with the Royal Shakespeare Company had not proved to be all that happy. When the tour was over at the end of January 1984, the idea was that everyone would stay on and play in Stratford for the long season there. This did not appeal to Daniel one bit. According to Philip, 'For a start Daniel wasn't in awe of the RSC at all, but in view of the personality clash with Caird there was just no way he wanted to stay on. Apart from anything else, to fit in with the RSC you have to be prepared to institutionalise yourself and Danny's like me in that respect – he wouldn't want that.'

Considering Daniel's terse pronouncements that he cannot abide the hypocrisy of people who suddenly clamour to shake his hand simply because he is now worth 'a bob or two', it's not hard to believe Philip's assertion that his friend had little patience with the snobbery and elitism existing in the RSC. It would seem that he was not averse to openly expressing this impatience either. But the Company still offered Daniel a year's contract at Stratford: an offer which he took perverse delight in turning down. Perverse in the sense that he was turning his back on regular paid work at a time when he had nothing lined up. It was a renegade streak which would surface again, more than once, in the future.

Making this stand may have momentarily given him a buzz of self-satisfaction, but it also bounced him back among the ranks of the unemployed again, this time for almost the entire first half of 1984. Determined to stay physically fit this time, Daniel immediately put his energies into running and cycling and joined the charity football team known as the Showbiz Eleven. This motley crew of celebrity soccer enthusiasts were more often than not found lumbering around the boggy football pitches of north London on a Sunday morning, training, rather than playing any matches.

During this period of professional inactivity he also moved house again. After quitting West Hampstead, he and Sarah, without Simon Dunstan, now took up residence, complete with roof garden, in trendy Queen's Gate in South Kensington. This locale proved handy when research began for his next project, one which was to bring him back to the bosom of the BBC. This was the five-part serial *My Brother Jonathan*, to be produced by Joe Waters and directed by Anthony Garner.

Based on the book by Francis Brett Young, the story had already been dealt with in a 1947 black and white film starring Dulcie Gray and Michael Benison. It follows the life of Jonathan Bakers, a small-town doctor working amidst abject poverty in the slums of the Black Country who has ambitions to become a famous surgeon. Daniel starred in the leading role. Years later the options open to him to research a role would be far greater, but for now he had to make do with reading as much as he could. His lone figure, lost in study, became a familiar sight around the public lending libraries of South Ken. Filming the serial would keep him busy from June through to August, for transmission the following autumn.

Then, come November, Daniel reprised his role of the Transylvanian Count Dracula in the play written by Christopher Bond, and again he sported his blond spiky hairstyle. This time the play was directed by Bond himself and performed at the Half Moon Theatre in London's Mile End Road. The cast also included the Scots actor Peter Capaldi, Bob Mason, Judy Holt and Richard Ireson. It was a bloodthirsty prelude to the festive season for a man hungry for success.

By the end of 1984 many fellow actors and directors, as well as others familiar with his work, were already unanimous in their praise for Daniel's strong physical presence, intelligence and ability. Although he had by now proved himself on television, his triumph, particularly in *Another Country*, led some to believe that Day-Lewis was headed for an impressive stage career. Daniel himself, though, had other ideas.

CHAPTER FOUR

YOB FOR THE JOB

'The jewel in the jacksee of south London.'

JOHNNY, *MY BEAUTIFUL LAUNDRETTE*

The first film role that Daniel really desperately wanted to secure was that of a gay south London punk called Johnny in Hanif Kureishi's drama *My Beautiful Laundrette*. The modestly budgeted £600,000 film was to be made by Working Title Films in co-operation with Channel 4 Television. It was produced by Tim Bevan and Sara Radclyffe and directed by Stephen Frears, whose future films would include *Danielgerous Liaisons*.

For *My Beautiful Laundrette*, Frears had chosen the familiar face and voice of Saeed Jaffrey for top billing, joined by Roshan Seth, Shirley Anne Field and Gordon Warnecke. The latter would play Omar, an attractive young Pakistani. Johnny, previously his school friend, would become his business partner and eventually his lover. The six-week shoot was due to begin on 25 February 1985 in three London locations – Stockwell, Vauxhall and Kingston.

When Daniel got wind of the part of Johnny at the end of 1984, he was immediately fired up to get it. Exactly what it was about the character that so attracted him is not entirely clear. Portraying the working-class tough had given him problems in the past in John Osborne's *Look Back in Anger.* Although Jimmy Porter and Hanif Kureishi's Johnny were hardly comparable characters, perhaps he saw a similar challenge in taking on the role of a young south London lad, outwardly rough and unattractive but in private tender, loving and a homosexual. At any rate he was determined to convince the director that he was the right yob for the job.

Frears was already acquainted with Daniel's track record on stage and television and was certainly prepared to consider him. Nor were they strangers to each other. A few years before, the two had met when Stephen was auditioning for an actor to take on the role of the late playwright Joe Orton. In August 1967 Orton's murder made headline news after he was beaten to death by former lover Kenneth Halliwell. The film was to be *Prick Up Your Ears*, written by Alan Bennett, and Daniel had been one of the actors chasing the Orton role. Unfortunately, as had happened more than once in the past, he seems to have adopted the wrong strategy for his audition by dressing like a hooligan and talking with a pronounced working-class accent. Frears was not in the least impressed and in the end cast Gary Oldman instead.

This time Daniel was up against Oldman again for the part of Johnny, as well as having Kenneth Branagh and Tim Roth in the running. It was hot competition and he grew more and more feverish to win through. But, once more, the all-important first impression he made on Frears appears not to have been particularly encouraging. At the time Daniel was appearing as Dracula at the Half Moon Theatre, which meant he came before the director complete with his blond crew cut. This prompted Stephen, who vividly remembered his last outrageous appearance, to remark with some acerbity on Daniel's preoccupation with weird hairstyles. It was not a promising start.

On top of that, Daniel remembered a barbed remark made when he had last appeared before Frears about him being the Poet Laureate's son. Having lived with this 'handicap' long enough, he now resolved to somehow prove to the director that he could be a thoroughly nasty piece of work if he put his mind to it, thereby, he hoped, convincing the reluctant Frears that he could pull off the National Front thug required for *Laundrette*.

To achieve this, he began bombarding Stephen with letters filled with colourful threats. Years later a legend would grow up that Daniel finally threatened to break Stephen Frears's legs if he did not give him the part. Whether he actually did or not, Frears caved in on the grounds that, if he was prepared to go to such lengths, then he deserved the part for that reason if nothing else. The director would frequently say of actors, 'A good part – it's like sex to them. They can smell it,' and in this case Daniel's hawklike nose had not let him down, for the role of Johnny in *My Beautiful Laundrette* was to become his film breakthrough.

The ninety-seven-minute film is both funny and violent in parts. Its variety of themes include the male–female inequality in Indian culture, the strength of family ties and the divisive greed of Thatcher's Britain as well as thugs, drugs and racism. This last is seen from both sides as Johnny is white working-class, and for a time ran with fascist groups. This later catches up with him when, in a reversal of roles, he experiences prejudice from Omar, whose success ultimately lends him the upper hand.

In the past, Daniel's ability to get under the skin of his

character to an impressive degree had often been recognised and remarked upon, especially by his director or co-star at the time. But this performance was the first of the startling series of total character immersions for which he would become famous.

Yet, the part itself, though a prominent one, was, all the same, a supporting role. The film's plot revolves around Omar (Gordon Warnecke making his movie debut), who goes into business with the help of his uncle Nasser, played by Saeed Jaffrey. Nasser has given Omar the job of managing a rundown laundrette called Churchills in a poor district of the city – art director Hugo Luczyc-Wyhowski converted a shoe shop at 11 Wilcox Road in south-east London at a cost of £10,000 for the shoot. With Johnny as the labourer, Omar sets out to transform it into a luxury establishment, renamed Powders in neon lights. There are washing machines which actually work, plush sofas strewn with *Vogue* magazines and music floating gently in the background – a veritable palace.

Daniel's portrayal is a revelation from the tips of his blond-streaked hair to the heels of his brown bovver boots. Marking a complete departure from the privileged Englishman, the streetwise Londoner has firmly arrived. The raw Cockney accent is entirely believable; it also never falters and he carries his fascist attire well. He has surprisingly little dialogue and that almost always delivered in words strictly of one syllable, yet he makes a strong impact on the film. Johnny is trying to straighten out and regularly warns those who think he will cave someone's head in just for the asking that he 'doesn't do no rough stuff, no more'.

Although Daniel allows his bony hips to suggestively give the odd swagger, he never resorts to overdoing any mannerisms intended to portray homosexuality. Yet the fact that Johnny is gay is communicated both effortlessly and instantly. At the same time, Daniel occasionally gives more than a hint of being very capable indeed if motivated, which produces a curiously unsettling, certainly engrossing, cocktail.

The gay love scenes between Johnny and Omar broke new ground for mainstream cinema, with frank close-ups showing Daniel and Gordon Warnecke engaged in a graphically deep and prolonged French kiss. It seems that after shooting these testing scenes both Daniel and Gordon promptly rifled packets of extra-strong mouth fresheners. Individually, both were at conspicuous pains to strut about re-asserting their true masculinity. Clearly conscious on set of the peculiar professional demands on him, at the same time Daniel was completely clueless that he was partaking in something so potentially controversial. The love scenes themselves are cleverly filmed and also extremely tender. One scene in particular, had it been a female whose clothes Daniel was slowly peeling away, would have been considered highly romantic, if not instantly dubbed 'steamy stuff'. Daniel may have had to resort to drastic measures to ensure that Frears cast him as Johnny but, in every sense, he earned the part which was to make his name.

The filming took roughly seven weeks at various London locations, and cameos from some of the outdoor night shoots remain in Daniel's mind to this day. For Daniel there can be little substitute for location work. In contrast to even the most authentic-looking studio set, working in real surroundings gives him a feeling of involvement with the place which helps him to imagine his role all the more vividly.

'Studios,' he has said, 'don't have ghosts.' And it is precisely ghosts, atmosphere, a heightened awareness of the past as well as of the present that he looks for most. Even if the forces he feels counteract what he is trying to achieve, the invisible energy and mental stimulation required to combat this creates a demon with which he enjoys wrestling to bring it under control. One scene for *Laundrette*, in which Johnny and Omar meet for the first time since school, shot under Vauxhall Bridge in the early hours of an overcast drizzly morning, proved to be a moment when it all came together.

At this point Daniel was still staying at his Queen's Gate flat. Unknown to him, a near neighbour was the film's star, Saeed Jaffrey, to whom Daniel carried a message from his mother on the first day of filming. Says Saeed, 'I first met Daniel when we were shooting *My Beautiful Laundrette*. He had the punk hair, complete with a centre blond streak like a badger, and he absolutely looked the part, but the only thing was he spoke with such a public school accent.' He goes on, 'About the first thing he said to me was that his mother sent her love and at first I didn't understand, but then I discovered that his mother was Jill Balcon, the radio actress. She and I had worked often together in the past. When I realised he was Jill's son, this made me feel even closer to Daniel.'

The schedule itself was hard work, with Stephen Frears, as Saeed calls it, 'keeping the motors running'. Frears superbly handled a script fertile in opportunities for a host of fine performances. There are excellent lines for everyone, which was invigorating for the entire cast, but credit for the film's overall success appears to sit foursquare on Frears's shoulders. Saeed explains, 'He's what I call a "gardener" director in that he chooses the plant or flower and, once planted, he lets it grow. He's not restrictive at all. If you like, he gives the plant the right amount of love, attention, water and sun it needs and the result is a spontaneous blossoming on screen.' Of Daniel's work on the film, Saeed firmly joins the growing ranks of those who remark on the absolute truth he brings to each role, adding, 'And the truth is so very intense and beautifully observed that it is played to a magnetic degree. He also has an incredible ear for accents.'

It was a role so far removed from his real self – the sort of role which always seems to attract Daniel most – that even more than before he found it necessary to isolate himself during the times when he was not filming. His desire to keep himself separate was not going unnoticed. 'Yes, it was apparent then,' agrees Jaffrey, 'and we entirely respected his desire for privacy. He needed to conserve his energy, to concentrate one hundred per cent on his role.'

As it happened, off-screen behaviour was in general different from the norm during the making of this film, as Saeed explains. 'Well, it was unusual in that mostly when work was over, when normally everyone would gather in a restaurant or pub, this time we didn't. We all went home. I think we *all* found it necessary to conserve our energy this time.'

It was to be *My Beautiful Laundrette* which would send Daniel's stock soaring, paving the way towards his future fame. At the same time the inevitable myths began to gather around him. Handles such as 'Day-Lewis the reluctant star' would mushroom in due course and often date back to his film break in *Laundrette*. According to Hanif Kureishi, his friend was forever saying he wanted to go back to making furniture and that there were frequently 'great depressions'. And Daniel has himself talked of work on this film as having been rewarding, but in the same breath called it agonising. Interestingly, though, a contradiction has emerged. Saeed Jaffrey, with whom Daniel had struck up a warm friendship, distinctly remembers a very different scenario.

He says, 'There was one day when we were filming the party scene. It was in a house in south London which was supposed to be my house in the film, and during a break there was a bunch of us standing around and I started talking about my time at the Actors Studio in New York, where I trained alongside Jon Voigt. We were talking about a lot of things, then I started telling Daniel and the others about the time I met Marilyn Monroe. She was introduced then, of course, as Mrs Miller and she clearly appreciated the Eastern courtesy of being addressed as a married woman because, she said, some people had often been particularly discourteous to her.'

He continues, 'Anyway, on Marilyn's skin, when you saw her close up, there was a wonderful kind of faint golden-coloured fluff and, when she responded to something which appealed to her, this fluff would rise, just lift gently. It was a rare and beautiful sight. Natural, too, and whenever it happened anyone looking at her couldn't help but stare. Well, I was trying to explain this, and Daniel was listening avidly to every word, when I looked round and by chance caught a look on his face which I will never ever forget. It was in his eyes and it said, "Lovely story. Some day people will talk about me like that." Of course, it has come true, but I don't mean that it was in an egotistical way at all. It was a look I would describe more of destiny, of knowing his own destiny.' Far from a desire to fight shy of reaching the heady heights of the business then, Daniel had his sights very much set on great things.

When filming finished in mid-April no one really realised that *My Beautiful Laundrette* would be heading for much better things. Originally intended as a made-for-television film, it took everyone by surprise when at that year's Edinburgh Film Festival it was enthusiastically received by the critics. Such was the acclaim, in fact, that it was decided to put its television release on hold and to offer it instead for cinema pick-up.

'It was discovered by all the critics there,' confirms Saeed.

'Daniel, Stephen Frears and myself were at the festival and we had a special time. I'm not talking wild drinking sessions or anything like that. It was a time of friendship, communicating. We found we liked the same things, like art. I asked Daniel afterwards what he was going to do with himself and he said he was going to go somewhere and paint to relax.'

While at the festival, Daniel met up with director John Schlesinger who had cast him sixteen years before in his very first film appearance. The boy vandal seemed to have matured into the morose adult thug with alarming ease.

But, as well as being reintroduced to old acquaintances, Daniel also made new friends while making *Laundrette*. One of those was actor Roshan Seth. Like Saeed, Roshan had appeared in *Gandhi* in which Daniel had also had a small role. But the difference in the importance of their casting meant that their orbits had not collided in 1981. As Omar's father, Papa, who remains mostly in bed, the opportunity for Roshan and Daniel to actually play opposite each other was limited to one scene.

This was at Powders' grand opening. Papa, muddled in his mind, mistakes the time and turns up when practically everyone, including his son, has gone. Johnny is still there clearing up. It is the first time Papa has met Johnny since he witnessed him taking part in a hideous National Front rally years before. Johnny's contrition and unease in the presence of a remarkably dignified and intelligent man who had known him since childhood was perhaps a small moment, but it was also one of the most telling in the film. It is one of those screen moments when Daniel conveys perfectly a deep and unreserved remorse, without uttering a single word.

For Roshan it was a special moment in reality too. He says, 'That single scene in the laundrette between Papa and Johnny was sufficient time for me to know that his spirit had touched mine. He looked into my eyes and I looked into his and we knew that a connection had been made that neither of us was capable of speaking about.' He adds, 'I ran into Daniel many years later. I cannot now remember the occasion but again he knew that I knew, and I knew that he did. It's hard to explain, but perhaps this is the essence – we smiled when we met.'

My Beautiful Laundrette, essentially an art-house film, attracted award nominations in both Britain and America, where it grossed in excess of $5 million at the box office. Hanif Kureishi unexpectedly found himself in the running for an Academy Award for Best Original Screenplay, as he did in the BAFTA awards, and Saeed Jaffrey secured the film's other BAFTA nomination that year for the Best Supporting Actor. Saeed lost out to the late Denholm Elliott for his riveting performance as the world-weary journalist in David Drury's political thriller *Defence of the Realm*, but he has this to say, 'Daniel was sitting with me at my table during the ceremony that night and I couldn't help feeling that he should have been nominated too.'

If Daniel did manage to snatch time after filming to disappear to some idyllic spot armed with paints and canvas, it would not have been for long, because shooting was about to begin on his next project – a Merchant Ivory film, *A Room with a View*. The character whom Daniel wanted to play in this adaptation of the E.M. Forster novel was Cecil Vyse. Saeed Jaffrey remembers when Daniel went to see the director.

'It was during the time we were filming *Laundrette* that Daniel went to see James Ivory. He was after the part of Cecil and yet he went dressed as Johnny – the full outfit. I wasn't there myself, but I know both James and Ismail Merchant and, having been told how the meeting went, I quite believe it.' He reveals, 'The story goes that James took one look at Daniel as this punk with streaked hair and said in his very American twang, "Oh yeah, Daniel, but you know you don't look the part, huh? I'm looking for an aristocrat here, y'know?" and Daniel replied in a really plummy English accent, "Listen to my speech. Is it not aristocratic?" Adding, when Ivory hesitated, "Trust me. I *shall* be that part!"' It had to have been his easiest audition to date because it worked and he was cast as the bloodless, almost sexless, Cecil Vyse.

The film itself was to be a lush screen adaptation of the book. By 1985 Merchant Ivory Productions had already had the project under consideration for three years. Initially the National Film Development Fund had provided the finance – some £15,000 – for Ruth Prawer Jhabvala to write the screenplay, which she did, but it was then sidelined so that they could concentrate on the production of the period drama *The Bostonians*, starring Christopher Reeve and Vanessa Redgrave. It was on the back of *The Bostonians'* success in America that the *A Room with a View* project got under way.

It was to be the first Merchant Ivory feature filmed in the UK: a six-way co-production with Merchant Ivory, the NFFC, Channel Four, Goldcrest, Curzon Films and Cinecom. Raising the necessary finance had not been easy. Budgeted at $3.5 million, it was the most expensive collaboration to date between producer Ismail Merchant and James Ivory. In fact, production had actually begun before the vital financial arrangements were finalised at the Cannes Film Festival: the only place where all the investors could find the time in their busy schedules to meet.

Based on Forster's 1908 comedy of manners, the film deals with Edwardian upper-class behaviour at home and abroad. The strong cast includes Helena Bonham Carter, Maggie

Smith, Judi Dench, Simon Callow and Denholm Elliott. Daniel's character, Cecil Vyse, is the fiancé of Miss Lucy Honeychurch, played by Helena. He is not the film's hero – the role of George Emerson would be taken by Julian Sands, who, with the Ronald Joffe film *The Killing Fields* under his belt, was fresh from completing Mel Brooks's *The Doctor and the Devils*.

The fact that Daniel did not want the romantic lead, and indeed infinitely preferred the role of Vyse, was something that the director found frankly fascinating. Daniel's reason, he told Ivory, was that Vyse was 'a man whose skin I could occupy in some of my worst nightmares'. Having read the novel, Daniel was drawn to Cecil almost entirely because he appeared to be someone who spends his life effortlessly, but unintentionally, alienating others. It would have been easy to portray him as a one-dimensional prat, but Daniel detected something deeper and the challenge of infiltrating this man's mind held a peculiar fascination for him.

The great-grand-daughter of the former Liberal Prime Minister Herbert Asquith, Helena Bonham Carter, then eighteen, had starred in the Trevor Nunn film *Lady Jane*, based on the life and brief reign of the teenage British queen. Helena is an actress whose beauty – she was named the Face of the Eighties by both *Vogue* and *Tatler* magazines – seems to belong to another age. She appears almost exclusively in period films, to the extent that no Merchant Ivory movie now feels complete without her.

In *A Room with a View* she is the female lead – a well-off young lady travelling through Italy accompanied by Charlotte Bartlett, her infuriatingly fusspot chaperone, impeccably played by Maggie Smith. In the Pensione Bertolini in Florence their rooms disappoint them by not having the expected view on the Arno. Two other guests, a father and son, offer to swap their accommodation, which has splendid views, for the ladies' rooms – they are George Emerson and his slightly seedy but well-meaning father (Denholm Elliott).

Worry over his son's melancholic behaviour leads Emerson senior to encourage Lucy to take an interest in George. Julian Sands called Forster's George Emerson 'not a particularly well-drawn character', and during shooting expressed the desire to ensure that he did not look like the conventional juvenile hero. In fact, young Emerson seems a bit of an oddball, but Lucy finds herself inexplicably drawn to him and they end up in a brief but passionate clinch in the middle of a cornfield.

The shooting schedule lasted roughly ten weeks, four of which were spent in the Tuscan countryside around Florence, before the production moved to the Kent countryside in England. All along it was dogged with bad weather which delayed filming and at times put the schedule back by several days. It is in the second half of the film, set in the fictitious English village community of Summer Street, that Cecil makes his entrance. Perching precariously with Lucy on a garden seat in the grounds of the Honeychurch home, he is proposing marriage to her. The pair are watched from inside the house by Lucy's mother (Rosemary Leach) and her less than impressed brother Freddy, played by Rupert Graves.

It was a long time since two consecutive performances by one actor had seen such startlingly opposite characterisations as the surly, streetwise Johnny and the preening, prissy Cecil Vyse. They established beyond doubt Daniel's enormous versatility and the unique depths of his strengthening abilities. Acclaimed actor Simon Callow, co-star of Mike Newell's romantic comedy *Four Weddings and a Funeral*, agrees. 'I stand by the belief that Daniel is the nearest we have today to

Charles Laughton. There is in Daniel, equally, this need to break himself down completely and recreate himself as the character required for the particular film, play or whatever. It's a facility in Method acting which can be a glory and also a burden. One wonders if it's always the right way, but every actor is different and what he needs to do to achieve his goal is equally different.'

As Charles Laughton's biographer, Simon is an authority on the late actor. He continues, 'It was Daniel's performance in *My Beautiful Laundrette*, rather than in *A Room with a View*, that brought home the comparison to Laughton for me. According to what Daniel told me, he based his portrayal of Johnny on a friend of his at a tough school he once went to. He certainly had a very strong idea of how he was going to play him and it was a lovely piece of acting – a triumph. The best performance by an English actor since the war, I would say.'

As to why Daniel had preferred the role of the repressed aesthete to that of George Emerson, Simon offers this insight: 'Well, it is interesting that he opted for Cecil. But, you know, to get hold of a romantic lead, really the essence of it and to get it right, it can be very rewarding but it is also surprisingly hard to do and to pull off, and I think perhaps Daniel was shy of it at that moment in his career.'

The full impact of Cecil does not hit home until, having secured Lucy's acceptance, he makes his triumphant entrance through the French windows into the drawing room to tell her mother and brother the glad tidings. Richard Mayne likens Daniel's Cecil in looks to a clean-shaven Lytton Strachey, the intellectual Victorian biographer and critic. With his jet black hair slicked close to his scalp, sporting a pince-nez and pencil moustache, his ludicrously exaggerated accent makes everyone else, even the genteel Bonham Carter, sound dead common.

Indeed, as Daniel struts his way through the film on his stork-like legs, his eyebrows continually flexing in unison with the curl of his simpering lips, he presents a figure of almost fascinating horror.

Forster believed Vyse to be a man trapped by his intellectual complexity and blind to what real life had to offer, yet never without grace-saving dignity. The Cecil that Daniel put together for the film certainly embodied the author's intent in spirit, but in practice he appears to have created a creature, not for the first time, entirely of his own imagining.

Simon Callow says, 'The first time we came face to face in Kent, Daniel was in costume and his Cecil was certainly not at all what I expected. It's not really the Cecil as in the book. Daniel had evolved not just a physical look but an internal performance as well, which is not all that usual on a film set. Personally I think it was a brilliant performance but I have to say I think it was assumed, put on, as opposed to his other roles.' He goes on, 'What I mean is, it was more a theatrical manifestation – very impressive and striking, but I can remember wondering whether James Ivory had colluded with Daniel on this and I don't think that that was the case. I think it was entirely Daniel's manifestation and everyone just accepted it.'

Cecil Vyse is often mistakenly thought of as being the vicar in the film. In fact, that role belonged to Simon, who played the good-hearted Reverend Arthur Beebe. It is he who unwittingly gives the first hint to Cecil that Lucy could be a girl of hidden passion. Certainly Cecil was a stranger to the word. He has a ring on her finger and the official engagement party in full swing before, strolling with her to a nearby wood, he shyly asks permission to kiss her. She agrees, but he forgets his pince-nez, which promptly squashes up between their faces as he tentatively presses his pursed lips to hers. Mortified, he rapidly returns to maintaining a decent distance from his fiancée. To spare him any further embarrassment, Lucy walks away. She cannot help but compare Cecil's clumsy effort with the memory of a wild warm assault from George Emerson.

As Fate has it, though, the Emersons – through Cecil's unwitting interference – rent a cottage in Summer Street, much to Lucy's initial dismay. Soon, unfortunate comparisons become all too obvious between the romantic, often dishevelled George and the immaculate and precise Cecil. Every insufferable utterance from Cecil's mouth systematically undermines Lucy's confidence in her decision to become Mrs Vyse.

In the end she summons up the courage to break off their engagement, telling Cecil when goaded that he is incapable of real love. Incredibly irritating though Vyse has proved himself to be, Daniel injects into the character a touching inadequacy which reaches out at such moments as his botched kiss, and now again at being jilted. He displays the struggling confusion of a man floundering to accept his fate while at last sensing where he has gone wrong. It is poignant that it is only at the moment when he is losing Lucy that Cecil wakes up to his faults. But it is too late to save their relationship – a fact he accepts with such painful dignity that it is not only Lucy who is left feeling like a criminal.

Daniel is not out to draw attention to himself and yet he is very hard to ignore. When he read both the book and the script he felt a strong sense of compassion for the character, recognising in Vyse all the unattractive qualities that most people would hate to believe themselves capable of possessing. What he set out to do was to convey that compassion to his audience, drawing forth a tangible sympathy for a character all too easy to dismiss as a spineless wimp.

Watching Daniel work held a few surprises for Simon Callow. By now his intensity was deepening, his need to stay within the confines of his character even greater. That he was already in costume the first moment Simon clapped eyes on him seems significant. Says Simon, 'Basically, if it is something that a person needs to do, then that's that. It can be rewarding to be so intensely lost in a role, assuming that role one hundred per cent, but you can also perhaps lose the objective sense of the character and so perhaps lose out in bringing some new and valuable raw material to it.'

He continues, 'Listening to Daniel, he is as fiercely intense as his reputation claims, but what many people don't know is that he is also very funny and will come out with great gales of clapping laughter too. Of course, he goes into such detail, studies things, and it was really quite fascinating to watch first hand. He would take enormous care over the most minute of things, for example, his scene swatting away some bees outside in the garden. The amount of work he put into that simple scene, when he was only in the background, was incredible. Most actors don't work that way.'

He goes on, 'But, getting back to his intensity, I did discover something which I found very interesting. I came across Daniel reading Kafka because he was about to do the Alan Bennett play and I couldn't help but notice how incredibly slowly he was reading. Daniel told me, "Well, you know, I don't read many books because I'm dyslexic." Therefore, when Daniel reads he concentrates, as I saw, furiously and knows every word, every nuance in the book – taking every single thing in. And inwardly I immediately wondered just what effect this had on his acting. I firmly believe that it has a very direct bearing on the way he acts. He encounters the character in such depth and then translates that into what he does with it. That's not to say he always gets it right and I'm sure Daniel would be the first to agree with that, but it is completely genuine, which is all anyone can ever hope for. He doesn't do anything lightly and perhaps, occasionally, he should.'

A Room with a View was not the first time Simon had met Daniel – that happened years before at the BBC's Broadcasting House in London when Daniel, then still a drama student, was with his mother. Their paths had fleetingly crossed in the intervening time, but it was in Kent in 1985 that they really got to know each other. Says Simon, 'The first thing that struck me, apart from Daniel being already in Cecil Vyse's costume, and I think it's what strikes anyone who meets him, is his powerful presence. It's partly physical, yes – he's tall, dark and good looking, but it's more an inner life that he exudes that's complicated and intense.'

Although he had already gained a reputation for isolating himself during breaks in filming, while shooting *A Room with a View*, Daniel would make it his business to seek Simon out. Says his friend, 'One day I was listening on my Walkman to some music and Daniel came up and sat down beside me on the bench and pulling one headphone away from my ear asked, "What're you listening to?" I told him, "Bartók." His face immediately clouded over and he demanded, "How can you? How *can* you like Bartók?! It's rotten music, disgusting music!" and he went on and on about it. He was like a man possessed and I thought, My goodness, how very refreshing to be so passionate about a string quartet! He left the subject alone after that, but for some reason his anti-Bartók attitude has stayed with me. I found myself wondering later if it was something spilled over from Cecil, but I don't think so.'

By the time the six weeks filming in Kent was over for Daniel, it was almost time to concentrate on his return to working with the BBC. At this point he had completed two films, unaware that they would both attract high acclaim, and his performances in particular would have a profound effect on audiences both in Britain and the States and, therefore, on his career. For the moment he was just happy to have another project lined up to get his teeth into. In July he found himself heading north to Bradford, ready to start shooting a short seventy-five-minute film for the BBC's Screen Two season, scheduled for transmission in February 1986.

The film was *The Insurance Man*, based on one of two plays written by renowned playwright Alan Bennett about the life of the novelist Doctor Franz Kafka. The play's title comes from the fact that Kafka, who first studied law, was an executive in The Workers Accident Insurance Institute in Poric Street, Prague at the turn of the century. Directed by Richard Eyre and produced by Innes Lloyd with whom Daniel had previously worked on *How Many Miles to Babylon?*, its cast included Trevor Peacock and Robert Hines, who play the central character Franz as an old and young man respectively. Alan MacNaughtan – another connection from *Babylon* – Toby Salaman and Tony Haygarth also appeared. Daniel played Kafka in middle life.

Filming began on Tuesday, 9 July 1985, with Alan Bennett in attendance for the entire month. Bradford proved an ideal location because of the well-preserved nineteenth-century warehouses still standing in a neighbourhood known locally as Little Germany – a throwback to the days when the area was alive with German merchant traders. On the first day of filming in Manningham Lane, a nearby scorched and blackened gate bore tragic witness to an horrific blaze which had swept through one stand at Bradford's football ground only weeks before.

The film begins in 1945 to the trump of mortar fire and

bombs blitzing Prague. Franz (Trevor Peacock) visits his doctor (Alan MacNaughtan) to receive some X-ray results. The doctor is reluctant to reveal the bad news about Franz's diseased lungs and instead begins asking probing questions about his work history. In flashback the story reverts to 1910 and so Daniel appears.

He plays Kafka as an extremely busy and conscientious inspector who speaks out passionately on behalf of all sufferers. With his winning personality, he displays great charm and sympathy. Daniel had been studying for this role, which would bring him warm critical praise, for months – as far back as during filming for *A Room with a View*, when Simon Callow had happened upon him slowly, carefully digesting the book on Kafka. His absorption by now, however, had deepened dramatically. It seems that it was during this particular production that onlookers really first noticed that Daniel had taken to remaining in character even when the cameras had stopped rolling.

In the diary he kept during the filming of *The Insurance Man*, Alan Bennett describes seeing Daniel walking along bent forward slightly and holding his neck at an awkward angle. According to Bennett, such a gait was perfect for the role as Kafka and matched the man's physical description to a T. The significant point was that this was off set at night, when filming was long over for the day.

After two weeks, shooting switched to Liverpool, this time making use of St George's Hall. This massive building built on the plateau in the middle of the city was a common rallying point for protest marches. It was a location Daniel would revisit some years later in one of his most powerful films, *In the Name of the Father*. By that time his practice of staying in character would be legendary.

The spell in Liverpool saw the filming schedule to its end. It was followed by a return to London and to his girlfriend Sarah Campbell. In completing *The Insurance Man*, he effectively ended his work in television. Although he had chalked up his share of successes in this field and had enjoyed working with some of his directors and co-stars, the medium itself never seemed likely to hold on to him. Even the mechanics of working on the small screen at times had aggravated him. He disliked the way what he has called the 'Dalek'-type cameras would glide around him, annoyingly containing him in one spot with barely an inch of leeway for movement.

The restrictions this placed on his freedom of expression often interfered with his creative process. The world of film on the other hand represented a wider, fuller and more liberating environment and by the end of 1985 it was towards this that he was determined to head.

CHAPTER FIVE

SEX APPEAL

'Life's so light.'

TOMAS, *THE UNBEARABLE LIGHTNESS OF BEING*

One intriguing trait of Daniel's is his willingness – sometimes determination – to lose himself in the professional wilderness of a thoroughly forgettable film. One such film is *Nanou*, an Anglo-French co-production shot entirely on location, mainly in the industrial area of Lorraine in France. The project had been on the go for three years and involved producer Simon Perry whose most recent success had been the Michael Radford film *Nineteen Eighty Four* with John Hurt and Richard Burton. Before that, Perry had chalked up the warmly received *Another Time, Another Place*, the powerful wartime romance about Italian prisoners of war in Scotland penned by one of Scotland's most famous authors, Jessie Kesson.

Regardless of other options open to him after the Orwell movie, Simon had committed himself to working on *Nanou* with newcomer Conny Templeman, just as soon as her time was up at the National Film School. Marking Templeman's debut as a feature-film screenwriter and director, this low-budget film starred French actor Jean-Philippe Ecoffey and a young Imogen Stubbs, who had been chosen from a casting shortlist of over a hundred girls.

It is a dismal offering. Nanou, the heroine, is played by Stubbs. She is an English student travelling through France when she meets a Frenchman called Luc (Ecoffey) on a train. On impulse she decides to throw in her lot with him and embarks on a tense, almost masochistic, relationship. On a flying visit to their daughter, her parents mention an old flame, Max, urging her to return home to England to see him. As Luc dominates Nanou in all things, he prefers that she invite Max to France instead, and she intends to, but before she has the chance, he arrives out of the blue.

As Max, Daniel enters the film halfway through. Nanou returns to the crummy flat and finds him sitting at the top of the staircase, with his head in a newspaper. Well-bred and elegant, every inch the cultured Englishman, he is a total contrast to the moody, scruffy and inarticulate Luc. The Frenchman had falsely given Nanou's parents the impression that their daughter and he were engaged to be married. Clearly unhappy at the thought, they have sent Max on a mission to try to lure Nanou home. Why she does not go with him with indecent alacrity is a complete mystery.

Daniel doesn't have a lot to do in this slow-moving tale except look tall, dark and handsome. He is also scarcely on screen for ten minutes, yet his arrival lights up an otherwise third-rate film. Max was Daniel's third outing in a supporting role and one not widely seen. This was a marked contrast to the startling attention he was about to receive in America.

On 7 March 1986 in New York *My Beautiful Laundrette* and

A Room with a View opened simultaneously in the States. To US audiences, Daniel's was considered to be the most striking star debut for many years. Individually, his parts were strictly speaking supporting roles, although both were masterly performances in their own right. But it was the timing – the fact that, at exactly the same moment, Daniel was seen in such disparate roles – that made such an impact. People scratched their heads in sheer disbelief that the gaunt gay punk and the absurdly correct Edwardian gentleman were flawlessly portrayed by one and the same guy. Not yet thirty, Day-Lewis – a name which to date hadn't meant a light at America's box office – was promptly hailed 'a chameleon' and 'the most accomplished leading man to have emerged in years', creating a universal buzz of excitement.

A Room with a View went on to win four BAFTA awards, including that of Best Film and Best Supporting Actress, out of a total of thirteen nominations and three Oscars out of eight nominations, guaranteeing its surprising success at the box office. However, it was the sudden explosion of Day-Lewis adulation which bewildered the actor himself. More than that, it also alarmed him. Far from wallowing in the sea of praise washing over him for his acting prowess, Daniel, by now back in London, determinedly blamed it all on an accident of timing. He firmly believed that the hype was in danger of earning him a reputation he was not quite ready at that point to live up to.

His wariness of being hoisted, unprepared, on top of a pedestal of the media's making, only perhaps to be toppled just as quickly, made him shy away from accepting the plaudits. In an attempt to deflate the situation, he admitted with blunt honesty that he had acted badly in the past, but that no one had taken the slightest notice at the time because he was not a star. It was equally likely, he maintained, that sometime he would act badly again once more. The pressures of instant stardom made him worry that, if he did fall on his face in the future, it would now be with all eyes upon him.

Such anxieties were, however, groundless, at least in the immediate future. For the day after those New York premières marked a distinguished return to the theatre for Daniel – this time in a National Theatre Company production at the Cottesloe Theatre in London. *Futurists*, written by Dusty Hughes and directed by Richard Eyre, previewed from 8 March 1986 and opened just over a week later, running in repertory until mid-June.

It was a new play, set during the 1917 Bolshevik revolution in Russia and the ensuing civil war. Daniel's character was the shaven-headed Volodya Mayakovsky. The cast included David Calder, Clare Higgins, Julian Fellowes, Roger Lloyd Pack, Fred Pearson and Jack Shepherd. Eyre, who had directed Daniel the previous summer in the BBC's *The Insurance Man* – which had been screened nationally in Britain at the end of February – dubbed him 'obsessional'. He observed that in his opinion Daniel is more comfortable in film work than on the stage. He may have been right. But to Daniel the distinction is not quite so clear cut.

Certainly, working on location appeals most strongly to him because of the lack of confinement that it offers, yet he also believes that the theatre provides him with the freedom to create his own reality. At any rate, his return after three years to the London stage as the crazy-looking, snarling Mayakovsky would be very well received. The reaction would be better even than the memorable reception his Guy Bennett performance had enjoyed in *Another Country*. His friend, director Ronald Wilson, calls it: 'An extraordinary performance. The character bore almost no relation to anything Daniel had previously done, except funnily enough it reminded me in a small way of his Dracula, for heaven's sake.'

Taking rehearsals into account, Daniel was engaged on *Futurists* for some six months. The play itself was a big hit, running to a full house all the way through. For the cast there was what Julian Fellowes describes as 'an unusual egalitarian spirit' which was extremely healthy. Julian played Tumin, in whose café everyone would meet. He says, 'It was an extremely agreeable experience all round. The most unusual thing was that there was a cast of, I think, about twenty people and about twelve of those were as leading parts. I mean, you had about a dozen actors with quite a lot to do, therefore there was no real main role as such, with the others subordinate to that, which is very unusual. It was great.'

It was Julian's first time working at the National and the first time he and Daniel had met. He says, 'The interesting thing is that this Day-Lewis phenomenon which has sprung up in the nineties, defining him as some sort of strange withdrawn and uncommunicative being, is not at all how I, personally speaking, found him. On the contrary he was diffident and very charming.' He continues, 'He was also extremely popular among the ladies. All through the run on any given night such and such a friend would take along their starry-eyed daughter, who was dying to meet Daniel, and time and again I'd have to go to the Green Room and say to him, "Oh, I know it's a frightful bore, Daniel, but there's another young lady outside waiting to see you.". And you know it didn't matter how often this happened, he came every time, very patient and genuinely delighted to meet the girl, sign her programme or whatever. He was unendingly gracious.'

For another star in the production there was much more to

Daniel than graciousness. Jack Shepherd, a highly respected 'veteran' of stage, film and television, now with his own successful TV detective series, *Wycliffe*, played Kolia Gumilyov, one of the other Soviet poets in *Futurists*, and he recalls, 'I could see that there was a definite ambition and determination mixed in with all that charm. As an actor he's very hard to summarise. He's certainly gifted. He attacks with a kind of rage and has to get so far into a role that he inhabits it almost completely, but, when it comes to trying to quantify him after that, he's very hard to pin down.'

About their work together at the National he goes on, 'The play was based around the Kronstadt Uprising, and the turning point of the revolution when Lenin decided to put down the sailors' mutiny rather than listen to any of their grievances, and it was from that moment that Russia died. That was the basic premise of the play. The victimisation all centred on the poets really, the people we were playing. As Mayakovsky, Daniel certainly wasn't relaxing, but then his character was a very aggressive and dangerous one – the kind of character that used to be called "the angry young man" and Daniel played it with a great deal of intensity.'

Whether Daniel was aware of it or not, he was riding something like the crest of a wave. In the background, the swell of recognition springing from the twin film releases in America, far from abating, was continuing to gather momentum. At home, the play's run was also proving very successful and, according to Julian Fellowes, Richard Eyre became more and more a great believer in Daniel. 'He also used him in some very unusual and effective ways, ways you'd never imagine,' he maintains. 'For example, Bill Douglas was the set designer and he had come up with these incredible curved sweeping staircases going up into thin air and things like that and altogether visually it was very strong. If Daniel had no dialogue, Richard started to have him just silently poised halfway up one of the staircases, and, although it's hard to describe it in words, when you actually saw it, somehow it created a really skilful happening on its own without anything else, just because of the way Daniel carried it off. I think a lot of us knew then that he was on his way.'

Speaking of moments behind the scenes, Julian goes on, 'The crew of a production can sometimes be difficult but Daniel was always very charming to the scenery people. He's very left wing and, without naming names, on that production there were those who had extreme socialist tendencies. The theatre, for all its grandeur, is an odd place for its strange mix of pomp, philosophy and politics.'

He continues, 'I remember one particular lunch when we had all congregated and it was at the time that there was some big Weizenthal war crimes trial going on and a discussion got up around the table about what it means to be Jewish. There were the usual two different opinions – the one which says that what happened in the war doesn't matter nowadays because it was all so long ago. And the other that it doesn't matter how long, that those responsible should be hunted down and brought to trial. And I said to someone who was busy maintaining that no one cares any more that that was easy to say if one wasn't Jewish, and suddenly Daniel immediately jumped quite ferociously in and agreed strongly, very strongly. It's an issue that's clearly very important to him.'

For Daniel it seems that working at the National Theatre on this play was an untypical experience. Jack Shepherd had been with the National since 1978, and would in fact leave that year, but he was well aware of an inherent problem there. He says, 'The thing is that people can disappear. Not if you

99

come in to a play in a leading part and leave as Daniel did. He was never in danger of being consumed by the bureaucracy, but it can happen. I left in 1986 and suddenly I found that I really had to start again for about a year. TV and film people seemed to have forgotten that I existed and that was a shock.'

Jack, as Daniel still did, played football for the Showbiz Eleven during this time. Daniel had never lost his love of the sport and thoroughly enjoyed taking part in various matches, even if he was unceremoniously barracked on occasion. Malcolm, security man at the Queen's Theatre who remembered Daniel from his days in *Another Country*, recalls, 'Yeah, I turned up on the touchline to watch him play. He stood out a mile, of course, because his head was all shaved and as soon as I arrived I began giving him a hard time, shouting and swearing abuse at him. He was running down the side of the pitch at the time and just about fell over the ball. It gave him the shock of his life!'

Although a solitary person by nature, Daniel does occasionally enjoy socialising with the circle of people he is working with at the time. He and Jack Shepherd got on very well together throughout *Futurists'* run and after the last performance they joined forces to put on an 'end of term' show for the cast and crew. 'We did a cabaret,' says Jack, 'which included myself, Daniel and Fred Pearson. Daniel was extremely funny in it. Part of it involved an old age pensioners' whistling team and he based his character, so he told me, on someone he knew well – an old man as light as paper he called him. It was a very funny character anyway and he thoroughly enjoyed himself.'

Besides dabbling with painting, Daniel enjoys playing the Irish tin whistle. His love of Ireland only increased as time went on. Together with his deepening disenchantment with

Thatcher's Britain it would lead to him, around this time, applying for, and being granted, Irish citizenship on the grounds that his father was Irish-born. His future career would include two films made in Ireland about two very different Irishmen from either side of the North-South divide, both under Irish direction. For many, they would encapsulate his most powerful performances as an actor. But for now he could not know what lay ahead of him, except that he was under consideration for the lead role in a British-made film called *Withnail & I*.

This Handmade Films production about Britain in 1969 followed the antics of two out-of-work actors in the dying days of the hippie movement. Daniel was originally interested in being cast by director Bruce Robinson in the lead role of Withnail – a hollow-eyed character whose fingers seem forever fused around the rim of a whisky bottle – alongside Paul McGann as Marwood, the 'I' of the title. But then an offer came which he found too tempting to turn down – the lead in what promised to be an important Hollywood film. Richard E. Grant, making his film debut, took the part of Withnail instead. It was a successful debut too, as *Withnail & I* went on to become a cult comedy.

Bruce Robinson remembers this time clearly. 'I met ten actors in all who were being considered for the role of Withnail and, of those, Daniel and Richard were the two I was most interested in.' He explains, 'This was of course only the preliminary stages when I was more or less just making it my point to meet each actor individually for an informal chat. Daniel and I had a meal together and a good yak. He is one of the few real stars this country has but, as often happens in this business, it just wasn't to be. Sometimes an actor's availability doesn't match your needs, or you can't afford him or something. But in this case I think some of the reason it didn't work out for my film was because it came down to the fact that the director and producer of *The Unbearable Lightness of Being*, in which he had been offered the lead, already had several good films to their credit then and I hadn't, and perhaps it was felt by himself or his agent that it would be safer for him to choose that way.' He adds, 'Whatever it was, Daniel didn't do *Withnail*, but I was more than happy with Richard.'

The only similarity between the film which Daniel had turned his back on and the one chosen in its stead was that it too was set around the end of the sixties. Only this time the setting is Czechoslovakia and the Russian invasion of that country on 21 August 1968. *The Unbearable Lightness of Being* was to be based on the 1984 bestselling novel by Milan Kundera. With a $17 million budget, the three-hour film project was in the hands of Chicago-born director Philip Kaufman and Oscar-winning producer Saul Zaentz, whose company has been responsible for such movies as *One Flew over the Cuckoo's Nest*, *Amadeus*, *The Lord of the Rings* and *The Mosquito Coast*.

Co-writer of the screenplay for the hugely successful *Raiders of the Lost Ark*, Kaufman loved Kundera's book, even though it has sometimes been dubbed dense and meandering. Together with Jean-Claude Carrière, he set about scripting a workable screenplay as well as embarking on its casting. The film, an adult love story, would include several bedroom scenes and a willingness to appear nude was a prerequisite for all three main characters – a factor which did not prevent many prominent American stars from going after the parts.

Philip spent months searching for the right actor to take on the role of the central figure. This is Tomas, an extremely talented neuro-surgeon who for most of the film is also completely sex mad. At this point, as the focus of so much media attention over America's continuing love affair with *My Beautiful Laundrette* and *A Room with a View*, Daniel had been coaxed into making a rare television appearance on one of Britain's breakfast magazine programmes. Shaven-headed as Mayakovsky, it was hard to equate him visually with Johnny and harder still to see him as Cecil. Among the millions of bewildered viewers that morning, though, was Philip Kaufman who, idly channel-hopping in his London hotel room, was stopped short by Daniel's interview. He immediately got on to the phone to make enquiries as to where he could contact this young actor.

Although the book describes Tomas as a man of middle age, when Kaufman studied Daniel's screen tests he decided to forget the decade-plus discrepancy and cast him in the role. It was a costly decision, at least time-wise, for he than had to spend several extra weeks recasting the other characters accordingly. To many this would be a testament to the Day-Lewis ability but typically Daniel does not see it that way. In fact, *Unbearable*, his first film in a starring role, is a part of his career he prefers now not to be even reminded of, claiming that he finds it too bleak to think about.

Perhaps part of his discomfort with the film lies in the fact that its steamy bedroom scenes instantly elevated him to the status of sex symbol – a label he shrinks from with genuine distaste. The two ladies with whom he spent the three hours romping around on screen were played by Swedish actress Lena Olin, seen more recently with Richard Gere in the romantic drama *Mr Jones*, and the intense twenty-three-year-old French-born beauty Juliette Binoche. Juliette was acclaimed at Cannes as being the 'Discovery of 1985' and Daniel would, it was reported, become romantically involved with her during work on the film.

Despite the increasingly high profile he was now attracting as an actor, Daniel still managed to keep his personal relationships strictly out of the public eye. But, while they were working for the eight months in France, it is claimed that he and Juliette, who plays his screen wife, fell in love behind the scenes. Certainly there was a chemistry between them professionally. This affinity had played its part in her landing the role in the first place, for originally she had appeared before Kaufman to read for another, much smaller part. It was late in the day, as shooting was due to start soon and he already had the role of Tomas's wife filled. On impulse, however, as Daniel happened to be with him, the director asked Juliette to read for Tereza. She and Daniel did a single scene together, and it was enough to convince Kaufman to change his original thinking and take on Binoche as the female lead. According to Philip Kaufman, Daniel shared his stunned reaction and was equally convinced about the girl's suitability.

As part of his preparation for the role of a neuro-surgeon, Daniel sat in on some real-life brain operations, watching the surgeon's every move. For the entire eight months of filming, come hail or shine he would rise at the crack of dawn every day, don his trainers and set out on an eight-mile run. During any breaks in the schedule he parked himself in the director's apartment, studying the script, analysing his character, querying his feelings and motivations, fiercely determined to infiltrate the skin of this apparently shallow, yet really complex character. According to Kaufman he had never worked with such an intense actor. It was at times hard to separate Daniel in his mind from Tomas, and vice versa.

The film revolves around Tomas, and his relentlessly lascivious behaviour. From his opening line, 'Take off your clothes', delivered in a monotonous, even bored, tone, he purrs his way seductively from one day to the next, radiating sexual threat to practically every young female he encounters. He also has a steady lover in Sabina, a free-thinking, sensuous artist played by Lena Olin. Then, on an out-of-town trip to perform an operation, he sees, subsequently follows and moves in on Tereza, a naive country girl who serves in a café. To him it is simply a dalliance for the sake of it, but Tereza follows him to Prague, turning up uninvited on his doorstep. Inevitably, within minutes she is flinging off her clothes for him, but unusually she ends up staying the night in his flat.

The film is set just prior to the Russian invasion and is a intermingled mesh of romance and politics. As filming in Czechoslovakia was impossible, streets in Lyon in France doubled for Prague. By splicing the film with original black and white newsreel footage, director of photography Sven Nykvist, who received an Academy Award nomination for his work on this film, made it seem for a moment as if Tomas and Tereza really did form part of history.

It is a strange film which could have been excellent had it been an hour shorter with less sex and more substance. Both Kaufman and Zaentz went to great lengths to achieve the right degree of authenticity. Having searched in vain through the US Army for genuine Russian tanks in working order, some were finally traced to Israel. The cost of transporting them to Lyon, however, proved astronomical. Replicas were frantically built instead, but they failed to come up to standard and in the end the French Military Museum at Saumur came to the rescue by renting out their Soviet hardware.

All uniforms, props and the 1968 Skoda car Daniel drives as Tomas were the genuine article too. Daniel was even fitted with a gold dental crown, popular then among trendy Czech men. As far as possible, author Milan Kundera was consulted. When shown a selection of the French streets under consideration for locations, mixed with photographs of Prague, even he was unable to tell the difference.

There are moments in the film when one's optimism rises. Scenes that capture the darkening political climate, the erupting street violence and the people's rebellion were well done, even when set incongruously against jauntily familiar sixties music. But these are not enough to rescue the film, and its impoverished plot is totally overwhelmed by what looks like erotic sex simply for its own sake.

Daniel acts his part very convincingly. His accent is subtle, the fruit of hard work with dialect coach Elizabeth Pursey. Elizabeth, who has worked with many stars, likens her professional relationship with any actor to that of a medical consultant's with a patient. As such, all specific details are confidential, but it is safe to say that, for the duration of the film, it was an intense experience. 'It is like being a very good tailor,' she explains. 'You don't mind showing the cloth and displaying the end product, but the fitting is a private matter.'

She goes on, 'Part of my work with actors is to show themselves back to themselves, and it's a delicate process which requires building up a great deal of trust. Every actor deals differently with dialect and, in bringing the acting truth into the new shape of the dialect, it doesn't always come off. With Daniel, he possesses enormous acting truth. He is also quite sensitively tuned, which meant in his case that it did come off. It made it a great pleasure to work with him. When you work with a splendid actor it is a privilege but it must also be a private thing.' Between working at RADA, Elizabeth spent six months altogether on the film. 'Saul Zaentz and his team were quite amazing to be involved with,' she adds. 'They came to the set every day. You didn't have to explain to them what the problems were. They could see for themselves, which made it easier to get through them.'

But, as well as having had Elizabeth's help in sounding the part, Daniel, complete with felt Fedora, also looks it. As the film progresses he changes from the wolfishly smooth predator, projected with an ease so effortless as to be almost smug, to a man who has matured emotionally and is often in torment. He plays the womaniser as an engaging and likeable villain, strangely reminiscent at first of Michael Caine's thoroughly amoral Lothario in the mid-sixties screen comedy *Alfie*. And, when he disappears from the film at one point for an almost unbearable stretch of time, there is palpable relief when he returns. His performance has been called mesmerizing by some, opaque by others.

The film itself came as a surprise in some ways. In October 1985 the all-American matinee idol Rock Hudson had died of AIDS. Since then, the media and entertainment industry had given increasing prominence to the deadly, sexually transmitted disease. The free-love boom of the sixties, mirrored by films like *Alfie*, had given way to stern warnings against the dangers of casual sex. This was being reflected on screen by the trend away from bed-hopping heroes.

The sex scene, while not entirely done away with, was now considered by many to be politically incorrect. Then, between late 1986 and the summer of 1987, films such as Jim McBride's *The Big Easy*, *No Way Out* with Kevin Costner and Sean Young, as well as Adrian Lyne's *Fatal Attraction* brought back steamy sex in New Orleans, the back seats of limos or even against the kitchen sink. *The Unbearable Lightness of Being*, however, was thought to be about to outstrip even that in the sizzle stakes. The word was out during production that it was shaping up to be the most sexually explicit movie of them all.

Although the love scenes between Tomas and the two main women in his life are meant to be central to the story, Daniel was known to be concerned from the outset that there would be no gratuitous nudity. Before all the intimate scenes were filmed, it was the director's task to rehearse with his actors exactly what was required of them and how they could best achieve it without crossing that line.

Often Daniel and Juliette would spend hours sitting in Tomas's apartment on a soundstage at Studios de Boulogne, so that they could try to inhabit their surroundings and thereby their roles. Even on a closed set with none but vital personnel present, love scenes which have to be faked yet look realistic are among the most difficult and delicate to shoot. As *Fatal Attraction* and *Disclosure* star Michael Douglas, a veteran of the sex scene, recently observed, they can be extremely stressful as they represent one of the rare areas in screen acting where practically everybody is a judge. They require a lot of trust from all concerned.

Juliette Binoche, with her dark cropped hair, trusting eyes and elfin cuteness, exudes a sweet and innocent appeal, whereas Lena Olin's voluptuous ripe beauty was more mature and striking. And between the two of them they keep Daniel, as Tomas, busy with much raunchy, room-wrecking sex.

His first love scene with Juliette, when she surprises him by suddenly seizing the initiative, has almost a spoof element to it – certainly as far as some of Daniel's expressions are concerned. It was not the first time he had appeared on screen without his clothes, but it was the first time he was supposed to be indulging in highly charged, passionate encounters. While professionally he did what was expected of him, earning himself a reputation as a sex symbol in the process, it is debatable how comfortable he was with any of it.

Daniel himself makes few comments on the film, beyond maintaining that it is too bleak to think about, but others had their own reasons for disquiet. One of those is actor and author Simon Callow. In 1986 Simon had translated Milan Kundera's novel *Jacques et son Maître* and so was familiar with the writer's work. He says, 'I cannot understand the casting of Daniel as Tomas and neither, I know, could Kundera. Tomas was supposed to have been at least forty-five years old, maybe older, and to have lived an extraordinary lifelong obsession with women and yet he would return night after night to his wife. That was the very essence, the whole premise of the character and pivot of the story of Tomas and for that to work he had to have *lived*, to have been well into middle age. I just don't think it works when you try to portray that with a person of barely thirty. Of necessity, it changes it entirely. As far as Kundera was concerned, he just said, "Well, a book is a book and a film, a film," and left it at that but it was undoubtedly odd casting.'

Odd or not, although neither Lena Olin nor Juliette Binoche were well known in America and this was Daniel's first Hollywood film outing, when the movie opened the following year it did so to rave reviews. Unfortunately, though, the box-office receipts would not go on to reflect this and the film received less than a third of its original investment. By the time it was voted Best Film of the Year by the US National Society of Critics, it had already vanished from the cinema circuit.

By now the pace of Daniel's working life was incredibly hectic. At times the shooting schedule for *The Unbearable Lightness of Being* had required him putting in fifteen-hour days. And yet less than two weeks after it ended, in early spring 1987, he left France and flew to New York to start work on his next film. This was to be a complete departure from the roles he normally took on – the lead in a screwball comedy called *Stars and Bars*.

Based on the novel by William Boyd, it would be directed by Irishman Pat O'Connor, director of the 1984 British film *Cal*, an attempt at tackling the Irish Question which starred Helen Mirren and John Lynch. *Cal* had been O'Connor's debut feature film and since then he had been determined to be selective in the projects he undertook. *Stars and Bars'* producer was to be Sandy Lieberson and the film had begun life as a pet project of leading British producer Sir David Puttnam.

Says David, 'I bought the rights from William Boyd at least two years before the film was made and also got William to write the screenplay – we had about five drafts before we were done. Pat O'Connor, with whom I'd just been working, came on board and I tried to set it up, but I failed time and again. But then I became head of Columbia Pictures and suddenly I was in the position to get it done.' On a $6.5 million budget, filming was due to start on 17 March 1987.

The lead character is Henderson Dores, a very English art expert who has emigrated to America believing it to be the land of opportunity. A hapless, harmless gentleman, he is destined to fall head first into a series of almost Keystone Cop escapades. Co-producer along with Sandy Lieberson was Susan Richards and in her search for the luckless Henderson she first set about rounding up a handful of British actors well known for their slapstick comedy. They did not disappoint, but neither did they hold any surprises. Then they came to Daniel. Says Puttnam, 'As soon as I saw Daniel's screen tests, for me, there was no one else in the running – it was always going to be Daniel from that moment on.'

Since 1978 David has had an arrangement with Warner Brothers whereby he passes talent tips on to them. In that time those tips have included Kenneth Branagh, *Schindler's List* and *Quiz Show* star Ralph Fiennes as well as Daniel Day-Lewis. He explains, 'I first saw Daniel on stage in *Another Country* and was very impressed. But it was at his screen test for *Stars and Bars* that I *really* saw him. I think he is a wonderful actor. He's completely watchable and very subtle, the kind of actor who, when you look at him, lights up. Some people have that quality, and Daniel is one of them.' He adds, 'Of course, I knew his grandfather, Michael Balcon, very well so there was a relationship between Daniel and me already there to start with, which was nice.'

Personally, Daniel dislikes being compared to other actors, and certainly film critic Barry Norman with his breadth of knowledge of movies and their stars down the years maintains, 'He doesn't resemble any other actor which, in my opinion, is a very good thing.' But David Puttnam has his own view. He says, 'He reminds me slightly – and I do mean just slightly – of a young Al Pacino around the time of, say, *Serpico*. Like Pacino, Daniel has a very different approach to acting.' In contrast to the *Godfather* star, others have since likened Daniel as Henderson Dores to the Lancashire-born light-comedy star from an earlier era Rex Harrison, with his knack of beautifully underplaying a part. But there was nevertheless in general, astonishment to see Day-Lewis undertake such a role. 'I don't know why,' says David. 'And he showed he does have a flair for comedy.'

Harry Dean Stanton, Laurie Metcalf, Will Patton and Joan Cusack joined Daniel in this ninety-minute tale, which kicks off with Henderson Dores newly arrived in America. He is very much the Englishman abroad – he talks differently, is ultra-well-mannered at all times and is desperate to become Americanised. Being an expert in impressionist paintings, when a rare and priceless 1908 Renoir surfaces in Luxora Beach,

Atlanta, he is sent by his boss on a mission to try to obtain it from the ramshackle Gage family for the best price he can. He promptly finds himself stranded in a nightmarish hick town at its very worst.

Susan Richards has said that one of the reasons Daniel made such a mark at his screen test was that he had absolutely no inhibitions, which is certainly true. He was most definitely not concerned about jeopardising his increasingly impressive screen image in taking on such a crazy role. Daniel plays Dores as the complete Englishman, softly spoken and gentle. Much put upon and at times taken complete advantage of, he is unfailingly proper in his pinstripe suit and tie, striving to remain elegant throughout the many mishaps which befall him. Not dissimilar from David Niven, outwardly he exudes an 'Englishman remains cool under fire' aura, but inwardly he is panicking worse with every passing second. As the film goes on, and his troubles multiply as the situation spins totally out of control, he arouses sympathy galore for the frantic innocent that he is, while at the same time being ingenuously funny.

Work on the film, though, was not so hilarious – sometimes nineteen-hour stretches at a time, and this was hard on the heels of the exhausting *Unbearable* schedule. Near the end of the film, back in New York, Henderson is abducted by gangsters and held hostage until he hands over the Renoir. No one believes that it was burned and the bad guys force him to strip so that they can torture him into confessing the painting's whereabouts. Left alone to consider his plight, however, Henderson manages to escape.

Sparing Daniel's blushes as much as possible the scenes that followed were shot from only the most sympathetic angles as, painfully thin and wearing only shoes and socks, he climbs out of a window in pouring rain and drops down to the street below.

From a nearby skip he finds himself a cardboard box to lash about his waist. In this, he sneaks out into the busy night-time streets. Jogging through Times Square, free and safely among people, his real awareness of America takes shape when he begins to find it amusing that not a single soul bats an eye at the spectacle he presents. Indeed, as he has 'Maxi Pads' emblazoned on his rear end, he blithely tells a passer-by that they are his sponsors, which produces a chorus of good-luck cheers.

Those Times Square shots were filmed late at night in May 1987 and marked Daniel's New York acting debut. It was difficult for the production team to keep the very busy Manhattan intersection of Broadway and 45th Street clear for long enough to shoot and much of the time Daniel lurked in the background, wearing only an increasingly soggy cardboard box. He looked like any other shivering down-and-out and, as such, remained unnoticed by the growing knot of onlookers busy craning their necks in every direction but his to try to discover which star was filming there that night.

During work on *Stars and Bars*, Daniel's reputation for being a deeply solitary person increased yet again. While on location in Georgia, although the rest of the cast and crew all stayed in the same hotel, Daniel preferred to spend the six weeks living alone in an isolated cabin in nearby hills instead. The only time he joined the others socially was to take part in the Sunday football matches. While he was in character, too, it was a brave man who disturbed him. One publicist, who ran foul of the Day-Lewis temper by interrupting him at the wrong moment, claimed Daniel went off like a rocket, screaming wildly at him in front of everyone, much to his embarrassment.

Daniel's desire to shut himself off so much – to remain locked into Henderson at all times – stemmed from his unshakable belief that to bring the required authenticity to a character it is vitally important to maintain the insular world within which that character exists. However, this time there appears to have been an extra need for 100 per cent concentration on his character, caused by the speed with which he had had to switch from his previous role in *The Unbearable Lightness of Being*. This was exactly the sort of challenge which was earning Daniel the respect and acclaim of US and British audiences and critics alike, but it was not without its problems for the actor.

With less than a fortnight between finishing one film and beginning work on the next, there had not been enough time for Daniel to exorcise Tomas from his mind. Even when shooting began on *Stars and Bars*, he had felt that Tomas still hung around him, cluttering up his mind. While in front of the cameras he acted, performed and thought as Henderson, but off-set his task was being insidiously interfered with and undermined by memories of how Tomas thought and felt. Daniel described it once as the characters being like two men in his head, sitting silently opposite one another in a waiting room. He had not had enough time to let go and it worried him.

As Simon Callow observed, it would perhaps be healthier if Daniel was less intense, but for Day-Lewis there is no easy compromise. He has been quoted as saying that the problem with acting is that 'you always believe you're a fraud'. In spite of all the lengths he will go to to personify the character he is portraying, ultimately he considers it to be an utter falsehood – a sham. But even so he appears at times to resent having to offload the identity he has spent such a lot of his time and effort assuming, while being perfectly well aware that he cannot carry around all the emotional baggage left over from all his screen characters. The very degree to which Daniel inhabits his roles means there is a considerable amount of emotional baggage too, and by the time shooting for *Stars and Bars* was over in June it was hardly surprising that he still had the ghosts of both Tomas and Henderson to be rid of.

Perhaps it was this that led to his almost panicky reaction to the spotlight he found himself in when *The Unbearable Lightness of Being* opened to such intense initial success. Suddenly he was the focus of rabid media attention, snapped wherever he showed his face.

Photographs accompanying the tidal wave of PR interviews began emerging, highlighting the deep-set, brooding eyes beneath black bar brows, the hair swept back from a broad forehead to curl on to his shoulders. The sex symbol tag easily matched the wolfish, predatory image conveyed, and was wholly consistent with the film he was promoting. The reaction it provoked, though, was unlooked-for and somewhat bewildering. While most actors would have lapped up every second of it, Daniel packed a bag and ran.

There may have been other factors at work behind his sudden flight, for there were also changes in his personal life to contend with. The demands his career now made on him, with lengthy location shoots, must have meant that he had very little time to commit to one person. Then there was also his frequent need for personal space, for the freedom to seek his own company alone. But, whatever the cause, his long-standing relationship with Sarah Campbell, the girl he had been with since school, broke up around this time.

When he moved out of the Queen's Gate flat they had shared for over three years, he went to Europe, where he travelled for several months incognito, blending in at student hangouts, sleeping rough in Avignon in France. He may not have known exactly what he needed, but he did know that he had to escape from the pressures he had felt closing in on him for some time, and from the scrutiny of family, friends and fellow actors. He preferred the company of strangers, so with no project lined up in front of him and no woman waiting at home he wandered unrecognised around the continent, in no particular hurry to rejoin the rat race.

It would not be the last time that Daniel would vanish suddenly and unexpectedly, and in the years ahead he would acquire an unrivalled reputation for the deftness of his disappearing acts. No one knew where he would go, what he would do and when he could be expected to return. It all added to his burgeoning reputation as a loner, fuelling too his own uncertainty about the profession he had chosen.

When discussing the character of Tomas, the brilliant surgeon who was reduced by the Soviet regime to farm labouring work and found it surprisingly worthwhile, Daniel confessed to a private desire to get up one morning and discover a reason not to go on being an actor. 'Maybe on my deathbed,' he mourned, 'I'll know whether or not the thing I spent my life doing was keeping me alive or killing me. I certainly don't know now.'

CHAPTER SIX

CLASS ACT

'Looks can be deceiving.

CHRISTY BROWN, *MY LEFT FOOT*

David Puttnam says of *Stars and Bars,* 'A lot of people didn't like it, but I did.' $8 million had been invested in the film but it returned only $100,000 in box-office receipts. Coming on top of the commercial failure of *The Unbearable Lightness of Being,* this was not news designed to boost Daniel's confidence when he returned from his spell abroad. However, he was about to meet some people who would have a major effect on his career.

While attending a party in Dublin in the spring of 1988 with *Stars and Bars* director Pat O'Connor, Daniel was introduced to producer Noel Pearson, the artistic director of The Abbey Theatre in Dublin. Pearson had started out by managing the Irish folk group The Dubliners, and went on to make his mark producing hugely successful stage musicals including *Joseph and the Amazing Technicolor Dreamcoat.* Genial and laid-back, he has since become Ireland's most successful theatrical entrepreneur, but behind the easy-going manner lies a hard-nosed businessman. By the mid-to-late eighties he had set his sights beyond the stage, on the screen.

For some time he and fellow Dubliner director Jim Sheridan had been putting on a variety of stage productions in New York. One day the two met in a bar and got talking. Both decided that they were bored rigid with their work and were looking to broaden their horizons. They began to toss a few ideas around and, among them, there was one in particular which they kept coming back to. It became the basis of a possible film project – one which would take them both back to Ireland to work.

With the costs of staging plays and musicals now ranging between two and four million dollars, both Pearson and Sheridan knew they could make a good film more cheaply. Especially when taking advantage of welcome new tax incentives which had recently been introduced by the Irish Government in a bid to stimulate the growth of film production in their country. By the night of that Dublin party, Jim Sheridan, in conjunction with playwright Shane Connaughton, had already started scripting a film from a book written by the Irish writer Christy Brown, called *My Left Foot*. Christy had been born severely handicapped with cerebral palsy, an impairment of muscular function caused by damage to the brain before or during birth, but he had overcome enormous difficulties to become an accomplished artist and writer. *My Left Foot* was his autobiography.

Noel Pearson had known Christy personally. They had first met in a Dublin pub several years before, when Christy was drunk. Some time later they met again when Noel attended an exhibition of Christy's paintings. During the reception afterwards, Noel discovered a rapport with the artist. Christy invited the producer home that evening, where they talked long into the night. From this sprang a lasting friendship. Like Jim Sheridan, Pearson would be making his screen debut with this project. In fact, Shane Connaughton was the only one of the trio to have a shred of cinema experience, but despite this they were all convinced that Christy's story would make a terrific film. During the party Noel enthusiastically began telling Daniel the tale of the remarkable Dublin man and of the entire Brown family – Daniel was all ears.

Just over a month later, at his new home in west London's Brook Green, he received a film script to read and consider. He had not entirely forgotten the story he had heard at that party, but it was not at the forefront of his mind, so at first he didn't connect it with the script. Then, among the accompanying papers, he saw that the proposed producer of the project would be Noel Pearson and suddenly it clicked.

In the time since making *Stars and Bars* Daniel had had steady offers of work, but so far nothing had touched the necessary chord. He wasn't absolutely sure what he had been waiting for, but as he settled down to read the script he soon knew that this was it. He was so blown away that he immediately made up his mind to take on the lead role of Christy Brown, despite the fact that the producers were experiencing a few hiccups in sorting out the film's finance.

Several factors combined to produce instant and deep attraction to the role. Certainly Christy's life story was very moving, but it was what lay at the core of the character that was guaranteed to snare his interest. That is, the tale of man's lifelong battle to find ways of properly expressing himself in every aspect of his life. Many actors decide on a part by asking themselves: ultimately, do they want to say these lines or not? This may enter into Daniel's thinking too, but his first reaction to any role is on a purely personal and emotive level. In this case, all his instincts led him to believe that he had a complete and immediate understanding of this real–life person, whom he had never met, called Christy Brown.

Clearly, too, the kind of depth of feeling that was going to be required to portray Brown answered a very real hunger inside Daniel at this time. He would be more sure of it after filming finished, but even at the outset his gut reaction was that, whereas he still considered most acting to be a sham, this time the work would be both justified and worthwhile.

At the end of the day the intimate scale of the project, on a relatively modest budget, was also a factor which appealed to him. The fact that it was intended to be predominantly an Irish production undoubtedly weighed heavily in the scale too. That Jim Sheridan, whom Daniel affectionately calls Shay, would be making his debut as a feature film director far from put Daniel off. On the contrary, again going on instinct as much as anything, he was convinced that Sheridan was capable of making great films. He has described the effect of Jim's personality on him the first time they had met as being bewitching. The fact that Shay was new to this particular field brought out a protective streak in Daniel, whether Jim needed it or not. At any rate, considering that Sheridan would later cite Daniel's rampant enthusiasm for the project as having been one of the most potent forces in its favour, it all augured well for a solid and highly productive working relationship between the two.

Shortsightedly, few people among the money men behind the film industry recognised the potential of *My Left Foot*. Pearson had been on the trail of finance since March, but had been met time and again with a negative response. This lack of interest could have resulted in the end of the project had it not been for the Irish television company Radio Telefis Eirann (RTE) pledging £150,000, and the eleventh-hour intervention of Britain's Granada Television. The latter weighed in with a sum to equal the amount which Noel had by now managed to put up in equity, bringing the budget to a final total of £1.7 million. What the Manchester-based TV company dubbed the 'unlikely hero's story' became a Granada film in conjunction with Palace/Ferndale Films. The Noel Pearson production promised to bring together a fine blend of fresh talent and proven experience, both in front of and behind the camera.

The cast which Pearson assembled included such well-established names as Ray McAnally and Brenda Fricker, as well as, in a cameo role, Cyril Cusack, then Ireland's most famous living actor. They were to work alongside the fresh new blood of actresses Fiona Shaw and Ruth McCabe as well as the youngster Hugh O'Conor. The crew boasted executive producers Paul Heller and Steve Morrison, line producer Arthur Lappin as well as the experienced cameraman Jack Conroy. The nine-week shoot at Ardmore Studios as well as on location in and around Dublin was set to start on 19 July 1988.

The script which Sheridan and Connaughton put together was inspired, even if its first page contained elements which Daniel found decidedly daunting. The film's opening scene sees Christy selecting an old 78rpm record from a rack, removing it from its paper sleeve and placing it on the turntable of an old monogram record player, which he then switches on before lifting the arm and positioning the stylus on the revolving disc. He does all this with the toes of his left foot. It is a long shot, filmed in close up, and, when Daniel read it through, at first it thrilled him, seizing his imagination with its sheer uniqueness.

Then, seconds later, it dawned on him that he would have to actually perform this task with his own left foot. Stunned, he wondered, 'How the fuck am I going to do this?'

By and large Daniel works on the premise that, if at this early stage his critical faculties come into play, then the part is probably not for him. Suddenly, he was not wholly convinced that he was the right man for the job. But, just as quickly, he stubbornly chose to ignore his doubts. Later on he would receive help in handling the peculiar extra demands of this role. For now, with the responsibility of portraying a real person in a feature film for the first time, he had to go right back and study the life of the man who had so much inspired both producer and director.

Christy Brown was born in 1932, into a working-class family. He was raised in Dublin, one of twenty-two children of whom thirteen survived. A cerebral palsy sufferer, the big toe of his left foot was the only part of his body over which he had any control. While his brothers and sisters went off to school every day, Christy remained at home with his hardworking, seemingly permanently pregnant, mother. His education was derived mainly from reading comics until someone introduced him to the works of Charles Dickens when he was in his mid-teens.

At eighteen, he belatedly began receiving treatment for his condition. The film would show that he felt uncomfortable at the clinic where all the other patients were much younger. Believing it to be a waste of everyone's time, he refused to go back. But the clinic's founder and his staff were to become hugely important to Christy's development, as was his large and loving family. As he grew older, the family built him a room in which he would spend most nights banging with his foot on his typewriter, or painting.

He also began visiting the pub a lot and developed quite a

drink problem. His art work, he considered, provided him with money to eat and booze. But writing was his outlet, the conduit through which he could best express his innermost feelings. He was a man who yearned to live life to the fullest but who had to battle with enormous frustrations and disappointments. Sadly these sometimes led him to contemplate suicide. Although from a practising Catholic family, he did not class himself as being particularly religious. He was often very irreverent in his humour, possessing a sharp intellect and a cutting wit which hid a much softer inner core.

In 1954 his autobiography was published. This slim volume he would later decry, with typical self-mocking humour, as his 'happy cripple book'. But it was not until he began writing novels in 1970 – his first being *Down all the Days* – that he considered himself to be a true author. In all he went on to produce five books. He thought of himself as an outgoing person by nature, but at the same time he was really a lonely and very isolated man. Any criticism of his literary work would have him brusquely brushing it aside in public, but privately reaching for the bottle. If the attack hit home badly, he would combine drink with sleeping pills.

Tragically, he was still a young man of just forty-nine when in 1981 he died from choking on some food. He left behind his wife Mary, whom he had met at his brother Sean's London flat during a party. It has been said that Christy would have been grimly amused at the idea of a tall, fit and handsome young actor physically contorting himself out of all recognition to pretend to be him for a film. This may have been true, but the Brown family were to be of valuable assistance to Daniel in his quest not just to project Christy's character, but also, for the duration of the film, actually to *become* the man. To do that meant embarking on his most exhausting preparation to date.

For *My Left Foot* Daniel set about learning how to write and paint literally with his left foot: an incredibly difficult task for which he received help from real-life disabled painters and writers. Through sheer determination, he mastered the art so completely that all the drawings in an album produced in the film were actually done by him with his left foot. He also spent two months of 1988 studying cerebral palsy sufferers and the therapy techniques employed with them at the Sandymount School and Clinic in Dublin. This is the clinic Christy Brown himself had attended. Daniel's approach to the school came as a complete surprise to the headmaster, Tony Jordan.

Says Tony, 'About a month after Christy Brown died I held a memorial service here at Sandymount for him. His family and friends were invited and afterwards I promised that, in time, I would organise a Memorial Day in Christy's honour with readings of his work, a special mass and so on. The Brown family were all very keen on this because really in the ensuing years he was in danger of being forgotten.' He goes on, 'Well, I was in the middle of planning this event for May 1988 and I hadn't known anything at all about any film being made. One morning, then, right out of the blue, there was a knock on my office door and this chap came in dressed from head to toe completely in black. He told me his name was Daniel Day-Lewis and that he was involved in making a film of Christy Brown's life. Well, to be honest I didn't pay much attention at first because there had often been talk of people making films which had never come to anything. And his name, I'm afraid to say, didn't mean anything to me either. Although the funny thing is, I'd seen *My Beautiful Laundrette* but I'd no idea that the guy in my office was the same one who had been in the film.'

A busy man and sceptical of, if not flatly unimpressed with, talk of films, Tony Jordan was loath to waste time on the polite stranger but at the same time he was curious, so he asked who was intending to make the film. 'When he told me it was Noel Pearson,' says Tony, 'then I realised it was a serious effort after all and I'm afraid it was only at that point that I invited him to sit down. Then I thought – the name Day-Lewis? I said to him, "You must be related, then, to Cecil Day-Lewis," and he quietly said that he was. I went on, "You're probably his grandson," and he replied, "Well, actually I'm his son". I looked at him closer and said that I'd have to check my English literary history when I got home, but he explained his father had been married before and that he was the younger child of Cecil's second marriage to Jill Balcon. 'Anyway,' admits Tony, 'it was all, what you might say, a rather tricky start!'

Tricky or not, it was a start. Daniel explained to the now attentive headmaster what precisely he was hoping for. In essence, this was to be able to come to Sandymount on a regular basis to observe the pupils and staff in their work. His wish was happily granted. Says Tony, 'It was quite a coincidence, as it happened, because here was Day-Lewis reading everything he could get his hands on about Christy Brown which, of course, is precisely what I myself was doing right then as part of my preparations for the approaching Memorial Day. Once he learned that most of Christy's family would be coming to this event, he was very anxious to attend too and to bring Noel Pearson and Jim Sheridan with him. Quite rightly he saw it as a great opportunity and environment in which to meet them.'

After all the hard work in making the necessary arrangements, the day of the Memorial arrived amid much anticipation. The chance to talk to and get to know some members of Christy's family meant a lot to Daniel, but what he did not know was that there was an extra surprise in store for him. Tony explains, 'One guest that day was Dr Han Collis, the widow of Dr Robert

Collis, who was the founder of Sandymount. He was also Christy's physical, and every other kind of, mentor. Christy attended this centre which, of course, is why yer man Day–Lewis wanted to come here for his research. In fact, Christy was one of the first students Robert Collis brought here.'

'Anyway,' he goes on, 'sadly Robert was killed in an accident in 1975, but Han, as I say, had been able to come to the Memorial. Day–Lewis had been busy being introduced to various people all day but, when I said I wanted him to meet Robert's widow and said her name, he froze. He was absolutely flabbergasted. His first words were – and they were a long time in coming – "Wait till my mother hears this!"'

Tony explains, 'Robert Collis had been married to someone else when his association with Han had begun and out of that relationship had come a baby. Collis was not yet divorced, which meant Han was expecting an illegitimate child which was very much frowned upon back in those days. He was trying hard to find places where he could entrust Han during her pregnancy until his divorce came through, when they could marry, and one of the places she stayed during this time was at Crooms Hill with Daniel's parents. The Day–Lewis family often spent holidays in Ireland anyway, but, after that, they and the Collis family would often get together. At one time they had been very close. Daniel's mother, though, had completely lost contact with them over the years and hadn't even known if Han was dead or alive and here he was about to meet her in person. He just couldn't get over the coincidence. He was just stunned.'

For Daniel when the day was over and the crowd dispersed, it was ultimately the contacts and acquaintances which had been newly forged that were most important. The coincidental link between Christy's mentors and his own parents only strengthened an affinity with this project which went beyond anything he had experienced before.

He made arrangements to stay locally so that he could cycle or walk daily back and forth to Sandymount. Professionally speaking, the benefits were to be incalculable. News of his impending arrival provoked two very differing reactions, as Tony Jordan recalls. 'The female members of staff, of course, unlike me had known instantly who he was and by the time they discovered that he was due to start coming to the campus on a regular basis, there was such an air of excitement among them.' Tony's own reaction, and that of his wife, was a very different matter.

Daniel's recently released film *The Unbearable Lightness of Being* was showing at a nearby cinema. As *My Beautiful Laundrette*, in which Daniel played a gay punk, was the only example of his work they had seen, they decided to go and see his latest movie, buoyed up with enthusiasm and fully prepared to like it. They were totally unaware of its heavily erotic content. Tony recalls, 'Half an hour into it and my wife and I left. It was a dreadful film, shocking. I remember, as we stood up and walked out of the cinema, thinking seriously to myself that if that's the kind of stuff he's involved with, what on earth was he doing coming to Sandymount?!'

The libidinous Czech surgeon, however, bore no relation to the quietly unassuming man who turned up at the clinic to begin his work. 'He came and went for about eight weeks,' recalls the relieved headmaster, 'and during that time we got to know him very well. It was at this stage that he really impressed us, probably most of all by his extreme sensitivity. He didn't want to be obtrusive and it was vital to him for people not to feel that he was staring at them, or even to be conscious that they were being watched. He was desperate that

I, and the others in the staff, ironed this out before he started. Actually we're used to people coming and going here, but he was determined to observe and absorb, but not in the way that would intrude on the pupils. Or the staff too, for that matter.'

As Daniel went about his study he made a lot of friends among both trainees and adults. Tony recalls, 'Mary Keirnan was a senior pupil here at this time, learning to use her left foot to type and to work a word processor and Daniel studied how she went about this very closely.' He adds, 'He also grew very close to another pupil, Helen Curtiss, who unfortunately has since died. In fact, Day-Lewis would have been at Helen's funeral, but he was in Japan at the time so he sent a beautiful flower display instead.'

In spite of the Jordans' joint dismay at the cinema, Tony has no difficulty in pronouncing 'yer man', as he calls Daniel, to be the genuine article. 'It gets to be in this job that you can tell the difference,' he maintains, 'and there's nothing put on with Day-Lewis. He's a lovely fellow.' Daniel's naturalness and general ease also struck Tony.

'While he lived in Sandymount during this time he could literally go about openly. I mean I'd be putting the bins out at night and he'd stroll by out for a walk in the night air or race by on his bike. And even though he's a much bigger star nowadays, he still goes about like that because that's the kind of place this is. I remember a couple of years ago, I was walking on the beach and Day-Lewis had just been filming *The Last of the Mohicans*. Well, one minute I had the place to myself, then all of a sudden this madman on a bike appeared and it was yer man charging downhill like a wild thing, his long hair streaming out behind him. It was almost as if he was still in character, his concentration was so total. I didn't speak to him as he flew by, there'd have been no point. He still looked like he thought he was in the *Mohicans*.'

The fact that Christy Brown had not been all sweetness and light appealed strongly to Daniel, incurably drawn, as he is, to portraying life's flawed individuals. He had been deeply moved by what he had experienced at Sandymount, touched too by the warmth and generosity with which he continued to be embraced by the Brown family after their meeting at the Memorial Day. It was also a role into which he knew he could sink his teeth deep.

But at the same time, he was – as others connected with the film were – very conscious that Christy's physical disabilities themselves must not become what the film was about. How the disabled had, in the main, been portrayed in films to date was a contentious issue to many. In Christy's case, his story was all about rising above, and achieving in spite of, his physical impairments. Therefore, the film ought not to focus just on how twisted Daniel's body looked in a wheelchair.

In deciding on his approach to any part, Daniel tries to avoid, if possible, falling into the trap of adopting a rigid system. In any case, as far as this film was concerned, no previous formula would have been appropriate and by the time shooting approached he was still preoccupied with the immense physical demands which would be placed on him. In his desire to transcend these demands, to the point where his portrayal of disability would be so near perfect as to appear normal behaviour, he was also very conscious that success would elude him if his mental energies were targeted solely on technical perfection. He had set himself a tough agenda and initially everything did not quite fall into place.

To help him surmount these problems on a day-to-day basis, well-known artist and photographer Gene Lambert was brought in to act as script adviser. Gene holds strong views about the way in which disabled people are represented on film and takes a highly critical attitude towards most attempts to do so. But the opening sequence when Daniel, as Christy, lets his head roll round to stare the viewer right in the eye was sufficient to let him know that this one was going to be different – refreshingly devoid, he felt, of the usual cheap use of sentimentality.

Daniel's dilemma was clear. He felt a deep sense of responsibility to be as accurate in his portrayal of the real-life Christy Brown as he could. This – there was no avoiding it – meant transforming himself into a man whose body is permanently contorted, whose head lolls and whose speech, at least at first, is slurred. But at the same time he did not want to deliver a performance so dramatic and realistic that it became a freak show. That feeling had only deepened through working with Gene Lambert. Then something else struck him. For all the obvious physical hurdles he knew he had to overcome, so determined had he been to immerse himself in Christy's mind that Daniel had never actually considered that the film was about a crippled man.

There were certainly others, however, who had considered precisely this fact. When the news broke that Daniel Day-Lewis was to play Christy Brown, it caused a furore among the disabled actors in Equity, the British actors' trade union. That year Equity had just opened a register of disabled members with upwards of a hundred names on it, including those with cerebral palsy. These members understandably demanded to know why an able-bodied actor should be cast to simulate paralysis, when there were so many available who could portray it for real.

For one disabled performer in particular it was just another log on the fire of a long-running intense frustration. Accomplished actor Nabil Shaban, whose career has encompassed playing Jesus in *Godspell*, Haile Selassie and Hamlet, was outraged. He says, 'I heard about *My Left Foot* before it was made, as you do obviously through the grapevine. What happened was that a friend of mine who is also a friend of Daniel Day-Lewis was visiting one night. He casually dropped into the conversation that a film of Christy Brown's life was in the offing with Day-Lewis in the lead. He didn't think I'd be upset by this news but I just hit the roof and was determined to try to do something about it.'

He goes on, 'I immediately started a campaign to protest about it even though I kind of knew it was probably too late, with contracts having been drawn and so on, but I wanted awareness drawn to this whole deplorable practice of what is nothing less than body fascism.'

Besides writing to the film's makers, Nabil also contacted literally hundreds of other people, including pressure groups around the world, referring in his letters to the 'obscenity of *My Left Foot*' and the 'grotesquely inappropriate casting of Day-Lewis'. He admits, 'I tried to create as much controversy as I could. I called on disabled people to boycott the film, to picket any cinema showing it and to hassle the distributors at every turn.'

His was a legitimate grievance with which Daniel personally had sympathy. But the harsh commercial truth of the matter remained, as far as those involved with making the film were concerned, that had they not drafted in Daniel then the film would not have been made at all. Casting anyone else, they considered, was therefore not a possibility.

Perhaps, even if subconsciously, the anger of Nabil Shaban and his fellow actors influenced the lengths to which Daniel went to immerse himself in his role, for at times they verged on the extreme. His preference for staying locked into the world of his character for as long as he could sustain it had been strengthening all the time. Now his obsession was out in the open for all to see.

One of his ultimate objectives was to prevent the viewer from remembering for a single second that he could actually get up out of the wheelchair and walk off for some lunch or a smoke. Not that he did anyway. From the moment filming began each day, Daniel remained wheelchair-bound in the real Christy's chair, his head and limbs painfully twisted to simulate cerebral palsy. He racked his voice, too, in his quest to stay 'paralysed' for up to ten-hour stretches at a time. Each morning he insisted that he be carried across the lengths of lighting cables to reach the set, remaining as Christy even during the long periods between takes when he was not required. At every mealtime, in the scrum of the canteen at Ardmore Studios, he insisted on being spoon-fed. If no one would oblige him, he literally did not eat. It was behaviour which spawned various reactions.

At first many were overawed and impressed at such immense dedication, but then admiration, perhaps understandably, wore thin among some of the busy crew because of the number of times they were expected to carry Daniel about. Saeed Jaffrey remembers cameraman Jack Conroy telling him that the last straw came when they were expected to cart Daniel up several flights of ladders to shoot some particular scenes. This extra burden was also a drain on everyone's time, which led to more irritation. But, if anyone entertained the notion that it was all, or even partly, an eccentric affectation, they were entirely wrong.

For Daniel, the task had been to break himself down and rebuild as another person – this time one whose physical impairments put huge extra demands on the actor's ingenuity and imagination. To turn himself into Christy Brown required

...aniel Day-Lewis with his sister Tamasin and their parents. The family ...e reading letters congratulating Daniel's father, Cecil, on becoming a ...oet laureate.

Daniel played the suave seducer Tomas in *The Unbearable Lightness of Being*. His role in this film assured his status as an international sex symbol as he set female hearts racing.

bove: *The Unbearable Lightness of Being* was his first starring role. He
pictured here alongside Juliette Binoche.

elow: Daniel played Christy Brown in *My Left Foot*, a true story about a
erebal palsy sufferer, severely handicapped from birth. He overcomes
e difficulties caused by his condition to become an accomplished artist
d writer, pictured below.

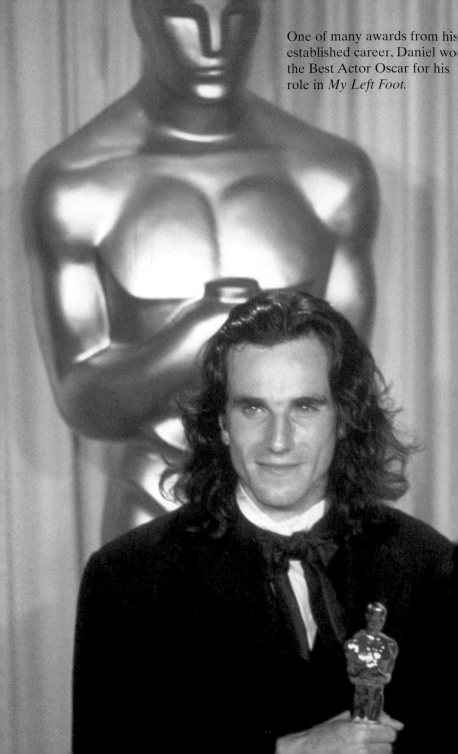

One of many awards from his established career, Daniel won the Best Actor Oscar for his role in *My Left Foot*.

…aniel is very particular about the roles he chooses to play. After much …rsuasion, he was impressed by director Michael Mann's passion for …*st of The Mohicans,* despite his own fears of the fame such a glamorous …e might bring him.

An introspective character who uses method acting techniques, Day-Lewis likes to live the lives of each of his very different characters.

aniel Day-Lewis with Cameron Diaz in *The Gangs of New York*. The
m centres on the bloody turf war between native Americans and Irish
migrants for control of the New York neighbourhood.

Above: During the making of *The Crucible*, Daniel met director, Arthur Miller's daughter, Rebecca Miller, an actress and director. The pair instantly fell in love and married in 1996. They are pictured here with Arthur Miller.

Below: The Ballad of Jack and Rose is co-written and directed by Daniel's wife Rebecca. Daniel, who plays Jack, is seen here with co-star Catherine Keener.

a new intensity in every sense and for Day-Lewis pulling any performance together already means a relentless concentration of energy, both physical and mental.

The process was interesting to watch. What had started as tolerance among the crew, gradually waned. The all-too-common habit of talking about someone in a wheelchair as if they were not there crept in. Annoyance at not always being able to understand what Daniel said, especially when they knew perfectly well that he could speak clearly, also began to surface.

There was a point to it all, however, and a benefit too, because, within the space of about a week, realisation had begun to dawn of the changes which had come over everyone and why. By analysing their reactions, they all realised that it led to a far better understanding of what they were trying to achieve than any amount of theory would have given them. The final result was a unique sense of involvement, a tight-knit production team and a performance from Daniel more powerful than had been seen on screen for years. It was a towering triumph, projecting with uncompromising frankness all the fury and pent-up frustrations of the man, coupled with his earthy, sometimes cutting, humour. Never once did he play for sympathy.

After the opening scene when Christy plays his classical record – a shot which took about fifteen takes before Daniel felt that putting on an LP with his foot looked like an everyday occurrence – he and his family are ferried in style to a stately home. Here, a benefit, at which he is the guest of honour, has been organised and it is while waiting in the library for his introduction that the story begins to unfold.

Christy as a young boy is played by Hugh O'Conor who, without one single line of dialogue, gives an outstandingly brilliant performance as a child locked in a silent world, unable as yet to talk. His family, particularly his father, are unaware that he does in fact understand them very well, but just cannot communicate. Brenda Fricker is marvellous as the mother, a strong and endlessly patient woman who is really the linchpin that holds the entire family together.

The Browns' two-bedroomed end of terrace house is overrun with children who all sleep in the same bedroom: boys like sardines in one bed, girls in the other. Daniel enters the film when Christy turns seventeen years old. It is his birthday and, as his family sit around the table wearing party hats made from newspaper, his mother brings in a huge home-baked cake with candles for him to blow out, which he has some difficulty in doing. Although permanently hard up for money, his mum is secretly saving up for a wheelchair, hiding the cash in a tin stuffed up the chimney of the coal fire.

Daniel saw the film primarily as the story of very ordinary, everyday family matters made complicated not only by Christy's cerebral palsy, but also by the problems inherent in growing up amid a large family living below the breadline in cramped conditions with no privacy, and coping with deep feelings of rivalry and the search for love and relationships. Christy's personality and achievements, his problems and frustrations are interwoven into the fabric of the film by a screenplay that deals honestly with issues less commonly addressed when the central character is a disabled person: most particularly his increasing awareness of his own developing sexuality.

Because Daniel takes over from Hugh O'Conor when Christy is a young man, it falls to him to depict his frustration at having been offered nothing but platonic love all his life. Although this eventually explodes during a charged restaurant scene when he memorably blasts, 'Fuck Plato!', there are threaded throughout the film moments of unspoken yet evident yearning, eloquently expressed by Daniel by simply a look or a grimace. This might be at the sight during the night of his older sister's bare back when the sheet inadvertently slips down in the bed across the room, or at glimpsing some intimate exchange between his father and mother. Daniel called the film a complicated story about simple things, but it included Christy's battle with the bottle, and at times with his rage against his father.

Rage is perhaps the emotion he imparts best in this role. His angry fierce eyes convey much more than words ever could; he brims with raw aggression. As he grows older, and his needs increase apace with his frustrations, Daniel's expressions deepen with a unique poignancy. But, alongside his anger, Christy has an enormous capacity for tenderness and there are moments when sudden joy breaks out. A fiery man, he admires spirit in others – as shown when, having locked himself in his bedroom on his return from the clinic, he swears at the female doctor standing on the other side of the door who is urging him to continue his treatment. The voice of Dr Eileen Cole, played by Fiona Shaw, unflinchingly comes back at him. 'With speech therapy, I could teach you to say "Fuck off" more clearly.' Christy doubles up with delight.

Professionally speaking, it is a performance from Day-Lewis which strips the senses raw. Often without a single word he communicates, by a combination of masterly facial expressions, subtle body language and barely discernible mannerisms, the whole gamut of life's emotions. As the story unfolds, Christy receives therapy from Dr Cole at home. She teaches him to exercise his lungs better and coaches him in the development of his speech. Because of their close working relationship he thrives physically, mentally and emotionally. It is through her contacts with an art gallery that his work begins to be recognised and she introduces him to the work of Shakespeare, encouraging him to learn speeches from *Hamlet*.

Along the way, perhaps predictably, Christy falls in love with her. He paints her portrait, which he keeps hidden beneath his bed, and awaits her visits with mounting excitement. Having already tried and failed to find a way to tell her of his feelings, he tries again on the night of his one-man art exhibition, during a meal afterwards in a restaurant. Unfortunately for Christy, she feels no more than platonic love for him. She chooses that very moment to tell him that she and the gallery owner are engaged to be married. The exhausting distress and rage that Daniel projects as Christy erupts hold an almost hypnotic horror.

The embarrassment of others around the table is very much secondary to Christy's own mounting trauma, made worse by repeated aggressive demands for more whisky when he is already drunk. Finally he bangs his forehead violently on the table. Eileen's fiancé loses his temper and tries to wheel Christy out of the shocked restaurant, but he has sunk his teeth into the tablecloth. Crockery and glass, wine and food cascade everywhere and Eileen is left rigid with tears of rage amid it all.

Shortly afterwards there is a silent, brief but harrowing scene when Christy, alone in his bedroom, attempts to cut his wrist by using an open cut-throat razor gripped between his toes. Yet it is the charged drama in the restaurant which for many stayed in the memory.

Describing the authenticity with which Daniel captured this utter humiliation, Pauline Kael of *The New Yorker* wrote that it was possibly the most emotionally heartbreaking scene she had ever experienced in the movies. 'Day-Lewis seizes the viewer,' she gushed. 'He takes possession of you.' This was something of a U-turn, since the same woman five years before had lambasted Daniel's John Fryer in *The Bounty*, saying with the lack of perspicaciousness peculiar to critics that Daniel Day-Lewis 'seemed like a bad actor'.

My Left Foot would achieve high international acclaim in time, but its initial reception was a very different story. It was naturally instantly popular in Ireland – a fact which meant a great deal to Daniel. On a personal note, when Christy's widow Mary attended the world première in Dublin at the Savoy Cinema on 24 February 1989, she was astounded at how strongly Daniel embodied precisely the powerful inner essence of her husband, so authoritatively that, for the duration of the film, even for her he had become Christy.

It was not, however, to Mary Brown that Daniel looked first for approval of his performance. Tony Jordan and some of Sandymount's pupils, including Mary Keirnan, whose typing skills Daniel had studied closely, were among the special guests attending the première. 'I was standing at the back of the audience when just at the end of the film yer man Day-Lewis came striding single-mindedly straight up to me,' reveals Tony. 'He was desperately nervous, wanting to know what I thought. To him, we were the ones to judge him best and I was happy to tell him that I thought he had brought off an almost perfectly authentic portrayal. He got as close as anyone possibly could get to truly representing Christy Brown. The only negative thing I have to say about it is that there was a tendency to be rather heavy-handed with the drinking and bad language side of him. Stage Irish I call it.'

There were one or two others who, according to Tony, had their own disappointments. He explains, 'The character in the film Dr Eileen Cole never existed. She was supposed to represent an amalgam of several people who helped Christy. Robert Collis was his mentor in every way – in his education and physical development but, more than that, he encouraged him to paint and write. In fact, he proofread Christy's first book and contacted the publishers for him – the lot. Dr Patricia Sheehan, who had played a very important role in Christy's development, was very much against the portrayal of Eileen Cole in the film.'

Leaving these details aside, however, the night of the world première was a time of celebration. At the reception afterwards, Daniel delighted the Sandymount contingent, some of whom, like members of the Brown family, had appeared as extras in the film, by singling them out. 'For all the fuss and goings on,' confirms Tony, 'typically, Day-Lewis paid a lot of personal attention to the pupils, which meant the world to them.'

Admiration for the film, though, was by no means universal and disappointingly it was turned down as an entry to the Cannes Film Festival. In Britain, despite having attracted strongly favourable reports before its release, it vanished so fast that it went straight to video within a fortnight. But then *My Left Foot* found its way to America, where it took off in an enormous way. Suddenly, the talk was all of possible Oscar nominations for this film which had struggled to attract financial backing.

Regardless of the film's reception, Daniel knew when he finished work on *My Left Foot* that it had been, quite probably, a unique experience of his life. And the pleasure this knowledge gave him was so intense that it was almost painful. For, tucked away at the back of his mind, he was aware that it might be something that would never again be repeated in his career. He also knew that this was how he wanted – needed – to work if he was to reconcile the internal debate about the worthwhileness of his chosen profession.

He maintained that making *My Left Foot* had not left him

hungry, but that it had left him very tired. This had been by far his toughest role yet. On a purely physical level, contorting his body for ten-hour stretches at a time, day after day, had left its mark, playing havoc with his protesting muscles and bones. Emotionally the experience had also been bruising.

As he had done before, Daniel began work on his next project punishingly soon, just one week after shooting ended in September for *My Left Foot*. As with the uninspiring *Nanou*, he had again opted to invest his time and energy in a foreign production – this time one which took him to Argentina.

At a previous London Film Festival Daniel had caught the film *The King and his Movie* by director Carlos Sorin. It was apparently on the strength of this effort that he agreed to star in Sorin's new film entitled *Eversmile, New Jersey* – Donald Sutherland had also, it is said, been considered for the role. The Los Films Del Camino Production was based on a screenplay by Jorge Goldenberg, Robert Sheuer and Carlos Sorin and produced by Oscar Kramer. Taking part cannot by any stretch of the imagination be classed as one of Daniel's better decisions.

Why he agreed to do this wacky road movie is puzzling. He was certainly in no physical shape to be rushing straight into another film, and indeed describes himself as being like 'dog meat' during the entire nine-week shoot. He had also lacked the time, once again, to shed his last character. In fact, he was still so immersed in being an Irishman that he is allegedly responsible for the lead character's nationality being switched from American, as in the original script, to Irish. *Eversmile, New Jersey* must go down as another of Daniel's forays into wilful obscurity.

His character is Dr Fergus O'Connell, a member of the Du Bois Foundation for the Development of Dental Consciousness. Eversmile is the name of the Jersey dental company which he represents. Daniel may have gained a reputation for never playing two characters alike, but, for most of the film, the voice of Christy Brown is heard time and again on screen. Fergus introduces himself as an Irishman from New Jersey but, when his accent is not a straight lift from Christy, he lapses from Irish brogue into standard English. At no time does he sound American – this, for an actor adept at accents, is surely a sign of his fatigue.

As O'Connell, dressed like a World War I flyer, complete with Red Baron goggles, he travels through Patagonia on a motorbike with sidecar. The travelling dentist's almost evangelical mission is to educate the ignorant and relieve suffering, all free of charge. Daniel plays the dentist as irrepressibly cheerful and doggedly undaunted in the face of fear and apathy. His passion for his mission can even lead him to erupt into violence and he is a man obsessed, if not possessed.

It is a dreadful film, not in any way relieved by the presence of his only co-star Mirjana Jokovic. She plays Estella, the daughter of a garage owner who comes to O'Connell's rescue when he has a road accident. Attracted to the stranger, she hides herself in the sidecar of the repaired motorbike and on the day Fergus leaves – the day she is due to marry a local man – she takes off with the dentist instead. The film also has odd religious overtones, and at one point Fergus lapses into a diatribe on the sectarian troubles in Northern Ireland. Treading a lonely path, he faces disillusionment and rejection, temporarily losing Estella to a vampish widow.

In a scene typical of the quirky movie, he finally rides up to the gas station where she works to find, as it is Christmas Day, that all the pump attendants are in festive costume. Circling Estella, who is dressed up as an angel, he calls to her to join him on the bike. She eventually does so, chased by half a dozen employees in Santa costumes. In the oldest cliché in cinema, the pair ride off into the sunset – Fergus driven by his new vision of a future without bacteria.

Not surprisingly *Eversmile, New Jersey* was deemed to be virtually unshowable and suffered the ignominy of being released straight on to video. Five years and three blockbuster movies later, when Daniel's star had safely risen, the film was screened as part of a special Day-Lewis series running at the Barbican in London. His friend Richard Marne, who caught the film, says, 'It is an absolutely awful movie, but leaving that aside the thing I couldn't help but be aware of all the way through was that, for those people who don't know him, it is the closest you'll get to seeing the real Daniel Day-Lewis – the citizen, the private man, his love of motorbikes and just how gregarious he can be.'

It seems a doubtful recommendation for, gregarious or not, it could be argued that Fergus O'Connell was on the brink of insanity. Certainly, by the time Daniel vanishes from the screen on his vintage motorbike, far from exuding any *joie de vivre* he looked very much more like a man completely at his wits' end.

CHAPTER SEVEN

BREAKDOWN

'My father's spirit – all is not well.'
PRINCE OF DENMARK, *HAMLET*

Much of the Day-Lewis mythology, building upon an already misleading media interpretation of his overdose at the age of fifteen, has centred on the moment in 1989 when he dramatically walked off stage during a production of *Hamlet* at London's National Theatre. Claims that he had suffered a nervous breakdown, that the effect was so traumatic that he could never bear to set foot on stage again would mushroom and multiply by the score until, according to the actor, he has read so many differing newspaper versions of what happened that there are times when he cannot remember the truth himself. Four years later, at the end of 1993, Daniel would eventually come out in the press and nail at least half of the myth – the half relating to just how devastating an effect it had had on him.

Hamlet, William Shakespeare's most famous play, is often

classed as the litmus test of an actor's career. Memorable Hamlets of the past have included Laurence Olivier, Richard Burton and Derek Jacobi. Kenneth Branagh is one of many who considers Hamlet to be an 'Everest of a role'. Max Beerbohm, founder of the Royal Academy of Dramatic Art (RADA), described the part many years ago as 'a hoop through which every eminent actor must sooner or later jump'.

But not every performer agrees with this opinion – and Daniel is one of those dissenters. Steadfastly determined not to be intimidated by the play's history, he denounces as 'all that theatre shite' the awe that a young actor is expected to feel towards the part and his illustrious predecessors in it. It was ironic, then, that this was a period in his life when many unhappy elements from his past would conspire to catch up on him.

Still not recognising his need to slow down, he embarked on rehearsals for *Hamlet* too soon after his return from South America. The National Theatre Company production would reunite him with director Richard Eyre who, just months before, had taken over as artistic director. The general consensus appears to be that Daniel, strangely enough, came to the play not altogether familiar with its plot and without being aware of the psychological minefield he might be entering.

The story goes that he quickly became obsessed with aspects of the play which he found in some way to parallel his own life. He promptly obtained from his mother a photograph of his father to hang prominently in his dressing room more, it is thought, as a challenge than a source of inspiration.

Whatever his intention, the reminder of Cecil would prove to create problems for Daniel. Since *The Unbearable Lightness of Being*, he had kept up a hectic work schedule, not just in terms of physical time and energy but, perhaps more debilitating, in mental energy. In his last four roles he had alternated between intensely serious characters and crazy, screwball individuals, all of which put intensely draining demands on him.

Because he had had no break between parts, trying to shake off both Tomas and Christy had at times been particularly hard. The process of continually having to shoulder aside their intrusions in order to portray the much more lightweight characters of Henderson and Fergus must have been very taxing. It would hardly have been surprising, in fact, if, along the way, something had got scrambled. But, although Daniel was inexorably heading for trouble, he could not afford to acknowledge it, even if he recognised it. He was certainly not himself, though, and the cracks would not be too long in beginning to show.

Hamlet was to be Daniel's first attempt at the role of the Prince of Denmark and his second time at the National Theatre. Built on London's South Bank, the building is one for which he has expressed an unusually graphic dislike, especially of its claustrophobic dressing rooms like concrete cells. It would be the third time he had worked with director Richard Eyre. The cast assembled for the play, which would last three hours and forty-five minutes, promised an impressive production. It included John Castle as Claudius, King of Denmark, Judi Dench as Gertrude, Hamlet's mother and the Queen, Michael Bryant as Polonius, Lord Chamberlain, and Stella Gonet as Polonius's daughter Ophelia, Hamlet's love. The Ghost of Hamlet's father was played by David Burke. The play had its first preview on 10 March 1989, opening six nights later.

Despite his determinedly unimpressed attitude towards the play's reputation, Daniel, with his fondness for tackling the most impenetrable characters, had found a worthy subject in Hamlet. Unfortunately, this time he had bitten off more than he could chew. It was to be a seven-month run in rep, often playing five nights a week. Run down to start with, he was to fight a losing battle with fatigue as time went on.

Generally accepted as being Shakespeare's most problematic play, variations in the execution of *Hamlet* can be profound. Daniel played his Hamlet as an apparently mad and certainly melancholy Prince, but in an unusually athletic manner. During his preparation for the role, someone described the character to him as being a silent man. This seems paradoxical since Hamlet talks incessantly throughout, yet it made complete sense to Daniel. As, in some ways, with Christy Brown, he was drawn to the role by what he perceived as Hamlet's complete inability to clearly express his thoughts and define his fears, even to himself, let alone to anyone else.

Looking the part came easily to Daniel. Tall and dark, his deep-set penetrating eyes were well able to project glittering but silent rage. His wide, thin-lipped mouth, curving with clever cruelty, would add to the saturnine image. And he had learned long ago how to use his hawklike profile to dramatic effect. *Being* the part, however – something he had become an acknowledged master at in other roles – proved an entirely different matter. Although his presence physically dominated the stage from the opening sequence, spiritually there was something disconcertingly elusive about him.

His greatest goal in acting, he says, is to be so completely immersed in his role that somewhere in the creation of that illusion he can lose all sense of himself. With *Hamlet*, a play so inextricably bound up with the relationship between a son and his dead father, it seemed that quite the reverse was happening. This time Daniel was being forced to confront himself in ways he had neither expected nor welcomed.

By his own admission, at thirty-two he was still weighed down by the regrets of his adolescence – the feeling that he had not achieved anything of which Cecil could be proud before he died. But, whatever unresolved feelings may have lain between Daniel and his father, by five months into the run at the National he had come to believe that Cecil was keeping a kindly eye on him.

There were, however, signs that problems were waiting in the wings. With discernible melancholy, during the inevitable round of theatre press interviews, he would talk of seeking self oblivion, of hovering close to the brink of an abyss and of having unearthed fears within himself, both old and new. One recurring demon was still the persistent doubt he harboured about the validity of being an actor at all – an agony he seems almost to wear like a hair shirt.

That was off stage. On stage, critics were quick to notice a problem too. Those who had hailed his earlier National Theatre appearance as Mayakovsky in *Futurists* as nothing short of electrifying found themselves searching desperately in vain for the same all-consuming passion from the Danish Prince. But the conviction did not seem to be there, and the opening-night reviews told of a lacklustre performance. Much as he had done before with *Look Back in Anger*, Daniel took the critics' remarks to heart. But this time he hid his feelings behind a show of belligerence, while privately casting about for ways to improve his performance.

Past attempts to strengthen his performances had proved successful, but this time the results were unpredictable. As the run progressed the notices proved mixed, deeming the play neither a brilliant success nor yet an unmitigated failure.

But, regardless of the opinions of audiences and critics, for Daniel himself this whole period of time was a daily grind. He would later refer to *Hamlet* as 'that dreadful play'. Leading up to each performance he would have to spend most of that day lying flat on his back in solitude trying to, as he puts it, clear his eyes. Intense torment is, of course, the emotion from which Hamlet never escapes throughout the play. His grief in the opening scene when his father, the King of Denmark, is being buried is compounded by the suspicion aroused in him by the surreptitious glances passing between his mother Gertrude and his father's brother, Claudius. When less than two months later the two marry, those suspicions of infidelity grow deeper. 'Frailty,' he curses, 'thy name is woman!' His state of mind becomes so bad that Ophelia's brother Laertes, played here by Peter Lindford, warns her to be careful of Hamlet's sanity.

Alerted by his friend Horatio that the ghost of the dead king has been seen walking on the battlements, Hamlet watches in the hope that the apparition will return. He does so, and with devastating consequences, for the spirit tells his son that not only had his mother committed adultery with his uncle, but, that he himself had in fact been murdered by Claudius. He charges Hamlet to avenge him and so a tale ensues rank with bitter treachery, revenge and slaughter. For almost four hours Hamlet runs headlong towards madness, his nerves stretched to breaking point by the ghost's visits – the second time of which is to the Queen's bedchamber where Hamlet, spilling out all his rage, grief and torment to his mother, straddles the terrified Gertrude pinning her down brutally on the bed and savagely kissing her.

In complicated plot and counter-plot, duels are fought with venom-tipped swords and poisoned toasts unsuspectingly drunk. Gertrude is killed by poison meant for Hamlet; Laertes is mistakenly poisoned by his own venom-tipped sword and Claudius is run through by Hamlet, who, having been slashed by Laertes's lethal sword, dies in the arms of the faithful Horatio. Performance after performance, Daniel went through these on stage traumas for months on end until one Thursday, late in September, something snapped.

A brewing storm is easy to recognise in hindsight, but more difficult at the time. Especially when intensity in Daniel was, for fellow actors, very much to be expected. Judi Dench, as Queen Gertrude, had the most important contact with Daniel during this time and she remembers the period with deep affection. Because of her acquaintance with Jill Balcon, Judi had known Daniel since he was a child. She had also starred in *A Room with a View* three years before, playing the part of Miss Eleanor Lavish, a lady novelist – for which she won the BAFTA Award for Best Supporting Actress. However, she and Daniel had not worked together then. She explains, 'As I only appeared in the first half of the film, all my scenes were filmed in Florence and none of them were with Daniel who, of course, comes into the film once it switches to England. So the first time we actually worked together was in *Hamlet*.

She goes on, 'He's – well, everyone knows how intense Daniel is. But I felt that he didn't seem as wound up during rehearsals as he is always reported to be now on his film sets. Having said that, once *Hamlet* opened that intensity was every bit as strong as he's famous for these days. I mean in the canteen beforehand he was kind of alright, I'd say, but once the play started he was locked into that performance totally. He focused in on it in minute detail.'

As is the nature of things, because Daniel did walk off mid-performance almost all the focus of his time in the play rests exclusively on that moment. But before that there had been a run of just short of seven months – a period Judi thinks of as having been very special. She says, 'As an actor Daniel is very different, totally unique. He was absolutely thrilling to work with. Sometimes when actors work closely together, the two of you will naturally adapt to each other and that's what happened with Daniel and I. Also, every night he changed it, even if only ever so slightly which meant you could never be complacent. You had to listen acutely to him throughout each performance and that was marvellous. For us it meant we were so alive to all the changes, which brought a wonderful freshness to it every time.'

Dame Judi Dench is a highly respected British actress. In autumn 1995 she made a piece of film history by being the first woman to portray the spy chief character 'M' in Cubby Broccoli's seventeenth James Bond movie *Goldeneye*. A veteran of many stage, film and television appearances, she has a well-earned reputation for investing poignancy in comedy while equally possessing the gift of leavening tragedy with humour. She made her acting debut at the Old Vic Theatre playing Ophelia, Hamlet's love, back in 1957 – the year Daniel was born. Thirty-two years later she was playing mother to Daniel's Hamlet – something she has very set views on.

Amidst the mixed reviews which followed the opening night, the one constant target for praise was Judi's performance. *Punch* magazine called her Gertrude excellent, extolling her combination of regal demeanour and earthy voluptuousness, while others showered her with 'magnificent', 'soft and sensual' and 'in peak form'. But, Judi does not see it that way. She maintains, 'The play itself wasn't particularly successful, nor yet unsuccessful. But leaving that aside, I wasn't happy at all with my own performance. It was a very personal thing but I just could not believe myself to be someone who could have given birth to Daniel. In contrast to me, Daniel's mother in real life is very dark and statuesque, and I was acutely aware of not being able to *be* that. I never felt that I looked like his mother. I trained as a designer and so I tend to see things very differently and I just know I didn't measure up.' She adds, 'I simply cannot shake the belief that somehow I failed in the part.'

It's not an opinion with which Daniel is likely to agree. The personal relationship between himself and Judi is one of deep warmth. Says Judi, 'Probably the most special moment during that time for me was when Daniel was talking about a poem his father had written for either himself or his brother. I can't now recall the name of the poem but it was about looking back, about school etc. Anyway, Daniel was talking about it and I said I admired it and all of a sudden he just said it to me. It sounds such a simple thing, but I can remember that moment so vividly and I always will. It was very special.'

She goes on, 'He is a very loving person when you get to know him, full of fun with a great sense of humour. But his responsibility to his work is of absolute paramount importance to him. It is to a lot of actors I know, but Daniel sets aside a great deal of himself for his work and that's something most actors don't.'

That Daniel perhaps sets too much of himself aside and too often would seem to be at least part of the reason for the dam breaking. That he had come to the play having pushed himself too far is something Judi can fully endorse. 'Yes, he was very run down, and especially so as the run progressed. On top of that, of course, *Hamlet is* such an intense part without adding Daniel's own brand of intensity to it. His tiredness or whatever it was, didn't detract from his performance at all. But off stage it was a different matter.'

Five months into the run, the company took the play to Dubrovnik in former Yugoslavia where they were to perform as part of a July festival. Daniel found great solace in these performances, essentially because the difference between

Yugoslav and British audiences was so profound. It was their sheer entrancement, their silent absorption of the minutiae of each show which cast a spell night after night. It gave Daniel a comforting depth into which he could allow himself to be drawn and in which he felt accepted and appreciated. When not working, however, he had taken to shutting himself off from the rest of the cast completely. Judi confirms, 'I can't recall ever seeing Daniel during the day when we were there. Not once. By the time we came back to London he was quite obviously extremely tired.'

That weariness wore on until a matinée performance one day in September. At the moment in the opening act when Hamlet first confronts the ghost of his father alone on the castle battlements, Daniel suddenly froze. The entire audience watched in startled disbelief as, after a few seconds of loaded suspense, he abruptly swung on his heel and strode off stage. In the years since that moment, a three-ring circus of conjecture has sprung up as to what exactly happened and why. That Daniel was physically exhausted is undeniable, but even according to the man himself, there was undoubtedly more to it than that.

He has admitted that suddenly, after playing the scene countless times without incident, instead of seeing the actor David Burke, he had had the most bizarre sensation that he was seeing and talking to his late father. He has openly admitted that he has long talked to his dead father every day as a matter of course, but presumably he had never before received a response. Apart from a single ambiguous allusion to Cecil having cast doubt on his career as an actor, Daniel has never admitted in detail exactly what it was he felt his father said to him on this occasion. Only that its effect on him was something he found perilously close to intolerable.

Regardless of how intensive the rehearsal period has been, or how long the run has lasted, during each performance the actor stands alone. Despite a packed auditorium and any number of fellow actors sharing the spotlight, that expanse of stage can be the loneliest place on earth. Concentration and imagination are considered to be the most important attributes an actor can have, but a fine balance must always be maintained. If for any reason the scales tip and the former wanes, while the latter catapults out of all proportion, then the results can be disastrous.

What's thought to be a useful device encouraged in the trainee actor is that, where fatigue or fear threatens during a performance, they must try to conjure up an imaginary bond with someone living or dead with whom there is a genuine personal link. Having forged this bond they should then concentrate on addressing that person instead. The effect is supposed to eradicate any feelings of self-consciousness or inadequacy. But, if Daniel did indeed conjure up his father's spirit that performance, it had the very opposite of a calming effect on him.

The actual moment at which Daniel ground to a halt certainly remains vivid to Judi Dench. She says, 'I wasn't actually on stage at that point, but was listening of course on the Tannoy and everything was proceeding as normal. Then, in the middle of Daniel talking to the Ghost, there was suddenly just this long pause, this complete dead silence. Naturally the first reaction for everyone was confusion, then as I recall there was an announcement, the curtain came down and Daniel's understudy had to prepare to take over.'

Daniel's understudy was Jeremy Northam, who otherwise played the courtier Osric. Says Judi, 'Michael Bryant went to Daniel and he was exactly the best person to go. I didn't go to him as I didn't want him to feel crowded – that was the last thing he needed right then. Instead, I went to Jeremy and I can honestly say I have never in my life seen anyone so completely white-faced. He was whiter than white and who can blame him. To have to suddenly get into costume and get out on stage in those circumstances in front of a by now thoroughly agog audience? Poor lad.'

As to what lay behind Daniel's startling departure from the stage, Judi says, 'I think Hamlet is such a challenge for any actor but for Daniel the emotions were just a little too close to home. I don't know. It's like if you can imagine two parallel but separate liquids, say water and blood. For Daniel, the water just ran red – the two mingled too well and suddenly it was all too much for him. Perhaps it would've been easier for him if it had been a film and not the stage in front of a live audience, but the demands on him at that moment were too much for him to take.'

More than Michael Bryant rallied round to support Daniel. The Scots actor and *Chariots of Fire* star Ian Charleson, who would take over as Daniel's replacement when a re-cast production opened again on 9 October, walked up to him later that day in the canteen and hugged him. He reassured him that, if he had in truth confronted Cecil's ghost, it was no bad thing to have faced it and come through the ordeal. His words were of obvious comfort to Daniel who must have still been very shaken by the experience. He left the theatre that night and was happy to do so; happy also in the knowledge that with his departure Ian would have the chance to take over a role he had very much wanted. Sadly, less than three months later, on 6 January 1990, Ian Charleson died of an AIDS-related disease.

The theatre has often witnessed actors walking off stage or being unable to go on in the first place, struck suddenly, often irrespective of experience, by stage fright. Others have simply abandoned a production mid-run, brought down by cruel reviews or overwork. In February 1995, the workaholic television star Stephen Fry caused a scare by going AWOL after only three performances of *Cell Mates*, a Simon Gray play in which he had been co-starring with fellow comedian Rik Mayall at London's Albery Theatre. His understudy Mark Anderson briefly stepped into the role of the spy George Blake before the production shut down.

But in Daniel's case many believed it was something more – that he actually suffered a nervous breakdown following this episode and that the traumatic memory has hung over him like an immovable black cloud, preventing him from ever wishing to set foot on stage again. The truth is that, in spite of its dramatic culmination, Daniel believes the experience of playing Hamlet to be something that he is glad he went through. As to never returning to the stage, although he is of the opinion that most theatre is bad, that too he condemns as a media myth.

The reality, he maintains, is that nothing has yet arisen that is sufficiently good to tempt him back. He also holds strong opinions on the snobbery within the business towards those who, like himself, do not put theatre work above all else. Judi Dench believes, 'I don't think Daniel wanted to be contained on a stage, if you know what I mean. I don't believe he wanted the stricture of four walls. Film is perhaps a medium he is happier in.'

Whether what happened to Daniel constituted a nervous breakdown or not, to conform with the National Theatre's insurance requirements he was obliged to take part in what he has called 'the fringes of analysis'. Hitherto it had not been his style to have a great deal of patience with any of his ailments. However, he clearly recognised the need to talk this particular.

problem over with someone. The fact that he had no choice but to enter into even the shallows of therapy, he now believes, helped him. The darker side of life is Daniel's confessed natural choice, but this time others were able to divert him from that bleak road – at least for a while.

Immediately after that night Daniel effectively vanished. His first call had been on a close friend, followed then by the Somerset home of his sister Tamasin who, since the day he ran to her side as a distraught thirteen-year-old from Sevenoaks school, seems to have been a natural magnet for him in his most troubled times. There, as part of his recuperation programme, he allowed her to steer him on to a healthier diet, obeying her instructions willingly with the exception of giving up smoking. He gave every sign of beginning to unwind, but then one morning Tamasin found that her unpredictable younger brother had flown the coop with little more than a change of clothes. He would go to earth for several months.

He left behind both general speculation and, for some, self-recrimination. Daniel had been living alone during the play's run, with no desire to socialise when he was not at the theatre. Even so, some people around him began to regret not having noticed the build-up of stress and castigated themselves for having done nothing to help. *Hamlet*'s director Richard Eyre went on record to say that in hindsight Daniel was the last actor he ought to have asked to play the troubled Prince, given that it ran a high risk of exposing his most raw personal nerves. And there was concern as well as understanding from his friends and fellow actors, especially from those with whom he had worked in the past. Director Ronald Wilson recalls, '*Hamlet* was certainly something I felt that Daniel was less successful in – I mean throughout the entire run. I liked what he was attempting to do with the part, but I didn't feel that he was vocally up to it. There was a tremendous energy about him, a vulnerable quality of youthfulness and certainly an attack. But I kept feeling that it should have been varied more and I could not understand why he wasn't directed to do that.'

He goes on, 'Daniel went at it full tilt, though, all the way through, and so of course it came to be that he was operating on a very needy, nervous and edgy plateau. The thing is, it worked in lots of ways but it's a role which puts enormous demands on an actor.'

This opinion is strongly endorsed by Daniel's friend, actor Alan MacNaughtan. He says, 'There is also a tremendous strain on being successful in this business and those strains become greater all the time. People tend to think that when you become famous that that's all right now. But it's not. It just means the burden gets all the heavier and becomes quite considerable. Daniel had been driving himself, as he does, at such a pace and he won't lower his standards or quieten down. It's almost a masochistic thing. It's certainly a kind of compulsion with him, but maybe there is something in it that lets him find the truth about himself.'

He adds, 'Hamlet is a play in which you can't totally fail. Almost always, even in the worst of performances, there emerges a few gems, a new slant. Even with what happened to Daniel, he didn't fail with his Hamlet.'

But perhaps the two men with whom he had previously worked who best understood were Simon Callow from *A Room With a View* and Jack Shepherd, alongside whom Daniel had appeared in *Futurists*. Simon had run into Daniel some weeks before his walk out and he reveals, 'I bumped into him in Colorado, where he was taking a break before his final stretch in *Hamlet*, and he was clearly under some considerable pressure. We talked at length and I know the role was giving him a great deal of grief. To go through that role and take it so seriously is dangerous anyway. Someone like Gielgud doesn't emotionally engage as Daniel does, for instance, and so it doesn't have the same effect on him. The hardest aspect of it was that Daniel was verbally uncomfortable with it and I think that was because he was so engrossed in what he was saying and feeling. He was feeling it all far, far too much.'

He goes on, 'You see, by nature Daniel is a mountain climber and not a skater. He's also not the kind of actor, or person for that matter, for whom words trip lightly off the tongue. And the thing is you need to find a line through a part like that, to find an arc along which to travel which is going to make the path easier. Olivier and Gielgud could do that effortlessly, but Daniel couldn't and was very locked into it in a dangerously personal way.'

What Simon also detected through his talks with Daniel was the private conflicts he was experiencing then. Says Simon, 'He spoke to me about his family background and there is, no doubt, a struggle within himself connected with his parents, his nationality and his class. There, too, there seems to have been no easy path for him and that, I feel, relates to everything he does in life.'

Jack Shepherd, for his part, understood only too well both the play and the actor. 'When Daniel assumes a new identity, he sheds his own with great determination and that's not an easy technical thing to do. It becomes a form of possession which I think results in this vibrancy that you feel from him. He is really committed, totally committed, as he was in *My Left Foot*, for instance. But there is a great deal of risk in this kind of possession because psychologically sooner or later it's going to have a serious blowback on you.'

As to Daniel's *Hamlet*, Jack goes on, 'Well, I managed to sneak snatches at it but I didn't see it all the way through, so I won't attempt to judge his performance as such. But I do understand the kinds of mental strain the part itself puts you under. It is certainly true that *Hamlet* requires enormous stamina. I've played it myself in Newcastle and it is an horrendously demanding role. The sheer amount of lines for a start is huge and the intensity is such that I think, if you have any psychological hiccups in you at all, then that is the play and the part that will bring them all tumbling out.'

He continues, 'It's extremely nerve-racking to act mad, to pretend to be mad when you're sane, and to pretend to be sane when you have in fact by then gone quite mad. You get very tired and yet overstimulated at the same time, which leads you into a highly stressful state where you become increasingly vulnerable and thoroughly drained.' Jack's illuminating description certainly seems to have accurately summed up Daniel's condition come September 1989.

The kinds of strain and pressure to which Simon Callow and Jack Shepherd attest have notoriously taken their toll on actors down the years. Many movie stars have turned to drink as a means of handling fame and meeting the demands it imposes of trying to better each performance. One reported casualty at the end of 1994 was Daniel's contemporary, *JFK* and *Dracula* star Gary Oldman who, in his determination to fight alcoholism, checked himself into a rehabilitation centre to dry out.

Ultimately, the idea that he might never return to the stage was not a prospect that Daniel found particularly upsetting. In fact, he is not afraid to say that, if the truth be known, the vast majority of stage actors would give their eye-teeth to transfer to film and that it is largely those on the periphery of the theatre who class it as a Faustian sell-out not to devote one's working life to the stage.

It's an old argument. Back in the seventies, Richard Burton confounded critics who accused him of wasting his talents by deserting the stage for some often dire films by confessing bluntly that he did so for the money. And his fellow Welshman Anthony Hopkins, when tackled on the same subject in a national television interview, owned up to a feeling of sheer euphoria each morning at the realisation that he would never have to play King Lear ever again.

Yet despite voices like these Daniel believes that snobbery within the theatre is, to a great extent, still prevalent. To a point, Jack Shepherd agrees with him. He says, 'The feeling of there being this elitism was certainly true up until, say, ten years ago. But there have been a lot of changes since then and now actors are encouraged very much to bow to the market place. It became, and really still is in a way, considered chic for quite rich people to do adverts and be comfortable with doing something purely for the money. I think, though, that, when you've left drama school, the theatre is considered to be where the real action is. It is certainly where a person discovers himself as an actor. It is very difficult, if not nigh impossible, I think, to discover yourself as an actor on a film set.'

Even Daniel recognises on occasions that those rare moments when everything has gelled on stage are what acting is really all about. Jack adds, 'If an actor is really only interested in self-presentation then they've sold out from the start. But I believe most actors are interested in culture, literature, language and society and that cements in the theatre and not in television or film. Of course, you get some actors – and this I can't respect at all – who are all charm and counting the money. Daniel certainly is not one of those. He has great looks and a lot of charisma but he doesn't, and never will, float on that. He wouldn't just take a part for the money.'

For now Daniel was not about to take any part for any reason, least of all money. He was in deep hiding, his whereabouts at one stage not even known to his immediate family, and had every intention of staying that way. But then something happened which he had not expected and could not have occurred at a worse time. Ironically, just when he wanted to drop out of sight into the darkest obscurity he could find, as the decade drew to a close he was about to be dragged into the brightest spotlight of his career to date.

CHAPTER EIGHT

THE LAST OF
THE MOHICANS

'Everyone gives in, in the end.'

GUY BENNETT, *ANOTHER COUNTRY*

Six weeks into 1990, Daniel had already picked up no less than eight Best Actor awards for his portrayal of Christy Brown in *My Left Foot* – including those of the Montreal Film Festival, the Los Angeles Film Critics Circle and the highly influential New York Film Critics Circle – when the 1989 British Academy of Film and Television Arts (BAFTA) nominations were announced on 13 February in London.

Again Daniel was short-listed for the category of Best Actor in a leading role, joining Kenneth Branagh for *Henry V*, Robin Williams for Peter Weir's *Dead Poets Society* and Dustin Hoffman for Barry Levinson's *Rain Man*.

Then, on St Valentine's Day, the 1989 nominations for the Academy Awards were revealed and again Daniel was in the running for Best Actor: this time up against Kenneth Branagh and Robin Williams once more, along with Tom Cruise for

Oliver Stone's *Born on the Fourth of July* and Morgan Freeman for Bruce Beresford's *Driving Miss Daisy*.

Even before the announcement detailing the nominations was made in Los Angeles, the British press were regarding Daniel's inclusion as a racing certainty. At the same time, however, some were claiming that, although he might be poised on the brink of superstardom, because of his 'breakdown' he was seriously considering turning his back on the acting profession for good. The film and his performance in it, together with those of both Brenda Fricker and Ray McAnally, had resulted in a flood of recognition. The resulting responsibilities knocked a hole in Daniel's intentions to opt out of the public gaze. On his re-emergence he had also found himself roped into a round of fund-raising activities to promote research into cerebral palsy. This entailed his attendance at various glitzy celebrity dinners throughout America. His duty to do everything possible to further both the film's success and also the charity was important to him, but so was his recovery and trying to balance the two could not have been easy.

The Academy Awards, nicknamed Oscars, awarded annually since 1927 by The American Academy of Motion Picture Arts and Sciences, are the most prized accolades in the acting world and Daniel was considered to be up against pretty stiff competition. Branagh, with his extrovert personality and passion for the stage, had emulated the 1944 achievement of the legendary Laurence Olivier in writing, directing and starring in a film version of Shakespeare's *Henry V.* Partly because of this, Branagh was being talked of by journalists on both sides of the Atlantic as the new Olivier.

And Tom Cruise had the advantage of being an extremely high-profile American actor in a film, moreover, which was already widely admired. Like Daniel, Cruise played a real-life wheelchair-bound character – Ron Kovic, a young soldier crippled in Vietnam who became a passionate anti-war campaigner – and he was widely tipped as having the Oscar in the bag. To listen to some American pundits, all he had to do was turn up to collect it.

Daniel was everything that Branagh was not, an introverted loner who had turned his back on the stage. Before picking up awards for *My Left Foot*, his credit list featured the unshowable *Eversmile, New Jersey*, and *Stars and Bars* and *The Unbearable Lightness of Being*, both of which had bombed at the box office. Even the film now receiving so much hype had originally been turned down by the Cannes Film Festival.

Yet, although Day-Lewis did not aspire to be the new Olivier, what had become abundantly clear was that, as an actor, he was a true chameleon and one with the elusive gift of possessing great sensitivity as well as authority. He also commanded respect and, just like Olivier, he was held in awe by many fellow actors. As Christy Brown, Daniel, with an instinct rare in so young an actor, had taken on a role few would have considered likely to swell their bank balance or smooth their path to stardom.

His incredible performance, in what was only his third leading role in a film, made many in his profession the world over sit up and recognise that they had just witnessed an acting achievement beyond their own capabilities. And on Monday, 26 March 1990, at the famous Dorothy Chandler Pavilion, it was Daniel Day-Lewis who stepped up on stage to receive the coveted gold-plated statuette from actress Jodie Foster, the previous year's Best Actress Award winner for her performance in Jonathan Kaplan's *The Accused*.

On completion of *My Left Foot* Daniel's expectations had modestly levelled out at hoping that it took off in Ireland.

When it did, the Irish love of the film, he says, filled his quota of pleasure. After that, anything else would be a bonus. By now his aspirations clearly ought to have risen considerably, yet, despite already being garlanded with awards, he had not truly allowed himself to believe that he would win the Oscar. The moment when Jodie opened the envelope and announced his name hit him like a ten-ton truck.

Wearing a black frock coat, with his unfashionably long hair curling about his shoulders, he cut a dashing, Byronesque figure, grinning wide with delight as he accepted the wild applause of the audience. Acceptance speeches from the brilliant spotlight of the Oscar podium can range from impassioned denials of worthiness, through cloying gratitude to political diatribes. Daniel kept it short, while maintaining, 'You have just provided me with the makings of one hell of a weekend in Dublin.'

In the previous forty-seven years, fourteen Oscars in the top categories of Best Film, Best Actor and Best Actress had been awarded to films dealing with various forms of disability, though only one of them had gone to a genuinely handicapped person – Marlee Matlin for her portrayal of a deaf-mute in *Children of a Lesser God*. In all these films, romance had been the mainspring of the story. *My Left Foot* was different. Unlike its predecessors, it focused first on the man Christy Brown, his personality and talents. Love and relationships, although important, took second place. *Foot* also secured four other Academy Award nominations, for Best Supporting Actress, Best Picture, Best Director and Best Adapted Screenplay. The night held a special pleasure for Daniel when Brenda Fricker beat off her competition to collect the award for Best Supporting Actress.

But, far away from the back-slapping of the Oscars ceremony, an old grievance was still burning back home among the disabled acting community. Nabil Shaban's was still the most prominent voice being raised against the Christy Brown casting, and indeed had been speaking out about it on British radio that very day. Despite the many appeals made to organisations such as The American Academy of Motion Pictures Arts and Sciences as well as BAFTA, it was clear that no notice had been taken of his lobby's protests. In 1995, Nabil said, 'Now, almost six years on, any cerebral palsy sufferer that I have spoken to hates the film and finds no virtue in the performance at all.' He adds, 'In 1989 I had appealed to disabled people everywhere to put pressure on the organisers of all the film festivals to have the *My Left Foot* entry removed and on top of that we wrote to the Oscar people, wrote to all those who gave out awards, in fact, to try to get them to stop pandering to this trend by rewarding this insult. We tried to influence them but I'm afraid we had little impact.'

Thousands of miles away, it was a situation Daniel was not unaware of. Even while being blinded by the blitz of flashbulbs, he took time during his interview with the world's media to reinforce his sympathy for the disabled actors' protest. Then, unable to do more, the issue was set aside and some serious partying got under way – Daniel, with the Irish contingent, quitting the official ball early, to drop in at various satellite celebrations held around LA. His numbed disbelief at actually winning the award was only slowly overcome by the feel of it clasped in his hands or cradled in his lap, until the soporific effect of alcohol finally left him sprawled contentedly asleep in a chair in the early hours of the following morning.

For a few days after the ceremony the first thing he saw as he opened his eyes every morning was the Oscar. He wanted it where he could stare at it, contemplating its meaning. Then he promptly wrapped it in a soft red shoebag and stashed it in an old suitcase. In the months straddling the Oscar ceremony, *My Left Foot* grossed in excess of $11 million in America: a success which continued in British cinemas, helped by the fact that, just over a week before the Oscars, Daniel had walked off with BAFTA's award for Best Actor.

While in Los Angeles his performance as Christy Brown had won over Tom Cruise's similarly wheelchair-bound Ron Kovic, in the 1989 BAFTA awards it was Christy versus Dustin Hoffman's autistic savant, Raymond, both afflicted, although by different handicaps. *Rain Man* had had its share of difficulties, having gone through four directors in as many years plus innumerable script re-writes, and during this time Dustin had concentrated on learning how to understand and operate within the limitations of autism. His hard work had, of course, already won him the 1988 Oscar. But his childlike, shuffling simplicity, although wholly sympathetic and engendering a spirit of natural protectiveness, proved no match for Daniel's Christy, determined, crusty and with a pair of gimlet eyes which defied a single ounce of pity from the viewer.

From the start, it seemed that the whole audience at the London ceremony was rooting for a Day-Lewis victory, so much so that, when the climax came three hours into the event, everyone burst into spontaneous, riotous applause at the mere mention of Daniel's name when the four contenders were announced by *Murder She Wrote* star Angela Lansbury. Such was the intense expectancy that one would have envisaged a mutiny breaking out had she opened the envelope and read out anyone's name but his.

The crowd's thunderously enthusiastic delight buffeted Daniel, dressed in the same poetic style as he would adopt for the Oscars, all the way up to the podium to collect his award. But that night belonged not only to him. Ray McAnally collected the award for

Best Supporting Actor for his performance as Christy's hard-working, hard-drinking and sometimes (at least outwardly) hard-hearted father, and the film also secured nominations for Best Film and Best Adapted Screenplay.

Being an Academy Award winner elevated Daniel into the ranks of highly bankable stars, prey to the silliest offers Hollywood could conjure up. More important to him, it meant the chance to work with top-notch directors and producers. It would obviously also increase his choice of films.

But, despite the natural pride and excitement he felt at having reached such heady heights, it had all been a rather overwhelming experience, especially coming when it did. The frenzied attention surrounding him steadily grew and was bewildering in its intensity. Being put on show and feted Hollywood-style is not something he is comfortable with at the best of times, but, having been prised reluctantly out of seclusion, he now hankered more strongly than ever for anonymity.

This particular luxury, however, would elude him for, some time yet, for although he managed to vacate Tinseltown within less than a week of collecting his Academy Award, he was bound for France. His responsibility to promote *My Left Foot* to the widest audience had not yet ended and he was faced with more public parading, in and around Europe. But before touching French soil he had one important stopover to make in Ireland first.

Sandymount's Tony Jordan explains, 'It was the Monday following his Oscar win. I had to leave the school sharp that day as I had a meeting elsewhere but on a hunch I said to my wife who works here too, "Look, just keep your eyes open this morning for yer man. I've a feeling he's going to appear." Nothing had been said or promised. It was purely a hunch.'

He goes on, 'Well, in my absence, not more than half an hour after I'd gone, in through the front gate walks Day-Lewis with his sister. He had a duffel bag slung over his shoulder and the Oscar was inside it. He'd taken it to Sandymount, not to show off, but to share it with all the pupils and staff whom he felt had helped him so much. He spent the whole day here; the Oscar passed from hand to hand and he patiently posed for photographs galore. It was a real treat and a very special thing for him to have done.'

After this barrow load of awards and honours Daniel's life was never going to be the same again. In the past he had had to chase work, which at times had come around in feast or famine style. Now the offers were flooding in and he had begun to be inundated with scripts and ideas. Far from giving in to commercial pressures, however, he showed no inclination to accept any of them. Just as before receiving the script for *My Left Foot*, nothing on offer rang the right bell and by now he had also made up his mind not to be part of another film unless he was granted a share of artistic control. He was not in any particular hurry – quite prepared to bide his time.

The film industry, on the other hand, was less patient, speculating madly on which project Day-Lewis would embark on next. Surprise was profound all round when, two months after collecting the Oscar, his one and only film involvement was announced and it turned out to be that of associate producer on a project called *Orlando*. Based on Virgina Woolf's 1928 novel and made by Adventure Films, it centred on a youth who lives for over 400 years, changes sex along the way and in the year 1600 is a court favourite of Queen Elizabeth I. Intended to be witty and entertaining, set in glamorous surroundings – St Petersburg stood in for medieval London – and with elaborate costumes, its central themes were immortality and class. The British actress Tilda Swinton starred along with Billy Zane and Quentin Crisp who played the Tudor Queen. Christopher Sheppard produced the film and Sally Potter directed as well as wrote the screenplay.

Potter's previous credits included *The Gold Diggers*, starring Julie Christie, and *The London Story*, and her unique script for *Orlando* instantly captured Daniel's imagination. He respected too her tenacity in pulling the project together. Reports quickly surfaced that Day-Lewis would himself appear in the movie – which, securing two BAFTA nominations along the way, went on to rank seventh in the Top Ten UK Domestic Films of 1993 – but he had never had any intention of doing so. He saw his sole role as that of using whatever contacts and influence he possessed to help the film find backers. Indeed, such was the low profile he preferred that he wanted his name left off the film's credits altogether. Beyond that, the impression given was that it would be quite some time before he returned to the screen. He avoided his agent and any attempts to pin him down to considering his future, and once more, with an adroitness now proving legendary, he faded from sight.

Exactly where he went and what he did, although much guessed at, remains by and large unknown. Daniel calls it classified information, but he certainly visited Ireland, spent hours cycling around the restful countryside, read a few books, travelled, and lived quietly in London. By now it was well known to his friends and associates that, if he decided to take off, then it was their lot to wait until the next time they heard from him, which could be any time.

If those handling his career were worried that it was a bad move to vanish from sight, Daniel himself was unconcerned. This could have implied that he either had immense self-confidence in his ability to pluck himself a plum role on his return or alternatively a sublime indifference as to whether he would ever work again. Certainly it was an unusual step to walk away just when he had reached such heights of international recognition.

When he embarked on his next film, it would be over two years since he had last worked on one. In between, his relationship with the woman with whom publicly he would be most linked over the coming years had been developing. In the past he had been assiduous in keeping the identity of his girlfriends out of the hands of the media. This time, secrecy had been more difficult because the lady in question was an actress, the French-born beauty Isabelle Adjani, whose name had previously been linked with Hollywood super-Romeo Warren Beatty.

Accounts vary, but some say Daniel had first met her in his pre-Oscar days, around the time he was appearing in *Hamlet* at the National Theatre. It is also said that she had been privately on hand to help his recovery after his dramatic departure from the stage at the end of 1989. Certainly they were together just a few months later, the following March, in Los Angeles during the time of the Oscars, although in an attempt to keep their association quiet they indulged in the usual cat-and-mouse caper with the gossip-hungry, ever resourceful, paparazzi. The exercise turned out to be the usual waste of time as they were eventually snapped, tellingly, walking hand-in-hand together.

Isabelle's father, an Algerian Muslim, was a garage worker; her mother was German. They met in Bavaria and later the couple moved to Paris, where Isabelle was born in 1955. With a blooming complexion, her cornflower-blue eyes made a striking foil for her inky black hair. She had become an actress at the age of fifteen and a leading lady by the late 1970s in such international films as *The Story of Adèle H*, *Nosferatu* and *The Brontë Sisters*. Considered the natural successor to Brigitte Bardot, with over twenty films to her credit by the dawn of the nineties, her star appeal in France was enormous. The bloody sixteenth-century costume drama *La Reine Margot*, based on the Alexandre Dumas novel, in which she starred as Margot, took the French box office by storm in early 1995.

Just a few years before, however, it had been a very different story and Isabelle had had her share of troubles. Around the time she made the much-maligned 1987 Columbia Pictures comedy adventure *Ishtar*, directed by Elaine May and co-starring Warren Beatty and Dustin Hoffman, she apparently became the target of an ugly whispering campaign channelled through some sections of the French press. Deeply distressing rumours abounded that she was suffering from AIDS and, worse, there were even claims that she was dead. Eventually, in a startling move to put an end to the mounting sensationalism, Isabelle appeared on live French national television for twenty minutes to prove that she was very much alive and well. It was a very bleak time in her life.

In spring 1990 her latest film was *Camille Claudel*. As well as co-producing, she starred as the ill-fated turn-of-the-century French sculptress, model and fiery mistress of Auguste Rodin, played by Gerard Depardieu. The film was directed by her ex-lover Bruno Nuytten, the father of her son Barnabe, making his directorial debut. It won five Césars (the French equivalent of Oscars) including that of Best Actress and was the official French entry at the 1989 US Academy Awards. However, unlike Daniel, Isabelle came away empty-handed, beaten to the Oscar by the veteran Jessica Tandy for *Driving Miss Daisy*.

As an actress, Isabelle's hallmarks are much like Daniel's – a propensity for identifying to an almost obsessive degree with her characters and, in the aftermath, experiencing difficulty in letting them go. Fiercely independent, she has confessed to some feelings of loneliness in life and in many ways perhaps appeared to be a female version of himself. Certainly she must have stood a fair chance of understanding the more intense and solitary aspects of Daniel's nature. At any rate, she came to London to live with him and over the ensuing years their relationship would come to be described by Daniel himself as one of the most on-off in showbiz.

It was over three years since, having broken up with his long-time schooldays sweetheart Sarah Campbell, he had lived on a permanent basis with a woman. But any illusion of even semi-domesticity was about to be well and truly shattered. Daniel's last day on a film set had been in Argentina in December 1988 and since then he had successfully avoided all attempts to bring him, in any shape or form, to another. But now he was about to be unearthed. Someone was on his trail, with a steely-eyed determination to secure his services for a blockbuster adventure movie of a type that had not been attempted for years. He also offered by far and away Daniel's fattest paycheque to date and the added lure of becoming Hollywood's next heart throb. The latter promise seems to have been enough to make Daniel sprint off in the other direction all the faster – at least for a while.

Michael Mann, the Chicago-born creator of the American TV cop series *Miami Vice*, starring Don Johnson and Philip Michael Thomas, was involved as director, producer and scriptwriter in a Twentieth Century-Fox Film Corporation project – a remake based on the James Fenimore Cooper classic novel *The Last of the Mohicans*. Mann's first task had been to pitch the idea to two men, development executive Riley Ellis and Fox's production president Roger Birnbaum. They went for it instantly, as did Fox's head Joe Roth, but, in handing Mann the green light and a $35 million budget, Roth was also adamant that the guy he wanted to see cast in the lead role had to be Daniel Day-Lewis. Roth already classed Daniel as one of the best actors in the world, even though by Fox's standards he had yet to star in a blockbuster-grossing movie.

Mann's pre-*Miami Vice* days had been spent as a scriptwriter, working on such popular television series as *Starsky and Hutch* and *Crime Story*, but he had viewed these purely as a means to an end, setting his sights on making movies. His most recent film had been the gory 1986 psychological thriller *Manhunter.* Now Mann set out on a manhunt of his own, to tempt the notoriously elusive Day-Lewis out of hiding.

It was a far from easy task. For four months Daniel resisted offers, blandishments and pressure alike. Mann envisaged his production as being an expensive and lavish movie in which he was convinced he needed what he called 'somebody as good as Daniel' to play Hawk-eye. The problem was, Day-Lewis had been turning down scripts right, left and centre and this one looked to be destined to suffer the same fate.

To many in the industry, a certain select few American agents have, for good or ill, replaced the all-powerful studio heads of yesteryear as the people who wield the most clout in the film world, and one of those mandarin agents is Sam Cohn. Cohn represented Daniel's friend, director Pat O'Connor, and the script for *Mohicans* carried Sam's personal recommendation. This fact played its part in drawing Daniel's attention to it time and again. But still it was not enough.

Family friend Richard Mayne explains, 'You have to be persistent with Daniel. You've got to keep at him and at him, if you're going to have any chance of breaking down his resistance to something. Being relentless is the key.' Michael Mann certainly could not be faulted in this department and when eventually a crack did emerge in Daniel's armour he plied the actor with as much information about the project as he could, in the hope that he could catch his interest.

His persistence paid off when, after four months, in October 1990, he managed to secure a business lunch with Daniel at a restaurant on London's Greek Street. It turned out to be a marathon four-hour affair, during which the director's passion for the project, plus the depth of his own research and knowledge of the period, impressed Daniel greatly. Even so it was not until afterwards, while walking down Shaftesbury Avenue, that Mann was finally sure that he had secured Daniel's agreement to star in the movie.

Daniel's resistance had been very real. He had read the *Mohicans* script several times in those four months, but he had put off meeting Michael Mann for so long because he believed that, once he had opened a channel of communication, somehow it meant he had made a commitment. His initial reaction to the idea was that the role of Nathaniel Poe (Hawkeye) was the very antithesis of the type of parts he wanted to play. Troubled and flawed individuals had been his stock-in-trade to date. This fearless frontiersman was an invincible hero – an archetype Daniel had difficulty seeing as something he could happily project. He recognises that there are other actors who carry off such roles with ease and frequently cites his admiration for Clint Eastwood, whom Daniel considers has got it together in both his professional and personal life in a way that he seems to wish applied to himself.

He was also perplexed as to why, considering his film credits – *My Left Foot*'s success aside – to date, Mann and the Fox executives should have chosen him to play such a character. In addition, after two years of not working in films, he had fully intended returning to a small-scale production such as *Foot* had been. That type of intimate atmosphere had suited him well. Whereas this project was clearly a very different kettle of fish.

And there was one other reason – a self-confessed resistance to fame itself. The screaming and obsessive attention from fans that he had experienced during the run up to and immediately after winning the Oscar was still vivid in his memory. To take on the part of Poe would be to assume the most glamorous role of his career to date, one which carried, built in, serious heart-throb status. That gave him great pause for thought.

However, when he re-read the script again, the opening sequence, when Nathaniel is hunting in the forest with his brother Uncas and father Chingachgook, hooked his imagination in a way he never expected it to. As he read on, although he still could not shake off the belief that this kind of role and size of production was not what he was looking for, gradually certain aspects of the hero's life and philosophy began to percolate into his brain.

He began by thinking that Nathaniel was a mysterious man, whose life was so far removed from his own that he would be unable to get close to him, and once planted this conviction grew steadily. Perversely, however, the stronger it grew the more fascinated Daniel became with the challenge it presented. It seems clear that the bigger the obstacle he builds in front of himself (and one wonders sometimes if it has now become subconsciously intentional), the more certain he is to tackle it. An undeniable appeal also lay in the fact that Hawk-eye is very secure within himself, strong and decisive.

Speaking of his own screen character, Martin Riggs, the burned-out cop in Richard Dormer's trilogy of *Lethal Weapon* films – the latest of which would be in the making at the same time as *Mohicans* – Mel Gibson once explained that the attraction of playing the crack-shot, all-action guy had lain in the fact that Riggs was the kind of macho hero all men secretly wish they were, but in real life know they never could be. Daniel was just as susceptible as Gibson to this brand of sheer escapism and in the end he wanted a piece of Nathaniel, even if only borrowed for a short while. So at last he signed a two-film deal with Twentieth Century-Fox, the first of which would be *The Last of the Mohicans*.

Production would begin mid-June 1991, but before that he had to make a return trip to the City of Angels in March, again to the Oscars, but this time as the current holder of the Best Actor award. It was his duty to present the statuette for the 1990 winner of that year's Best Actress award – which was Kathy Bates, for *Misery*. That done, Daniel headed east to Alabama to begin his preparations to play the hero created by James Fenimore Cooper.

The Last of the Mohicans, his best-known novel, was first published in 1862. Michael Mann based his screenplay on a combination of the novel and the action-packed 1936 film version by Philip Dunne, directed by George B. Seitz and starring Randolph Scott and Binnie Barnes; one of Britain's best acting exports of the 1930s to Hollywood. Essentially Michael saw it as the love story of a couple caught in the middle of a war. To bring the project together he roped in assistant director Ned Dowd, previously first assistant director on *Stars and Bars,* Hunt Lowry as line producer and Jon Landeau as executive in charge of production, before turning his attention to the rest of the cast.

Joining Daniel would be Steven Waddington, Maurice Roëves, Jodhi May, Eric Schweig, Wes Studi and Russell Means, the famous Native American activist who would play Chingachgook. Wes Studi, who would chillingly take on the fearsome Huron captain Magua, is a real-life Cherokee and Russell is an Oglala Lakota Sioux. The all-important responsibility of leading lady fell to the actress Madeleine Stowe, who later referred to *Mohicans* as being the very first film in which she was not expected to take off her clothes.

It was to be a four-month shoot on and around Lake James in Burke County, Western North Carolina and in the Appalachian mountains in Alabama, both areas standing in for New York state in the eighteenth century. Authenticity in all aspects of the film remained Michael Mann's watchword throughout and he went to some extraordinary lengths to ensure historical accuracy.

For the construction of Fort William Henry, first of all eighteenth-century plans were closely consulted. Then, having agreed with the relevant agencies a series of measures to limit and compensate for any environmental damage done, a huge land clearance took place, denuding acres of forest and levelling hills so that over a hundred tradesmen could construct a massive fortress on the hilltop site overlooking Lake James. Many local residents from the Asheville area worked behind the cameras and also helped to fill the massive 1,200 quota of extras in the film, but the Indian warriors were recruited mainly from real Native Americans – mostly Iroquois, from all corners of America, brought in to portray their fellow tribesmen of yesteryear.

Mohicans was to be the biggest movie filmed in Western North Carolina, an area rich in quite breathtakingly beautiful countryside. Settings used in this film would include Chimney Rock Park, Table Rock, Linville Falls and Gorge as well as Lake James itself. It was on Lake James that the escape scenes were shot, in which Nathaniel and the other main characters flee in canoes from a determined band of Hurons after having survived the spectacular ambush that follows the fort's surrender.

One Asheville resident destined to play a bigger part than the other locals was Michael Bigham, who was brought on board as the film's North Carolina Locations Manager. It was his responsibility to fulfil Michael Mann's various location needs and he certainly did not let the director down. Prior to contacting Bigham, who had previously worked on the 1990 film *The Hunt for Red October*, starring Sean Connery (part of which was also filmed on Lake James), the production team had been considering other US states as well as locations in Canada. It eventually boiled down to a decision between Canada and North Carolina. The choice of the latter brought an estimated $25 million into the Asheville area, as well as putting that part of America firmly on the map for tourism and future potential film-makers.

While most of the scenery was natural, one scene near the end of the film was to be shot in a fake setting. The waterfall under which Magua and his men followed Nathaniel, Cora and the others was specially built in a warehouse opposite River Ridge Market Place in Asheville. A mock cave was constructed, and then tons of water were recycled to create the illusion of a massive thundering waterfall. Still, Hawk-eye's dramatic waterfall jump, which predated Harrison Ford's much-vaunted leap in *The Fugitive*, looks impressively realistic.

With everything in place production-wise, Daniel's priority was to get himself into shape physically to meet the demands of his role as the eighteenth-century frontiersman. The cinema-going public had already seen more than his bare chest, and sights such as his hairpin thinness in *Stars and Bars*, when it was practically possible to count his ribs, made it clear that he needed to build up his six-foot-plus frame considerably. To this end he spent months under instruction from fitness trainer Richard Smedley. Richard reckoned Daniel had to acquire twenty pounds of muscle. He immediately put him on to a 5,000-calorie-a-day diet to complement the stringent workouts that were essential to beef up his chest, arms and neck. This would allow Daniel to carry off realistically the frequent shirtless he-man scenes required in the film.

As usual, having embarked on the project, Daniel's concentration was total, his research techniques once again reaching new dimensions. Altogether he spent six months in training, during which time he learned how to track and skin animals, build canoes and fight with tomahawks, often dressed only in a loin cloth and moccasins to better understand the part. His character, usually called Hawk-eye, but in this production Nathaniel Poe, has another name – *La Longue Carabine*, meaning the long rifle. In this case it was a 12lb flintlock, nicknamed Killdeer, which Daniel learned how to fire and reload, even on the run. Because a hunter in the wild would never have let his rifle out of his sight, he carried it literally everywhere including when he went out for his early-morning jog. He took his weapons training extremely seriously and was coached in eighteenth-century arms and combat at a Special Operations Unit in the Alabama region.

But physically looking the part and being able to wield a tomahawk like a pro was not enough for Daniel. Along with Michael Mann, who is also renowned for his thoroughness, he spent four weeks living in the woods with Native American experts on a wilderness survival. Perhaps it was partly because of this form of male bonding that actor and director related so well, but once the cameras started rolling there was a deep and natural understanding between the men which made communication complete and so much swifter. Daniel surprised some of his co-stars by never once challenging the various directorial edicts – a rarity which, at least for his leading lady, instantly set him apart from his frequently vocal American counterparts.

Daniel later joked that the main reason he took on the outdoor role was to be able to enjoy some fresh air for a change, but there was nothing lighthearted about his approach. He imagined his character's life to have been a combination of pure sensation and instinctive reflex, and he worked very hard to absorb this persona as deeply as possible in order to effectively become this man from another time. It had been a brave decision for an anti-hero like Daniel to take on the responsibility of a classic leading man, but in his looks and bearing alone he was to bring a decidedly aristocratic air to the buckskin-clad warrior. When shooting began on 17 June 1991, it had been two and a half years since Daniel had set foot on a film set.

The Last of the Mohicans is set in 1757, in the third year of the war between England and France for possession of the American Colonies. The action takes place along the frontier west of the Hudson River. Nathaniel, determined to keep out of the conflict, is heading west with Chingachgook and Uncas to winter in Kentucky. Along the way they call at the cabin of their friend John Alexander Cameron and his family, where they witness the British Crown round-up of volunteers for a colonial militia.

A group of those volunteers head to Albany, to seek an assurance from Colonel Webb that if their settlements are attacked by Indians in their absence they will be granted leave to return home to defend their families. In the presence of a newly arrived English major, Duncan Heywood, Webb agrees to this – a promise which is later reneged upon. Apart from bearing despatches, Heywood is in Albany to meet the daughters of Colonel Munro, Cora and Alice, in order to escort them to their father at Fort William Henry. It is while the company of soldiers led by Heywood are en route to the Fort, guided by Magua, that they are led by him into a Huron ambush on the George Road.

The film ran foul of the American board of censors for the violence of the battles between Indians and soldiers, particularly in what was supposedly a film for family viewing. Especially graphic are the repeated scenes of hacking bodies in half and vicious scalpings which dominate two ambushes. During the first of these, while his men are sliced down by the dozen, Duncan battles to protect single-handedly the two terrified and defenceless women. Just when all seems lost help arrives out of nowhere as first Chingachgook, then Uncas and lastly Nathaniel burst into view to save them, fighting off the band of crazed savages.

From the moment they meet, a clash sets in between Nathaniel and the pompous and arrogant major. Initially there is also a clash between Nathaniel and Cora who, unlike her timid sister, is spirited and speaks her mind. This comes quickly to a head when, Nathaniel and his companions having agreed to lead the trio to Fort William Henry, they pass by the Cameron cabin again but this time find it burned out and everyone killed by an Indian war party. Nathaniel's refusal to bury the dead leads Cora to accuse him of unforgivable indifference. His response to her insults is to advance on her menacingly, making her back away from him in fear as, without explanation, he insist the bodies stay as they lie.

Michael Mann saw the Cameron massacre scene as being a pivotal point in the film. How best to handle the resulting confrontation between the two leading characters was a matter of deep debate between himself and Daniel. It was only one twelve-word line of dialogue – the important issue was how Daniel said it. Mann described it as a moment of killing rage. Echoing an observation of actor Jack Shepherd's, he maintains that he discovered at this time that there is a unique kind of fiery anger inside Daniel which cannot be called up from the outside, but which emerges unexpectedly and entirely of its own volition.

Both actor and director agreed that the scene required controlled rage, but neither wanted the tired old muscle-flexing-in-the jaw method of delivering it. In the end, after several takes, as Mann had inwardly relied upon, Daniel's spontaneity suddenly took over. Finally, after the umpteenth take, he turned and strode downhill towards Cora. As he reached her, it was clear that he was applying great restraint in not laying violent hands on her. His eyes, often romantically described as being capable of smouldering a hole in wood, conveyed an undisguised and incandescent fury. It was original and believable and for Mann summed up best his determination to cast Day-Lewis at all costs. Specially pinpointing that particular moment he has since insisted, 'That's why I wanted him to play Hawk-eye. To elevate this whole movie, story, novel to immediacy.'

The central love story begins to evolve from there on. Cora seeks out Hawk-eye that night to make peace with him over what she discovers has been her misunderstanding. At the same time she learns about his past and in turn he sees her in a new light. Before they arrive at the besieged Fort William Henry, she has clearly begun to fall for this strange man, alien in every sense of the word to any other she had previously known.

There is only one real love scene in the film. This is when, having helped his friends escape the fort in flagrant disobedience of orders, Nathaniel seeks Cora out. High on a deserted section of the battle-scarred stone ramparts, against a starry night, they finally come together. As Tomas in *The Unbearable Lightness of Being*, Daniel had had more than his share of celluloid clinches, yet he had not always appeared entirely comfortable with them. Five years on, although mainly shot from behind him, his sensuously hungry kisses with Madeleine Stowe conveyed a highly realistic intimacy. Made all the more passionate for not being prolonged, this time they looked to present him with no problem whatsoever.

Indeed, Daniel's Hawk-eye, as well as being every schoolboy's hero, was all virility – blatantly intended to be the stuff girls' dreams are made of. Admittedly he rarely smiles in the film but, when he does, it lights up the screen. His buckskin clothes had been designed by Elsa Zamparelli, the same costume designer who had worked on *Danielces with Wolves* and, with his shoulder-length raven hair flying, he brought a rush of potent earthiness to his role.

During the sixteen-week shoot Daniel had for the most part stayed locked as usual into his character. While others plugged into their portable compact disc players or sat with their feet up smoking and chatting, Daniel would detach himself from the cast and crew and either squat by a tree, lost in his own world, or stalk about alone, staring fixedly at the ground. But not all the time. There were occasions when he joined the others in the rough and tumble designed to relieve the stress and boredom which can easily creep in on a film set. But even then the kind of compulsion which drives the actor came out in the man. Steven Waddington, who as Major Heywood was Nathaniel's adversary in the film, speaking of an off-screen boxing match he and Daniel took part in, has told of how relentlessly Day-Lewis pounded into him, unwilling – perhaps even unable – to stop, just for that moment.

It was not all unremitting intensity, however, as Madeleine Stowe revealed when she confessed to the antics that she and Daniel frequently indulged in. They often challenged each other to car chases at the end of the day, the cars being driven by their respective drivers. Stowe, with a stuntwoman driver in former rodeo champion Kellie Frost, invariably won, which drove Daniel and his driver, Sam Katanich, to resort to sabotage.

One day during the race Daniel, who was behind the wheel on this occasion (with his antique rifle sticking incongruously out of the open window), had been trailing as usual when Madeleine and Kellie saw him lose control, and Sam being tossed out on to the dirt. They braked, leaped out and ran back to Daniel and the 'wounded' man. Sam's bloodstains were faked, however, and, although both women twigged instantly, they had completely lost the advantage. Laughing uproariously, Daniel promptly leaped back into his car and sped off triumphantly.

It would appear that Madeleine found her British leading man an unusual actor to work with in almost every sense of the word. His innate courtesy to all cast and crew day in, day out struck her forcibly, as did the fact that the infernal flintlock not only graced the meal tables, but went with Daniel even to the washroom. A mutual professional admiration developed between the two and the chemistry between them worked very well on screen. For those working behind the cameras, however, the chemistry was not so good.

Just over a month into production, reports leaked out that grievances were stoking up over poor food, pay and working conditions on the film. At the outset a representative of the International Alliance of Theatrical Stage Employees (IATSE) had arrived at the set, seeking to negotiate the terms of a union deal on behalf of the crew but, it's said, he was turned away at this point by producers Hunt Lowry and Ned Dowd.

The discontent among the ranks promptly deepened and, in July, erupted when almost the entire crew went on strike. Picket lines were mounted at the set gates, initially manned by union members, then joined swiftly by crew members. Each day of filming lost meant the sky-high costs mounted and so did the tension. The crew ran a high risk of being fired en masse, but they held out, greatly encouraged when their numbers were swelled

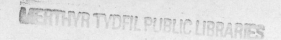

by many of the Native American extras. Such disruption was no good to anyone and doubtless unsettled Daniel and his co-stars, but luckily the dispute did not last very long and was ultimately resolved through negotiations with the IATSE. *The Last of the Mohicans* had begun life as an independent production, but as at 24 July it became a union shoot.

That was not the end of strife, though. There were other casualties at department-head level. Costume designer James Acheson, whose work had included *The Last Emperor*, left due to nervous exhaustion. *Out of Africa* hair stylist Vera Mitchell quit over differences relating to conditions, and then experienced cinematographer Doug Milsome left, allegedly not entirely voluntarily, just five weeks into principal photography. His place was promptly taken by Danielte Spinotti, with whom Mann had worked on *Manhunter*.

One by one these problems were ironed out, however, and the demanding shoot battled on its way. In the final weeks of filming it was clearly taking a lot out of Daniel. By this time he, Michael and Madeleine had developed a firm bond in which each helped the other in whatever way was necessary. Stowe has fond memories of when, on virtually the last day of filming, she was literally too tired to put on her own make-up. Daniel, exhausted himself, applied her mascara and eye-liner for her, while wearily telling the assistant director, urgently urging his presence back on set, that he was going as fast as he could.

Due to wrap at the end of August, filming overran until, after eighty-one days, shooting finally came to an end on 10 October. The production had also gone over budget to the tune of some $7 million, and the schedule had been tightened so much that latterly they were filming practically round the clock with scarcely time to eat or sleep. During the entire time on location Daniel had allowed no press interviews and very few observers on the set, all of which added to his reputation for intensity.

To a man, everyone was relieved to leave the Blue Ridge Mountains location which had been home for almost four months. Daniel, like the others, tossed his hiking boots on to a pile which, when doused in gasoline, became a symbolic funeral pyre. Michael Mann, heading for the nearest airport and the first fast-food joint he could find, graphically summed up the general feeling of release by growling, 'Fuck nature. I'm out of here.'

For Hollywood studios, the most important time of the year is the summer season. Forty per cent of their annual income is made over this period and so between late May and the end of August they each wheel out their big guns in the hope of blasting their way through the magic $100 million barrier. *The Last of the Mohicans* was originally slotted for a July 1992 release, to join battle in the box-office war with *Lethal Weapon 3* and Tim Burton's gothic masterpiece *Batman Returns*: both sequels to huge hits. However, it was bumped back and opened instead on 23 September – its debut taking place at the Beaucatcher Cinema in Asheville, North Carolina. It opened nationally across America two days later.

Its US publicity launch was impressive. Posters emblazoned with the caption THE FIRST AMERICAN HERO, showing Daniel in all his glory as Hawk-eye in full flight and armed to the teeth, plastered billboards in towns and cities across the country. Daniel was called upon for the first time in his career to open a big-budget movie in person, which meant an unrelenting round of promotional appearances and interviews. It reaped rewards, however, when *Mohicans* became the unexpected hit of that autumn, storming straight to the top of the US box-office chart in its opening week and grossing in excess of $43 million in its first month.

Everyone from investors to the marketing people were doubtless delighted, but, for Daniel, being used as the main advertising tool was more of a burden than a joy. In the aftermath of making the movie, exhausted once more, he is said to have suffered slightly from hallucinations and also claustrophobia for which, by the time September came around, he was receiving medication. In the past he had never given that many press interviews, but this time his schedule was packed.

During one of the first, conducted in a suite in Los Angeles's plush Hotel Bel-Air, he frequently went quiet and would reach for, and break open, a small glass vial. Honey gold liquid, which Daniel suspected was little better than a herbal concoction, would slip over his lips. Although he has since maintained he was joking, he explained at the time that the medication was designed to help him get over his deep-rooted disinclination of talking about himself. This was certainly a great handicap when one was the marketing mouthpiece to sell a film.

In America, his standing in the 1980s had soared due to the startling propinquity of two extremely diverse films. The sex symbol tag earned by his portrayal of Tomas had not been forgotten either, but he had also since acquired a reputation for being a tortured soul. The story of his premature exit from *Hamlet* had crossed the water amid all the hype, and the fact that it had been over two years between films all added to the aura of a man riven by doubts about his calling. Intriguing stuff as all this was, however, it was no match for a more powerful force. Suddenly all previous views of Daniel were being pushed aside and the label invisibly tattooed on his forehead was that of Hollywood hunk, whether he liked it or not.

Typically he did not like it, did not feel in many respects that he was ready for it. His half-brother Sean has openly confirmed that Daniel genuinely finds fame very hard to handle. But it went even deeper than that. The prospect, according to Day-Lewis, thoroughly depressed him. It was not the reaction one would normally expect, but then it had become abundantly clear that Daniel was not the stereotypical star.

In Britain he had by now achieved the standing of one of the country's finest actors, certainly of his generation. He was there in person when *The Last of the Mohicans* received its UK Gala Premiere on Wednesday, 4 November 1992 at the Parkway Cinema in Camden Town, north London, amid much excitement stirred up in the press. It was an event not only to raise money to help the ailing Parkway Cinema, but also to bring to public attention the plight of the world's vanishing tribes. Two days later the film went on general release.

The Last of the Mohicans secured only one Oscar nomination, for Best Sound, and a BAFTA nomination for Best Original Film Music, and not everyone loved the movie. Some film critics denounced it for being flashy, disappointing and lacking depth and substance. However, those views were in the minority and Daniel was once again among the nominees for the 1992 BAFTA Best Actor award. This time he was up against Stephen Rea for *The Crying Game*, Tim Robbins for *The Player* and Robert Downey Jr for *Chaplin*. Daniel lost out this time to Downey.

After *Mohicans* Daniel had very little time to let the grass grow under his feet for he was obligated to move on to what was planned to be the second of his Twentieth Century-Fox projects – an obligation he very much looked forward to in at least one respect as he was at last about to fulfil the second of his all-time acting ambitions. He could hardly wait.

CHAPTER NINE

DREAM COME TRUE

'Everything is labelled but everybody is not.'

NEWLAND ARCHER, *THE AGE OF INNOCENCE*

In 1921 the society novel *The Age of Innocence*, written by Edith Wharton, was one of the first winners of the Pulitzer Prize for fiction. In 1934 a film adaptation of the book was made by RKO, starring Victor Heerman. Fifty-eight years later a second film version was ready to go into production.

The name of Martin Scorsese, one of the leading directors of his generation, best known for the films *Taxi Driver*, *Raging Bull*, *Cape Fear* (all three starring Robert De Niro), was synonymous with dealing very effectively in masculine aggression and brutality. He was widely thought to be the least likely director to be at the helm of this sumptuous period romance.

Radical choice or not, Daniel was thrilled that the film he was about to embark on would mean him having the opportunity of working with the renowed filmmaker. Two years before, Scorsese's film *GoodFellas* had opened. This blackly comic mafia saga had teamed him up yet again with Robert De Niro, this time accompanied by Ray Liotta, and Joe Pesci in an Oscar-winning performance as the movie's hitman. Daniel saw *GoodFellas* a number of times in quick succession and promptly wrote to Martin, telling him how much he loved it. To join the likes of De Niro in being directed by Scorsese was an ambition he had nursed for many years.

His role in *The Age of Innocence* was to be that of the central character, Newland Archer. Joining him was an all-star cast which included Michelle Pfeiffer, Winona Ryder, Siân Phillips, Miriam Margoyles, Richard E. Grant and Jonathan Pryce. Filming began at the Kaufman Astoria Studios in Queens, New York on 24 February 1992. It was to see yet another example of Daniel's now legendary alchemic transmutations: a process which began long before the cameras started rolling.

As more details of the proposed film project steadily unfolded, it soon became apparent that Scorsese's production was going to put even Merchant Ivory in the shade with its sheer lavishness. Just as Daniel had studied E.M. Forster for *A Room with a View*, so he set about digesting Edith Wharton's tale of repressed love and denial amid the splendid but strict confines of New York high society in the 1870s. In doing so he discovered a stronger affinity with Wharton, whose work he had never read before, than he had found with her English male counterpart. The touching vulnerability of the upper-crust New Yorker he had signed up to portray appealed to him strongly; although it's true to say that he had his reasons for being predisposed to feel that way. Candidly Daniel has confessed that, had the director in this case not been Scorsese, in all likelihood he would not have taken the part. But it was, and he had, and so again he set out to assume a new identity: once more, one far removed from the last.

To do this he first had to lose all physical reminders of

Nathaniel Poe. This meant sacrificing the long flowing locks for a neatly barbered short back-and-sides, complete with side-burns, as well as shedding the twenty-odd pounds of muscle he had spent months acquiring for the outdoor hero. Lean drawing-room elegance was now the order of the day. It was vital to his mental preparation to immerse himself in the life and times of Archer, a skilful young lawyer and eligible bachelor from a prominent monied family. For those now accustomed to the Day-Lewis method, it came as no surprise to learn that, when, for the duration of the shoot, he checked into one of the few genuinely Victorian hotels New York has left, he did so as Newland Archer. In addition he would only receive mail and telephone calls if they were addressed in like manner.

Scorsese's connection with the project had tentatively begun twelve years before when Jay Cocks, a close friend and former film critic with *Time* magazine, had given him a copy of the novel to read. At the time Martin was immersed in making *Raging Bull* – a Hollywood biopic US critics voted the best film of the eighties – with Robert De Niro in his Oscar-winning role of World Middleweight Boxing Champion Jake La Motta, and he felt no affinity whatsoever with Wharton's restrained world of starched collars and boned corsets. Not bookish at the best of times, it was a further seven years before he finally got around to studying the work during a trip to London, where he was engaged to give a series of *Guardian* lectures. But, when he did read it, he found himself gripped by the raw sense of poignant self-denial, the exquisite romantic pain experienced by the principals involved and the subtle cruelty of genteel society which formed the backbone of the piece.

Originally it was intended to be a Twentieth Century-Fox film. Martin and Jay Cocks had agreed a deal with Fox whereby together they would write a script for submission in early 1989, which they did. They had also budgeted it at $32 million. Just days before *Cape Fear* premiered, however, Martin received the bad news from Fox's head, Joe Roth, that his company could not finance it after all. Even for a director of Scorsese's standing, obtaining the green light on a project is rarely straightforward.

With Fox bowing out, next in line loomed Universal Pictures who, although they adored the script, were not prepared to come up with the necessary budget. Finally, an acquaintance of Martin's who had worked with him on *GoodFellas* came to the rescue. Mark Canton was freshly installed as head of Columbia Pictures. It was when he offered the full finance that the film deal was clinched.

Shortly after this Martin, by chance, watched a video of *The Unbearable Lightness of Being* and was captivated by the way Daniel, as the womanising Czech surgeon, moved. There had been predatory stealth and grace mixed, to Scorsese's eyes, with a kind of almost choreographed elegance in the aloof way he carried himself. Then, in *My Left Foot*, he recognised in Daniel a depth of obsessive dedication which, he felt, mirrored his own work philosophy.

This combination of style and commitment led Scorsese, by now convinced that Day-Lewis was the man for the part, to approach Daniel in Los Angeles in early 1990, literally on the eve of his Oscar win, to ask him to take on the role of Newland Archer. Despite Daniel's long-held dream to work with the director, surprisingly he did not agree on the spot. Indeed, he only finally said yes the following year, just prior to leaving London bound for the North Carolina location of *The Last of the Mohicans*. Scorsese was delighted to have his acceptance. In fact, as far as casting was concerned, all three central figures were, rewardingly, his first choice.

A lover of old movies, Scorsese had been much influenced by

the 1949 Paramount film *The Heiress*, which his father had taken him to see as a child. Starring Olivia de Havilland, Montgomery Clift and Ralph Richardson, it had been based on a screenplay suggested by the Henry James novel *Washington Square* and it made a memorable impact on the boy. In that film, director William Wyler had meticulously recreated the Victorian era and its mores. With *The Age of Innocence*, Martin was determined that the period detail would likewise be exceptional.

In a complete departure from what he was used to handling, there were to be no guns, fists or blood-letting – this time all the violence was to be psychological, emotional and social. Having invited Daniel to his home, the pair watched *The Heiress* over and over again, discussing it, thrashing out what came out of it, privately each absorbing their own lessons from it. Where Henry James's strength had lain in portraying the psychological aspects of life, his friend Edith Wharton's had focused more on the reality of life's constraints, especially in connection with social change in old New York. The amalgamation of Wyler's film and Wharton's novel proved a powerfully evocative concoction. An exciting prospect, the project had been in the planning stages for over two-and-a-half years and was at last going into production.

The working relationship between actor and director was unusual from the beginning. On the evening that Daniel went to meet Martin in his hotel suite to discuss the film prior to shooting, despite being fully aware of Daniel's reputation, Scorsese was still surprised to open his door to find him already dressed from head to toe as Newland. During the months of filming Scorsese would always call Daniel Archer. In itself this was not unusual, as he was in the habit of addressing his actors by their characters' names. But in this case it went beyond that to the point where Scorsese had the unshakable feeling that somehow Archer had really come alive. It was something he was very conscious of on set every day, but it was in no way off-putting. On the contrary it seems to have instilled in the director a firm confidence and also a sense of fun.

Daniel felt much the same thing. Indeed, it is probably true to say that *The Age of Innocence*, his thirteenth film, was the first one he thoroughly and unreservedly enjoyed making. Every morning he woke up with a deep feeling of satisfaction and well-being at the thought of working with the diminutive director, with whom he had a rapport best described as therapeutic. It was the first time Daniel had accepted a role purely for the opportunity of working with a particular director and he had no regrets.

The film revolves around Newland Archer, who from the start is romantically linked to the daughter of another prominent New York family, May Welland, played by Winona Ryder. Born Winona Horowitz, she had made her mark in the late eighties in the comic fantasy *Beetlejuice* and the seriously weird black comedy *Heathers*.

Her engagement to Newland is announced at the annual Beaufort ball. The alliance is much approved by Archer's mother, played with her usual glacial grace by Siân Phillips. It was Siân's second innings as Daniel's screen mother; the first had been in the BBC2 film *How Many Miles to Babylon?* eleven years earlier. The match at first presents Archer with no trouble. He happily woos his fiancée in the fashion of the times by having flowers delivered to her every day. However, May has a cousin – Ellen, the Countess Olenska – who in contrast to May's demure, well-bred innocence is enigmatic, feisty and with an intriguing beauty. Having lived her married life in Europe, she is prone to unconventional thought and speech. The vital role of Ellen was ably adopted by Michelle Pfeiffer whose credits to date included *The Witches of Eastwick*, *The Fabulous Baker Boys* and *Danielgerous Liaisons* – for the last two of which she had been Oscar-nominated.

Winona Ryder had been the last of the main trio to be cast. Michelle, on the other hand, had captured Scorsese's attention years before. He admired greatly what he saw as her wide-ranging ability and has cited two of her 1988 films as being responsible for clinching his interest – her portrayals of a mafia widow in the offbeat *Married to the Mob* and a devout paragon of virtue in *Danielgerous Liaisons*.

It is the Countess's unconventionality, her outspokenness and independence which first attract Newland. She makes him laugh too, a reaction which appears to surprise him, and has a liberated spirit he loves, yet a vulnerability he craves to protect. As a lone woman separated from her Polish husband, she seems condemned to being ostracised, and initially his protection extends only to helping her be accepted back into polite society. Then, when she intends to seek a divorce, the legal firm for which Archer works is instructed to act on her behalf. Newland himself is appointed by his senior partner to advise the Countess.

As he learns just how intolerable her life with her husband had been, his respect for Ellen deepens – a respect which gradually turns to love. He then finds himself in a terrible dilemma. On the one hand he yearns for Ellen to be free of her marriage, but in all conscience he cannot possibly advise her to embark on a course guaranteed to render her a social leper. Also, he is very publicly engaged to one woman, while privately in love with another.

Emotionally torn, he and Ellen begin what is termed an affair although it is very restrained in its expression. The only real intimacy between Archer and Ellen is restricted to two scenes. In one, during a bumpy carriage ride in the snow, having been thrown suddenly into his arms, she allows him to slowly unbutton and push back the cuff of her kid glove to nuzzle the inside of her exposed wrist. In the other, at her house, racked with emotion he kisses his way caressingly around the back of her head, shoulders and neck before burying his face in her lap, then feeling his way lower to worship at her satin-clad foot. Yet so hungry is the viewer by this time for some degree of physical contact between the two tempted lovers that the effect is almost disproportionately poignant.

Theirs is a great love, doomed by the dictates of both conscience and of a society which is relentlessly forcing them apart. The helplessly desperate longing between them is all intensely played out in deeply painful illicit moments snatched behind the backs of their friends and relations. Such moments alone may be heaven, but their deceit weighs heavy.

Daniel's Archer is underplayed. In contrast to the panache of Nathaniel Poe who openly fights for what he wants, Newland, as befits a gentleman of his class and era, is not given to violent outbursts. Emotions are felt as deeply as they are hidden. The vulnerability this engenders is probably the strongest element throughout. The key to understanding the workings of this distant, powerful society and the havoc it could wreak behind its veneer of unstinting good manners lies with Daniel, rather than with the explanatory narrative. His expressive face signposts Archer's torment every step of the way. His jealousy of Julius Beaufort (Stuart Wilson), for example, is so unwitting at first that somehow Daniel manages to communicate it to the viewer while at the same time keeping it a secret from Newland himself. Although verging on tears at times, Daniel has no need to be so obvious to convey Archer's wretched longing and the unbearable thought of his future lifelong confinement.

Apart from fulfilling his ambition in actually working with

Scorsese, Daniel found the experience extremely rewarding in other ways. Although Martin held the reins very firmly, his style of communicating with his actors on set created the illusion of affording them an immense amount of freedom. Like Michael Mann before him, Martin wisely made the most mileage of Daniel's subtlety, his ability to convey so much with minimal means of expression, the merest hint of emotion made transparent by his cleverly controlled, sometimes rationed, body language.

At the end of the film, Newland is a widower of fifty-seven. Not old, yet he is aged beyond his years – the once-raven hair is steely grey and he walks with the aid of a cane. Still handsome in a faded way and certainly elegant, he is in France with his son Theodore, who is making his way to visit Ellen. Much to Newland's dismay, he discovers that not only does Ted know of the past affair, but also that he had learned of it from his mother before her death. In the end Archer refuses to go up to Ellen's apartment with Ted and stays instead on a bench in the street below. Although both he and Ellen are now free, he prefers his dreams and the memories of the love they had shared all those years ago, and after a while he gets up and walks slowly away – a final act of self-denial in this gentle tragedy of disappointment.

Daniel was acutely aware that to truly tune in to the mood of the movie required a complete detachment from today's behaviour and ethics as well as an understanding of the unbending rules of an earlier age. The role of Newland Archer is a subtle and complex one and for him one of the hardest tasks in getting under the character's skin was blocking out the present day. Martin Scorsese's pronouncement on the film was that his leading man met his goal entirely in both looking and behaving of the era.

The Age of Innocence is top heavy, by design, in period detail, having employed the services of various specialists in nineteenth-century dress and decor right down to table decoration. Scorsese also had as etiquette coach Lily Lodge, an acting teacher at The Actors Conservatory in New York whose grandmother had been a close personal friend of Edith Wharton. All is beautifully shot by German director of photography Michael Ballhaus, but for all the grandeur it is the performances of the three main figures, particularly Daniel's, which carry the film. From the opening sequence of unfolding red and yellow roses, there is scarcely a moment when Archer, appearing in the first minute consulting his programme during the opera, is not in the film.

This meant extra heavy demands on Daniel, and he coped by striving to isolate himself, if possible, even more than he had ever done in the past. He and Scorsese had talked a great deal before filming began about their objectives in the movie and how best to achieve these, but by mutual agreement when shooting began it was left to Daniel to get on with it. The visual demands were easily met. Descriptions like 'divine looking' and 'a fastidious study of a man of taste' flowed from the critics' pens, and, to complement the exquisite cut of his cloth, Daniel's accent is certainly soft and easy on the ear. He also smiles a lot, which in films is unusual for him. But it was the inside of the character on which he had had to concentrate most-how to conjure up his mind and motivation, his reactions when these were at odds with his breeding and how they should be unlocked and gradually revealed.

His performance of the tormented young lawyer required no outward props such as a wheelchair or a tomahawk; its essence lay in projecting the character's ingrained and indestructible sense of honour and duty, the intense hurt he endures behind a perpetual mask of impregnable correctness and which he dare not show. At one with Scorsese's understanding of the insidious barbarity inflicted by this society on anyone foolish enough to transgress its rules, Daniel saw his role as being that of someone with whom the viewer must emotionally engage in order to properly recognise and respond to the traumatic effect that the seemingly invisible, but systematic, attack of his peers has on him.

He clearly achieved his aim, for on the film's release many remarked on how effectively Daniel subtly, even tantalisingly, allowed the viewer the inside track on his thoughts and tortured emotions. How he arrived at that state came down to a combination of measures in his preparation, some familiar, some new. Firm in the belief that how one is dressed dictates largely how one relates to others, and vice versa, he set out from the start to recondition his every move and word appropriately. This meant that Daniel not only dressed as Archer, but strove to communicate on a daily basis as him too. A gentleman's apparel, particularly evening wear, was a matter of quite ludicrous importance in those days, and so the actor, who in real life is fond of dressing down, paid meticulous attention to ensuring that he was turned out at all times in the required impeccable style. He also spent weeks in the street practising precisely how to wield the required silver-topped walking cane, all in an attempt to create in advance the illusion of the world in which he would be required to live and breathe for the duration of the shoot.

Once work began, maintaining that state was not always easy. On a busy set, alive with reminders of the present day in the shape of modern high-tech filming equipment and a bustling crew, it is impossible to escape reality totally. The important thing was to hang on as hard as he could to his imagination. It has been said of Edith Wharton that she possessed a masculine soul as well as a feminine one and that this accounted for the acute definition with which she drew her male characters. Certainly Daniel considered her to have possessed an uncanny understanding of the male mind. He had little difficulty in twinning his perception of how Archer would react, with the dictates of the author, especially the longer he managed to remain in solitary contemplation when not filming.

Such a sight had become an expected part of any production in which Day-Lewis was involved. Actors had grown to respect and accept it long ago and this film's cast was no different. Pfeiffer and Ryder were happy to relax and unwind – stories leaked out of much giggling and larking around – but both his leading ladies respected their leading man's desire to keep himself separate at all times. In the background of much hilarity then, Daniel would be sitting almost out of sight, still in character, locked in his own world.

Michelle admitted that, although he was courteous in every sense of the word to all those around him, by the end of filming no one felt they had really got to know him. Madeleine Stowe had remarked much the same thing after the four months spent together on *The Last of the Mohicans*. That Pfeiffer personally considered Daniel gorgeous, she was gaily prepared to declare, at the same time highlighting the element of shuttered darkness he exudes which she feels adds to his mysterious personal appeal. But the fact that he is an extremely private individual who plays everything very close to his chest meant that he remained teasingly, after weeks of working side by side, a complete enigma to her and everyone else.

Although it was Pfeiffer's character with whom Daniel was in love on the screen, it seems that it was Winona Ryder, who would attract one of the film's five Oscar nominations for Best Supporting Actress, with whom he appeared to have the strongest chemistry. In time-honoured tradition, this notion was picked up on by the watching press. Soon the Day-Lewis name was romantically linked with that of Ryder's, even though his relationship with Isabelle Adjani appeared to be very much still on. Indeed, Adjani, then said to be still living in Daniel's London Brook Green home, has since been credited with having been instrumental in helping Daniel prepare for his role as Newland Archer.

One other cosy link with home had been that, for the first time in his career, there was to be a small family connection with this movie. Daniel's sister Tamasin was given a brief non-speaking role, in which she appears at Winona Ryder's side, admiring her engagement ring during the ball near the beginning of the film and then silently watches as Newland Archer elegantly approaches. Scorsese and his family got in on the act too. The fussy bustling photographer who later takes the official wedding photographs was in fact Martin, indulging in an Alfred Hitchcock habit of popping up in his own movies. Special guests to the Astoria soundstage when shooting was nearing completion included Scorsese's parents, who also took small cameo roles. Sadly, his father did not live to see the film's release the following year and, in tribute to his passing, Martin dedicated *The Age of Innocence* to Luciano Charles Scorsese.

Shooting ended in June and, although the time span between the completion and release of such a film can be around fifteen months, originally *The Age of Innocence* was intended to be released in the US a mere six months later. This was in the hope that it could qualify for consideration for the 1992 Oscar nominations. It was a timescale, however, which turned out to be wholly unrealistic.

At the beginning of December, after having studied what was in the can, Scorsese and Columbia Pictures were agreed that more time would be required to get it right. A year after filming finished, in June 1993, Daniel would return to the Queens soundstage at the Kaufman Astoria Studios to do looping work. Another release date in 1993 had had to be abandoned because of a delay in post production – not normally a good sign – but the film eventually premiered in America in October of that year and opened in Britain the following January.

Coming hard after *The Last of the Mohicans*, *The Age of Innocence* was seen as Daniel's second outing in the role of the smouldering romantic hero. Inevitably the image-building machinery began gathering momentum, producing predictions that Day-Lewis was heading for permanent membership of the ranks of Hollywood's most sought-after romantic leading men. But Daniel stubbornly refused to see the characters of Nathaniel and Newland as nothing but out-and-out dreamboats to feed female fantasies, insisting that the 'irresistible' tag, which had been rapidly lassoed and jerked tight around his neck, was utter rot and that frankly he felt between a rock and a hard place.

Says Richard Mayne, 'I had dinner with Daniel round about this time and he was acutely conscious of being at a crossroads in his career. He said he was very aware of being poised on a knife edge, balancing between the star thing and being an actor. In his own words basically he was asking himself, does he want to be a Mel Gibson or a Cyril Cusack. He wasn't sure he wanted superstardom at all.'

Doubts of a different kind preoccupied some of those watching his career. Simon Callow says of Daniel's role as Newland Archer, 'Such an awful lot of fuss was made of it, but I didn't see it really in that light at all. I salute his performance and to experience life in that class at the turn of the century is one thing, but it's not all that valuable unless you convert that into something else, some meaning.' He adds, 'I'm not criticizing for the sake of it. I've a feeling that deep down Daniel saw it that way himself.'

Film critic Barry Norman also holds particular views. He says, 'I think Daniel is a very fine actor indeed, very versatile and he genuinely pursues roles which appeal to him rather than for commercial reasons, which is hugely commendable. My only query is that there seems to me to be a coldness from him. I feel there is often a distance put there between himself and the audience. It came through, I thought, even in *My Left Foot*, surprisingly, and in the case of *The Age of Innocence* . . . It was a pretty unsympathetic role but I wonder if it would've added another dimension to Archer if Daniel had projected a warmth, added a real tangible sadness to the ending, in particular when he walks away rather than going up to see Countess Olenska.'

Barry goes on, 'Some of today's biggest Hollywood stars, most of whom couldn't hold a candle to Day-Lewis acting-wise, still project warmth, which is what communicates to the audience and, I believe, accounts for their amazing popularity. I don't know if superstardom is what Daniel is after, but the romantic lead would be his time and again if there was more warmth to him. Mind you, having said that, this distance wasn't there in *The Last of the Mohicans*. There was no barrier then so perhaps it is something he can choose to turn on and off to suit himself.' He adds, 'I feel that audiences respect and admire him, rather than empathise with him.'

Someone who had a different point of view was producer David Puttnam. Since making *Stars and Bars* with Daniel, David had been dismissed in 1987 as chairman of Columbia Pictures, the film company ultimately responsible for bringing *The Age of Innocence* to the screen. He found his faint personal apprehensions were laid to rest once he saw his former studio's movie. He admits, 'I confess I had reservations when I discovered that Daniel was going to do the Scorsese role, but he was fine in the part and totally proved me wrong.'

In autumn 1992, only weeks after filming ended for *The Age of Innocence*, the usual press reports began to circulate linking Daniel's name to various new projects. Some accounts associated him with starring in a film later to be called *Philadelphia*. Others stated that he was going to take the leading role in a £20 million production, based on a screenplay by Tom Stoppard, called *Shakespeare in Love*, which was then under way at Pinewood Studios in Buckinghamshire. This latter production was making the news because the female lead, *Pretty Woman* and *Sleeping with the Enemy* star Julia Roberts, was reported to have walked out on the film in October, allegedly because Daniel had refused to play the Bard, causing all operations to be suspended for the rest of the cast and crew

The project was certainly halted, but the specific reason is not even known to the playwright himself. According to Tom Stoppard's secretary, 'He doesn't know why the film was stopped. He wishes he did! All the discussions took place in America and then suddenly, out of the blue, all Tom was told was that it was no longer on, no explanations – nothing. It just wasn't happening any more, and,' she adds, 'it hasn't happened yet.'

As far as Daniel's involvement was concerned, the newspapers had got it wrong. It is true that he talked to the film's makers, but it was not possible for him to take on the work as he had already committed himself to something else.

With two major motion movies behind him, Daniel was now competing with the cream of the industry for the most sought-after roles in Hollywood. Tim Roth, Gary Oldman and Kenneth Branagh were once his rivals for parts. Now it was people like Tom Cruise and Tom Hanks. But Daniel had turned down the chance to follow up Newland Archer with another lawyer, this time in twentieth-century America in *Philadelphia,* and the part passed to Hanks. He preferred to star in a rough diamond of a project which would take him back to Ireland and reunite him in a working capacity with his friend director Jim Sheridan. Shooting was due to start early in 1993 and he had absolutely no desire to change his plans.

CHAPTER TEN

BEYOND ENDURANCE

'In the name of my father.'

GERRY CONLON, *IN THE NAME OF THE FATHER*

There had been so little time between making his last two films that embarking on a new one right then was the last thing Daniel needed. However, the rumours surrounding his intentions became fact when, in the first week of December 1992, his agent Julian Belfrage confirmed that he would be taking on the role of Gerry Conlon in a film whose working title then was *The Conlon Story* (aka *The Conlon Family*). The movie was part of a £7.5 million three-film deal which Jim Sheridan had struck with Universal Pictures and it promised to be a strong role and a highly controversial one – factors which alone were guaranteed to attract Daniel to it.

By now it had become almost mandatory for him to start off by resisting a role and, not for the first time, he initially considered himself to be the inappropriate choice to take on this particular part. However, a good deal of his reluctance stemmed from the straightforward reason that he was mentally and physically shattered. After finishing work on *The Age of Innocence* he had returned to Ireland and immediately sought refuge with Shay, staying at the director's home as a friend and guest. His 'mistake', as he frequently calls it, was to show genuine curiosity for the project Jim was then working on. Whether by accident or design, it was inevitable from that moment on that he would be sucked into it.

In spring 1990 Gerard Conlon had published his autobiography, *Proved Innocent*, in which he told the story behind his arrest, subsequent conviction and life sentence, of which he had spent almost exactly fifteen years behind bars, for a crime he did not commit. The book came out just seven months after his sensational release by the Appeal Court on Thursday, 19 October 1989, along with Paul Hill, Paddy Armstrong and Carole Richardson – collectively known as the Guildford Four. It was a frank, for the most part unvarnished, account of his life and experiences at the hands of the authorities.

As the true story of one of Britain's biggest miscarriages of justice, *Proved Innocent* could inevitably be expected to be of interest to film makers. Belfast writer Terry George, by then living in New York, prepared a screenplay from Gerry's book at the instigation of the actor Gabriel Byrne, who had plans to star in its film version. Together they approached Jim Sheridan with the idea. Sheridan had followed up his successful debut film, *My Left Foot*, with a project Daniel once discussed with Noel Pearson on completion of Christy's story, called *The Field*. This was another saga of an Irish family and their troubles, again produced in tandem with Pearson and this time starring Richard Harris, in an Oscar-nominated performance, along with John Hurt and Sean Bean. Since then he had been looking for a new project for some time. He liked the initial treatment George showed him, and on the strength of that alone he decided to become involved.

For two years Jim had been trying to attract the necessary backing to get the film off the ground – a search which had taken him the length and breadth of America without success. He found a heartening interest in the father-son angle but curiously little passion for the injustice side.

This then was the project in which Daniel expressed an interest while staying with Jim. Within minutes of hearing the basic outline of the story, Daniel felt a sensation akin to panic rising inside him. He well knew that he needed to rest and recuperate; he also knew that what he was hearing was already beginning to tug on him and would be dangerous to his resolve to take a long restorative break from making movies. He wanted to tell Shay to stop, but he didn't and by the time the director was finished Daniel was fired up with enthusiasm and desperate to read Conlon's book. As if neatly orchestrated, within days of Daniel finishing *Proved Innocent* the author himself turned up at Sheridan's house. Daniel warmed to Gerry instantly, to his needle wit in particular, and in many ways that was a bad sign for, exhausted or not, he knew then deep down that there was going to be no way out of getting involved in the project.

It was also bad news for Gabriel Byrne. Although, from the moment when Gerry *Conlon* had engaged his interest in the prospect of his autobiography becoming a feature film, Byrne had seen himself as being the person to play Conlon on screen, when the project passed out of his hands and into Jim Sheridan's, it became a whole new ball game. Sheridan set to work on Terry George's original screenplay and he has since admitted that he was writing with his friend Daniel in mind all along.

Tentatively, Jim offered the tailor-made role of the Belfast tearaway supposedly turned terrorist to Daniel, who, without waiting for him to finish, hastily cut him off mid-sentence with a blunt refusal. Sheridan, however, knew his mate too well. He was fully aware that, behind all his protestations, his interest had already been aroused; all the fire needed was a little oxygen to make it burn. Of a highly persuasive disposition anyway, Jim subtly worked on Daniel, pulling all the stops and wearing him down until he eventually caved in.

It was perhaps some consolation to Gabriel Byrne when he remained involved with the film in the capacity of executive producer. But, as it happened, Daniel's acceptance to star in *The Conlon Story* meant a lot more than the chummy director/actor team having the chance to work together again for, as Sheridan admits, it was actually the Day-Lewis name which at last secured the finance to back the film. During his search for investors, Jim had originally approached Universal Pictures in August 1992. They were certainly interested, but, when he was able to come back and tell them that he had Daniel's verbal commitment to take on the lead, the deal was consolidated.

Right then *The Last of the Mohicans* was doing huge box-office business in the States. Hawk-eye's face adorned everything from magazine layouts to the freeway billboards and the Day-Lewis name was on everyone's lips. Universal coughed up a straight $10 million for Sheridan to get his project under way. There was an element of risk in it for the film company. It was certainly a potentially explosive subject and it was identified at the outset as possibly also being a tough marketing challenge. But at the same time with Daniel on board, as well as the startling results that he and Jim Sheridan had already produced, it equally had Oscar material written all over it.

But, if riveting performances were anticipated by investors busy rubbing their hands in anticipation, the British press had other ideas. From the day it was made public that the project had been given the go-ahead, the film and its stars came in for a fair degree of flak. Daniel was singled out relentlessly by Fleet Street for his interest in Irish issues, as if that in itself constituted some sort of crime. At times the form this attack took could almost be described as a kind of defensiveness on the part of the English press – as if, every time Daniel extolled or embraced something Irish, somehow by definition that represented a slight on his birthplace.

It is a curious practice and something which at times irritates Daniel immensely, particularly because he sees some of the criticism as implying that somehow his love of Ireland is a kind of gimmick or affectation. A remark which frequently surfaces in the press from Stephen Frears, the director of *My Beautiful Laundrette,* that he knew Daniel before he was Irish appears, at least at face value, to have annoyed the actor intensely.

Emma Thompson, who would play the role of civil rights lawyer Jean Gareth Peirce, Gerry Conlon's solicitor, also came in for much early criticism. It was not new to her. Her earlier outspokenness about the Gulf War, first had drawn ludicrous accusations that she supported the Iraqi point of view in the conflict. Her involvement now attracted comments that she ought not to be working on what was, at times, being termed an 'IRA film'. But, as before, she shrugged the nonsense aside.

Much of the heat generated before and after the film's launch would centre on its mix of fact and fiction into that hybrid, faction. It was also a highly controversial topic to be handling, dealing as it does with a true story which included claims of police brutality, the revelation that vital evidence was suppressed which would have cleared Gerry Conlon at the original trial and the role of the IRA, of which Conlon and the other three were wrongly convicted of being members. But

213

Sheridan was not concerned with the political issues involved and instead saw it mainly as a human story of gross injustice, intermingled with a troubled father-son relationship.

The son, in real life, was a Catholic kid from the Lower Falls area of Belfast. With little money coming into the house – there was much unemployment in the district – the Conlon family was still a close-knit one and very much part of a warm local community. Strictly apolitical, Gerry was, however, clearly anti police. This stemmed he claims from having been roughed up by them as a young lad. A self-confessed petty thief from a fairly young age, by fifteen he was involved in regular riots against the RUC as well as having run foul of the IRA because of his persistent stealing.

Gerry was just twenty when an intensive IRA bombing campaign began to blast the peace on the British mainland into smithereens in the early 1970s, by which time he was himself in London, living in a hippy commune. His sole aim in life then was to drink and party as much as he could. Sometimes the high jinks fractured into arguments with others in the crowd. It was the night he and his old schoolfriend Paul Hill had a disagreement with one of the other young drop outs and left the commune that time-bombs went off without warning at two public houses in Guildford. These had been targeted because they were frequented mainly by off-duty soldiers from a nearby army training camp. The carnage left five people dead and seventy-five others seriously injured.

By unlucky coincidence, having run out of money and with nowhere to stay, Gerry hadn't fancied the prospect of another night sleeping rough. Thoroughly disillusioned with London he headed home, only to be detained by Special Branch detectives at Holyhead as he was about to board the ferry to Dublin. He was released that night and was at home with his family

watching the television news when he saw a report of arrests
which had just been made in connection with the Guildford
pub bombing. Among the nineteen suspects being shown taken
into custody, he recognised Paul Hill, even although he was
virtually hidden under a heavy blanket. With the £700 Gerry
had stolen from a break-in, he and Hill had gone on a shopping
spree, buying themselves identical gear. It was the sight of the
distinctively garish platform shoes stepping out of the police
van which made Conlon freeze where he sat. Hours later when
everyone was asleep, the RUC burst into the Conlon home in
a dramatic armed raid and arrested Gerry. What followed began
the worst nightmare of the young man's life.

To combat the rising wave of terrorism afflicting the country,
just two days before Conlon's arrest the British Government
had passed a controversial new law, – the Prevention of
Terrorism Act (PTA), which enabled the police to hold
suspects for up to seven days before being charged. These
were draconian powers in a democracy, but a measure of their
desperation. Gerry was arrested under these new powers and
in the days that followed he would, he claimed, be beaten,
threatened and starved of food and sleep. All this intimidation
finally led him to making false confessions due to sheer fatigue,
confusion and terror.

In the meantime, his father Giuseppe Conlon, his aunt
Annie Maguire and five members of her family had also been
arrested, accused of being the Guildford Four's back-up
support unit. Committal proceedings began on St Patrick's
Day 1975. Gerry, Hill, Armstrong and Richardson were, after
a costly trial which lasted weeks, eventually all found guilty
and given lengthy or life sentences. The film was intended to
centre on the period just prior to Gerry's arrest, the trial and
his subsequent imprisonment, as well as the crusade to prove

their innocence – a fight which would become a huge national public campaign.

While details were being finalised to secure Daniel's services for this charged drama, whose title by now had been changed to *In the Name of the Father* in the late Giuseppe's honour, in the lead up to Christmas Sheridan began casting for the other roles. Because one of the main planks in Jim's mind was the father-son relationship, casting the right Giuseppe Conlon was vital. The man who in the end landed the part was Pete Postlethwaite, an accomplished British actor who had also, appropriately, been Daniel's mentor many years ago at the outset of his acting life at the British Old Vic Drama School. This fact probably had a lot to do with why it was Daniel's suggestion to cast Pete. Paul Hill was to be played by John Lynch and the main senior detective, the fictitiously named Inspector Robert Dixon, by Corin Redgrave.

Shooting was scheduled to start on 8 March 1993 and Daniel bent his mind to preparation for his new film. His research techniques had long ago become a by-word for intensity – a fact which rarely finds favour with Daniel himself. He prefers not to divulge the lengths to which he goes to portray a character, believing that it is in the main irrelevant to the understanding or enjoyment of a film and also that it risks ruining the magical quality of the film itself. At the same time, he is just as curious as the next man about these things if they concern some other actor. But he also makes the point that there is a danger of too much emphasis being put on what he does in preparation than is relevant to the ultimate result. Nevertheless, the lust for details about what Daniel was up to this time in his research was as rife as ever.

Prior to filming, Daniel had several meetings with Gerry Conlon and his family, during which they talked in great depth.

It was a valuable period. Conlon gave Daniel a deep and very personal account, not only of events which had taken place, but of the whole gamut of emotions he had endured. Despite his horrific experience, he showed a remarkably resilient ability to inject some light relief into the situation. This caused Daniel some surprise.

All acting is a form of mimicry and an essential part of Daniel's preparation for any role involves studying people, which is something that in the past he had always been able to do unhindered. Since winning the Oscar, however, and certainly with the release of *The Last of the Mohicans*, the days were long gone when he could walk about in public and remain unrecognised. So here, too, he had taken to assuming a disguise.

Richard Mayne gives an example. 'A couple of years ago I had attended a debate at the Everyman cinema in London at which various people were speaking about the direction of, and standards in, film and television. The place was packed and afterwards everyone was standing about chatting in the foyer, when the moment I was alone this long-haired leather-clad greasy yob suddenly appeared at my elbow. I kind of took a step back and was just about to say something when I looked up and discovered it was Daniel.'

He goes on, 'Well, for at least three-quarters of an hour we stood in this crowded hall and spoke. I could see people giving me strange disapproving looks for speaking to this guy, because he really did look a sight, but the point is this place was crammed with so-called film buffs, including producers and directors, some of whom, I may say, had already worked with Daniel. And not one person recognised him standing there in their midst.' Richard adds, 'Probably that incident, more than anything I'd seen of his on screen, made me realise just how complete his ability is in taking on a persona. It goes way beyond wearing the clothes, styling the hair. He soaks himself in whatever character he is assuming and it transforms him fully – to the extent that, if he doesn't want people to notice him, you can be sure they won't.'

With this ability at his fingertips then, in addition to his meetings with Conlon, Daniel managed to spend time in Belfast, wandering the streets undetected listening acutely to varied and everyday examples of the Ulster accent. In this department, he also had the help of dialect coach Brendan Gunn, who speaks of his time with Daniel as having been 'a very intense experience'. Now events began to gather speed, although the dynamite implications of the subject about to be tackled did not fully sink in with Daniel until filming was actually under way, when the real hardships began.

In order truly to simulate the depths to which Gerry Conlon sank under the police interrogation tactics, Daniel went to what many considered unprecedented lengths for his art. The stories, for which a degree of exaggeration must be allowed, which emerged from the set included that for nights on end he refused to sleep, so that he could experience for himself the true effects of such fatigue, and that he insisted on eating slops – prison-style food. On top of that, while he lived for two days and nights in a specially built cell, it is said that a handful of locals were hired to kick and beat on his door every so often to prevent him from getting any rest or peace of mind. And, if not doing this, they were lobbing pails of icy cold water over him while shouting abuse: all in the drive to experience Conlon's misery as closely as he could.

Whether some of these tales are simply examples of the by then increasingly uncontrolled Day-Lewis mythology or not, it can be guaranteed that it was an intense time for Daniel. Each actor's way of working is a very personal thing and Daniel admits that his preferred method is not perhaps what every person can associate with, but he needs the totality of it both on and off set. When filming stopped for the day it was highly unusual for him to socialise with the others but, if he did so, it is said that not only did he maintain his Ulster accent at all times, but, that he insisted that he continued to be called Gerry.

Although Conlon came from Belfast, the filming of his pre-prison days obviously could not take place there. Arthur Lappin, who had been line producer on *My Left Foot*, was co-producer on *Father* and he reveals, 'The street scenes were shot in and around Dublin. Most of the scenes in prison were shot in an old prison called Kilmainham Jail and we also built a set in the courtyard too. Other prison scenes were shot at some working prisons around Dublin. In all the schedule lasted fourteen weeks, which included a three-week shoot in Liverpool.'

It was when they had transferred to Merseyside that problems began to hit the production. A local pensioner had given permission for the gable end of her house to be painted with a mural which showed a gunman with the words 'BRITS OUT' and, later on, the word 'IRA' was added. Precautions were taken to make it perfectly clear to the Liverpool public that it was all part of a film set – large, clear signs were erected to this effect and security guards were posted – but still it caused an uproar. The householder, herself an Orange Lodge member, was subjected to substantial harassment from locals – receiving abusive telephone calls which grew so threatening that the police had to be brought in. Loyalists also somehow got through the security cordon and destroyed the mural, which had to be painted all over again.

Elizabeth Lloyd, then a local drama student, who played an extra in *Father* remembers the problems surrounding this mural. She says, 'The lady apparently claimed that, while she gave permission for the film people to paint it, she hadn't known exactly what the mural would be of. It caused a big stink at the time and it all got pretty heated. People here, you see, thought that the film glorified the IRA, but I don't think it did at all.'

Although registered with a casting agency, Elizabeth found out about the film when the producers put out an appeal on Radio Merseyside that they were about to start shooting and were looking for extras. Sheridan had previously applied to Universal Pictures for a further $200,000 to enable him to hire 2,000 professional extras, but, as the budget had already risen, his request had been turned down. He had to make do then with wildly keen, but mainly amateur extras.

The climactic court scene when Emma Thompson as Gareth Peirce confronts Inspector Dixon with the previously concealed evidence which, in *Father,* results in the convictions of the Guildford Four being quashed was filmed at St George's Hall. This houses one of Britain's last remaining Victorian courtrooms. When Daniel, as Gerry, bursts out into the street, triumphantly pumps his fist in the air and strides towards his banner-waving, cheering sea of supporters, he emerges, however, not from St George's Hall but from the nearby Liverpool Museum. Its huge impressive doors double for those of London's Old Bailey.

Says Elizabeth, 'I was in the crowd outside, opposite the old court. The idea of the scene was that the extras had to charge forward, to crash through and run towards Daniel – to appear to mob him but not to actually touch him. The scene took take after take, then just when it seemed right I was accidentally pushed from behind and fell to the ground while the cameras were still rolling. It became absolute chaos. The people behind didn't want to come forward and those in front were turning back confused with all the commotion. I heard one of the film crew shouting "Stop! Stop! This is madness!" then two men dived in and pulled me off the ground and out. I'd been trampled and kicked on and was feeling very shaken.'

She goes on, 'By this time Sheridan was yelling again and I heard him bawl through his megaphone, "Would the lady just knocked over please come and see me," but I didn't go. I was in shock and I suppose I felt embarrassed, too. My back was aching and, after I'd been treated, a few people were standing about talking to me. Next moment I felt my left arm being gently squeezed and I was pulled round and this voice asked in a very concerned way if I was all right. I looked up and it was Daniel.' Elizabeth had watched him all morning, take after take, belting down the court steps towards the crowd she formed part of, but she hadn't been this close and it is a moment she says she will never forget. She explains, 'Well, I had watched *The Last of the Mohicans* just a fortnight earlier and, shock or not, I vividly remember thinking that I couldn't believe I was actually looking straight up at Hawk-eye himself.' Daniel repeatedly asked if she was all right, sympathising with the fright she must have had and all the while appeared to be trying to return her to some semblance of normality. After posing patiently with her when she roped in a passer by to take their photograph together, he returned to work for another dozen or so takes before the shot was considered in the can.

The impression Daniel left Elizabeth with was of a very shy man, a loner. His concern for the injured extra was the one moment he was prepared to break his concentration. Apart from that, between takes when everyone else was milling about, as Elizabeth verifies, he would be seen pacing up and down alone in the background totally self-absorbed, waiting only for

221

his cue. 'It was as if the rest of the world didn't exist,' she adds.

As it happened, the film's climax had to be re-shot in late September, almost four months after shooting had originally ended. Because of the intensity with which Daniel had inhabited the role of Gerry Conlon, together with the trouble he then experienced in letting the character go, it was not news he wanted to hear. By that time he was also in the process of moving house out of England and wanted nothing to do with films at that point. Sheridan, however, was not happy with the final cuts, and with less than a month to deliver the finished product to Universal Pictures, he had pressures of his own to consider and so insisted that it be re-done. Despite their personal rapport, Daniel confesses to having been rather difficult with Jim about the whole thing.

The emotions felt and certainly expressed by Daniel as Conlon in the final court sequence of bitter hatred and fragile fear must have been tough enough to portray to such intense effect during the making of the entire movie. To somehow conjure them up again from cold, when he had been trying desperately for many weeks to rid himself of the spirit of the character, was bound to be much more difficult. In order to put himself through that nerve-racking wringer again, Daniel had to feel for himself that it was truly necessary. Eventually, he could see that Sheridan was right and, having apologised, set about filming the re-shoot.

This resistance was, in fact, not the only source of hassle on this film. By his own admission Daniel had, uncharacteristically, not been very easy to work with throughout the entire period of filming *Father*. It is something he was constantly conscious of but, for the most part, apparently unable to do anything about. The fourteen-week schedule had been tough and he had embarked on the project in the first place at a point when he had really needed to rest. If he had wanted to find excuses for his behaviour, he would not have had far to look, but, still, displaying any signs of awkwardness was still a first for him.

According to Madeleine Stowe, Daniel's complete acceptance of directorial guidance during *The Last of the Mohicans* had been so pronounced as to be unique in her experience, and, while working with Scorsese, Daniel had been only too glad to put himself unquestioningly in Martin's professionally renowed hands. But *In the Name of the Father* had been gruelling. He called it a 'supreme act of trust' to let himself behave with less than his usual control in front of Jim Sheridan, but his faith held firm, for Shay in no way held anything against Daniel for it. When making *My Left Foot*, Daniel had felt very protective towards the director, then making his debut in the world of feature films. Now, five years later, the roles were reversed and it was Shay who provided a sense of security and stability for the, at times, frazzled actor by virtue of the fact that theirs is a very close friendship.

He is the first director, according to Daniel, who, far from being daunted by some of his more extreme preparation methods, instead actively provokes him to push the barrier of 'madness'. For his part, Sheridan echoed *Mohicans*' director Michael Mann's analysis that Daniel contains a kind of fire that springs from deep inside and which has little to do with acting a part, by acknowledging what he termed his huge, pure rage in *Father*. On a lighter note he also quite cheerfully eggs Daniel on, abusing him in the heat of filming on occasions as a 'fucking mad bastard' – a brutal denunciation which Daniel describes as a euphoric experience!

'Mad' behaviour, perhaps, but certainly dedicated and the film world's equivalent of the dream ticket had done it again with *In the Name of the Father*, producing a powerfully evocative film, guaranteed to provoke deep emotion. The soundtrack was impressive too, with music from Jimi Hendrix, Bob Dylan, the Kinks and Thin Lizzy. The dramatic theme music was the work of the director's friend, U2's lead singer Bono. Deliberately jarring, it kick-starts the nerves and gets the adrenalin pumping before slamming the film into gear.

Daniel makes his entrance balancing precariously on a rooftop, gaily stealing lead. Wielding a length of piping spread low across his thighs, he wildly begins to play air guitar to his own tuneless accompaniment. Outlined against the daytime skyline, darting in and out behind a fat chimney stack, he is mistaken for a sniper by the jittery squaddies patrolling the pavements below, so they open fire. Sobered instantly, he flies off the roof with his mate and runs for his life pursued by soldiers, first on foot, then backed up by thundering armoured vehicles, all to the hot exotic dissonance of Hendrix's 'Voodoo Child.'

It is a fast-paced and gripping beginning which sees civilians immediately rallying round to protect the two fleeing local lads, letting them hurtle through houses and rattle down rabbit warrens of back alleys, while women and children bang bin lids against walls to signal when the coast is clear. The incident is all that's needed to spark a full-scale street riot. Behind a wall of riot shields, the Brits advance, firing tear gas and rubber bullets, trying to isolate their 'sniper' from the mob, which in turn is busy pelting them with petrol bombs, bricks and corrugated iron fencing ripped from the ground. And at the forefront of this mob is Daniel's Gerry Conlon.

Daniel later revealed the flak he received from some unimpressed Irish women present at the filming over his disappointing lack of Hawk-eye muscles. He admitted apologetically that they had all fallen off within weeks of returning from the North Carolina shoot. Indeed, as he prances provocatively about in the face of the army onslaught, he is back to looking as thin as a yard of pump water. His appearance is made more spare by the then fashionable bell-bottomed hipster jeans, brown leather fitted jerkin and a sweater as tight as a bandage with his shirt tail hanging out; his straggly shoulder-length hair is a greasy slick across his brow.

Roughly ten years before, firstly as Guy Bennett, then as Romeo, he had effectively carried off the part of a seventeen-year-old on stage. In his mid-thirties now, he had originally wondered if he could still effectively pass himself off as a lad barely out of his teens. These opening scenes, during which he grabs the audience's attention despite the carnage erupting all around, disprove his doubts. His expression as he hurls abuse at the troops is disturbingly authentic in its fury and contempt, and his irresponsible enjoyment of the whole furore that his rooftop escapade has created, gives the viewers their first reading of Conlon's character. His high is only punctured when some IRA men get hold of him and lead him away to a quiet housing-estate courtyard.

Having previously warned him for his persistent stealing, and now livid that the riot he has caused has endangered an arms cache, the terrorists have Gerry, his mate and another young man lined up against a wall, with the apparent intention of kneecapping them. Rescue, however, is not far away, for Gerry's little sister, who had been watching the riot, has run to her father at his workplace in the nearby bookmaker's office to tell him that the IRA have got their Gerry.

Giuseppe, waving a white hankie, rushes to the estate only to find his son and the others with their trousers round their ankles – to save cloth getting into the wound. He breathlessly begs the gunmen to let them go, blaming their foolishness on their youth. Relieved when the gunmen disperse, Giuseppe then tackles Gerry on his persistent trouble-making antics. This is the first of many confrontations between father and son which become integral to the story. Every one is brilliantly enacted by both Daniel and Pete Postlethwaite, whose performance was to earn him a well-deserved Oscar nomination for Best Supporting Actor. As the best thing he can do, Giuseppe gets Gerry a passage on the first ship out of port to England. 'Go and live, son,' he tells him, but on board Conlon bumps into an old school mate, Paul Hill – a meeting which will change his life.

Daniel carries off the dishonest side of Conlon's character with believable realism. He projects a likely lad who looks as if he would rob the sugar from your tea, and he walks with a distinctly annoying, nervy gait. Although he is not an entirely likeable character at this stage, Daniel manages to create at least a neutral acceptance of Conlon for what he is.

It is during the scenes of police brutality that he commands the viewers' deepest sympathy. His portrayal is one which grows in passion as Conlon's fear and distress reach overwhelming proportions. The film includes scenes of officers pulling him limb from limb, wrenching his ears and hair as well as viciously beating him about the head. Daniel's overwrought state appears frighteningly realistic as he is gradually reduced to a crying, gibbering and exhausted young man, willing finally to sign anything as long as they will stop hurting him.

Two of his four early interrogators were played by Richard Graham, the thug Genghis from *My Beautiful Laundrette*, who was also a mutinous crew member in *The Bounty*, and Daniel's friend Philip Davis, with whom he had also previously worked on *The Bounty*. Owing to the crucial importance of this scene, everyone seems to have been very tense during the shoot. One of the interrogators later revealed that he had suspected that Daniel had at one point deliberately sabotaged the carefully choreographed mimicking of physical assault so that his blow actually landed on him – presumably in quest of injecting an extra sharp shock of authenticity. Whether or not it had the desired effect on Daniel, it certainly shook the life out of the actor delivering the heavy blow.

To Daniel, if one single scene in the film was to convince people how an innocent man can confess to a heinous crime he did not commit, it was the moment when, broken by repeated and savage interrogation, he signs a false confession. It was vital to him to portray, utterly realistically, a man so lonely, exhausted and terrified that he could lose all rational thought. To do that, he had to understand that state of mind for himself, which required him to experience his own version of Conlon's hell.

With a reputation for never playing two roles the same, there can obviously be little, if any, mental source material available to Daniel to draw on from his past performances. And indeed he has maintained that, on leaving a film behind, he lapses into a kind of amnesiac state about what triggers his reactions. Yet in *Father* there was an echo from the past and the link was *My Left Foot*. Christy's imprisonment had been physical and so too, although in a different way, had Gerry Conlon's. Both had been acutely frustrating. The difference was that Conlon's imprisonment, for Daniel, was also a spiritual confinement, and that touched the actor on the raw.

In keeping with his oft-expressed dislike of outsiders analysing his methods, he tried to insist that the measures he took remained unknown to the general public. But still more rumours leaked out – stories such as how, during shooting of the interrogation scenes, on the director's instructions, none of the other actors was permitted to talk to Daniel in between takes. Instead, they were to concentrate wholly on exuding a malicious menace towards him, strong enough to maintain the illusion of intimidation.

Before shooting began, as part of his preparation, Daniel is said to have visited the actual cell in Guildford Police Station in which Gerry was detained for questioning. For the film, these police station scenes were shot in the now disused and freezing Dr Steevens Hospital in Dublin's south side. The clinically cold tiling on the floors and walls helped to create the necessary atmosphere of bleak incarceration.

Daniel was 'held' there for two days and nights in conditions intended to simulate the isolation of his arrest and during this time, it's claimed, he subjected himself to intensive interrogation by members of the real Garda from the Serious Crimes Squad. If he required to visit the toilet, even, he was escorted by his cell guard, who would place a thick rough blanket over his bowed head. Together with those tales of the men then hired specifically to kick on the cell door at regular intervals, this treatment was designed to bring him to a pitch of mental fatigue and hysteria, almost nearing collapse. He succeeded to possibly an alarming degree, even by Jim Sheridan's flexible limits, for Shay described Daniel at this point as being so mentally abused and exhausted that he was virtually close to tears for this entire section of the shoot.

When first on remand and then for the duration of their time in prison, father and son are housed in the same cell – one of the major criticisms of the film on its release as this is not what happened in reality. However, bowing to the needs of condensing a life story into 133 minutes, placing the two together provided the opportunity for the problems between the men to be played out. Alone in their cell, Daniel portrays

Gerry as a son harbouring long-held grudges for seemingly trivial things, considering his present plight. His outpouring of bitterness over a football medal won as a child clearly comes as a surprise to his father and sows the seeds for many such confrontations. Leaving aside the visually compelling images of brutality, the personal interaction between them, and how, each in their own way, they overcome past and present grievances, is probably the most potent force in the film.

The relationship culminates in Gerry displaying a deep love and respect for Giuseppe, made all the more poignant by his death in custody. Daniel, from the first, felt unequivocally absorbed into each phase of its development, arriving almost instinctively at a core of understanding.

It cannot be true to say that he found many parallels to his own life and relationship with his father, for, although he often refers to his deep regret that Cecil had more than enough opportunities before his death to witness him make mistakes and at the same time never achieve anything worthwhile, Daniel was still a youth when he passed away. The sort of challenges experienced between a father and a son entering early manhood were lost to him. Even so he would vaguely allude to a faint personal association, particularly relating to a vibrant, healthy son watching a father's health fail and learning to acknowledge strange, occasionally resentful, feelings because of that.

This recurring accusation, that Giuseppe has been weak through illness all his life, is something which Gerry uses as a hurtful weapon against his father. But it is an element in the film which was introduced entirely by Daniel and did not come directly from the true Conlon story. Having spent a lot of time with Gerry and his family, he had absorbed everything he could of their past, their feelings and the events. There came a time, though, when he had to walk away, to cut himself off from the real Conlon and create his own Gerry, based as authentically as he could on the man, but also incorporating a line of his own to follow. This resentment of Giuseppe's illness is effective and forms the emotional pivot of the story when later, instead of attacking his father for his weakness, he becomes protective of him as he finally recognises Giuseppe's quiet strength and innate integrity.

It all gave rise to excellent performances from both actors, each one feeding off the other. Daniel's long-standing friend Pete Postlethwaite has admitted that their bond during this time was so total that he often had difficulty discerning whether Daniel was responding to him as himself, or as Conlon's father, and indeed if Daniel was being Daniel off screen or was still Gerry.

As well as changing in his attitude towards his father, Daniel's projection of Conlon alters subtly throughout the film. In the beginning there is an almost feral quality to him, very shifty and totally untrustworthy. Once he is arrested this turns to nervous energy and a look of being permanently freezing. As his internment progresses, his looks, perhaps improbably, improve considerably. His hair still slants across his forehead, tossed every so often out of his eyes, but the face is lean and strong and the eyes convey not so much a grim acceptance of his fate, as a steely determination to do something about it. By the end the unlikely hero, standing tall and proud, hell bent on justice, has the masses behind him, baying for blood.

The budget for *In the Name of the Father* rose to nearer $16 million, fully financed by Universal Pictures. Although the final scenes ended up having to be re-shot, filming originally finished in early June, at which time Daniel had to head straight to New York and the Kaufman Astoria Studios soundstage to do looping work for *The Age* of *Innocence*. There, he was immediately pounced upon by journalists already on the interview trail, even before Daniel himself had had a chance to see Scorsese's film all the way through.

Because of a delay in post production, *Innocence* would be released just weeks before *Father*, which meant that apart from anything else it was going to entail a great deal of spreading himself around for the individual publicity departments. He had little doubt in which direction most of the coverage would go. From his earliest television performances it had become apparent to those working with Daniel that he was one of a breed of actors, like Hoffman, Pacino and De Niro, for whom it is vital to jealously guard his own space both on and off the set. A self-confessed fear Daniel harbours is of turning up to start filming and feeling a stranger to the role. Beyond that, once having captured the character he firmly believes the chain must be maintained and never broken. The world he creates is as complete as he can make it and within those confines he can then shut out all that is not directly related to his characterisation. Although it represents no difficulty for most actors, the idea of jumping in and out of two completely unrelated lives is not something either Daniel feels equipped to do, or would want to do.

A studier of the human condition, his feeding ground is any public place where he can observe without being seen. The way in which someone walks, their manner and expressions, is absorbed, squirrelled away and analysed. More particularly, an interesting face seems to tell him a story. Sometimes, in an instant, he can even imagine that he knows what it means to see life with those eyes. When that happens it ignites a flame inside him, a passionate need to experience whatever being that person involves. While conscious that his interpretation of another's life may not always be totally correct and is perhaps incomplete, nevertheless when he faces the camera he deliberately blots out any questions left unanswered and operates solely with the tools he has accumulated.

Under scrutiny for years and unable to stem the press's avid fascination with his by now famous preparation techniques, Daniel seems to feel both threatened and disappointed by the attention this whole area of his work receives. Threatened in the sense that, if one attempts too rigorously to expose the mechanics of any art, then the risk is high of destroying the fundamental appeal of its magical illusion.

Daniel is also disappointed, because to him the point of all his work consistently appears to be missed. It is not the steps he physically takes to become a Christy or a Conlon that count, and nor does he simply assume some form of disguise. It is the complex mental framework he strives to build up inside which creates his screen character. His aim is to reach the point where his actions and reactions are as spontaneous as they would have been for that person, and not those of Daniel Day-Lewis merely acting a part.

Reports that he insisted on enduring repeated soakings while banged up in a cold cell on set for *Father* can, when taken at face value, very easily suggest a form of masochism. This charge has been levelled at Daniel's approach to acting, but this is not where he himself believes he comes from. Maintaining that he is searching for the pleasures that discovering a life alien to his own can give him, he considers any physical or mental suffering he may endure along the way simply to be a conduit towards that end.

His methods are not, he concedes, foolproof. Nor is there a set sequence of steps to take. Rather it is an intangible process, which frequently leaves him with no certainty that specific actions will automatically guarantee a successful outcome.

Mentally, it is a mire through which he has to grope his way forward. Every time the process is new and every time he must hope. And because he has had to suspend his real self in limbo for the duration of a film – a factor he once cited as being one of the most satisfying aspects of his work – to avoid feeling an imposter in his own life, there must follow another period of rediscovery when he has to let go and return to being himself again.

Once a film is in the can, still more confusion emerges for Daniel. Like a lot of actors, he often finds no particular pleasure in watching himself on screen. But what bothers him is the constant stream of what he calls 'very disturbing infidelities' which follows the end of a film. Embarking on a role assumes the proportions of a passionate romance and one of such intensity that, when the ruthless cut-off comes, the pain is all the more acute. With a depth of feeling surely unique, he inwardly rebels against the accepted process whereby, when a film is over and all the obligations of its launch have been met, one is expected to discard it and walk away.

Undoubtedly the degree to which he inhabits a role and therefore bonds with it carries much of the responsibility for these feelings. When pressed to analyse this compulsion, he has confessed that possibly it is his way of compensating for devoting his time and energy to doing something he has never quite been able to quantify the value of. Such soul-searching must lead, at least at times, to a deeply unsettled frame of mind.

Daniel's immediate future in the autumn of 1993 was hardly plain sailing either. Around this time, his passion for motorbikes landed him in trouble when he was arrested for speeding on the M5 motorway. In September, Devon Magistrates at Cullompton imposed a fine of £120 plus costs and a driving ban of one week, just as he was due to return to Liverpool to re-shoot *Father*'s ending. Less than a month later, he ran into another kind of bother.

In October Daniel, along with his friend actor Jeremy Irons, Jim Sheridan and a handful of others including actress Vanessa Redgrave, attempted to fly to war-torn Sarajevo to act as honorary patrons for an upcoming film festival there. They had journeyed as far as Ancona in Italy when they were unexpectedly prevented from boarding a United Nations plane bound for the Bosnian capital on the instructions, they understood, of the British Foreign Office. They were requested instead to return to their hotel. They had been granted press status for the trip but, it was claimed, this was abruptly rescinded with no proper explanation.

Frustration and annoyance was no doubt rife, especially for Vanessa who led the group, but, according to Patricia Ramsey of the United Nations Department at the Foreign and Commonwealth Office in London, there was no mystery behind the sudden about-face. She says, 'UNHCR (the United Nations High Commissioner for Refugees) has laid down clear policy guidelines relating to the carriage of passengers in these aircraft. Broadly speaking, the carriage of non-Yugoslav nationals is limited to personnel directly involved in the humanitarian or peace process or to bona fide journalists with accreditation from the UN Protection Force (UNPROFOR). Any proposed exception to this would require the support of the relevant government.'

She goes on, 'When Miss Redgrave approached this office about transport on one of the RAF flights participating in the airlift, she was told that the Government could not support her request because the criteria had not been met. Miss Redgrave and her party subsequently obtained accreditation as journalists from the UNPROFOR Public Information organisation. It's not clear why this was issued but, as soon as they became aware that press status had been granted to Miss Redgrave and her party, UNHCR took the view that it was invalid and took immediate steps to alert UNPROFOR.' She adds, 'Unfortunately UNHCR's decision did not reach Miss Redgrave and her party in time to stop them travelling to Ancona.'

At the end of the day it had simply been a trip to Italy for nothing, but for Daniel the mixture of politics and film work would rear its head again in just a few weeks' time. For now, though, *The Age of Innocence* received its American première and launch in October. Scorsese, in whom some had had doubts, thoroughly silenced his critics by delivering an immaculate production, which was lavish in every sense of the word. The film, however, which proved to stir the deepest feelings was *In the Name of the Father.*

Even before its release Jim Sheridan was flatly denying that it was inflammatory, sticking to his guns that it was all about family bonds and injustice. Daniel also firmly denied that *Father* constituted an anti-British film, determined to reinforce Sheridan's theme that the central issue was the gross miscarriage of justice. There was resentment that some sections of the press seemed to be attacking the Irish as being, en masse, the enemy.

But more than journalists were swarming around in agitated mood. Ulster and Whitehall politicians were deeply uncomfortable about the film, fearful that it could potentially be seen, however unintentionally, to support, or in some way glamorise, the IRA. Their concerns centred strongly on the effect it would have on the population of the United States. There, early showings of selected trailers had produced a tidal wave of emotion against the British police and establishment, resulting on occasions in audiences literally booing and hissing at the screen.

A more orderly audience attended the film's world charity première when it took place at the Savoy Cinema in Dublin on Thursday, 16 December 1993, with Daniel and Emma Thompson in attendance at the £100-a-seat bash. The proceeds, anticipated to exceed half a million pounds, were to go to the Very Special Arts Ireland, which works at encouraging better access to the arts for disabled people. Hundreds of onlookers crowded behind the pavement barriers, craning their necks to catch a glimpse of the star they had so firmly taken to their hearts, as Daniel accompanied the others in to the jaunty strains of 'As the Saints Go Marching In'.

Other celebrity guests that night included Bono and the intense shaven-headed Irish pop star Sinead O'Connor: another name with which the newspapers have at times linked Daniel romantically. Two days later it was Belfast's turn, held at the Queen's Film Theatre. Daniel was once again in attendance, this time accompanied by Jim Sheridan. A fellow guest here was Marie Jones, who plays Gerry Conlon's mother, Sarah. Going on general release in Ireland on Boxing Day, the film was expected to break box-office records.

Unlike *The Age of Innocence*, for which Daniel ended up undertaking minimal publicity engagements, he threw himself headlong into the PR merry-go-round required to help launch *In the Name of the Father*. This meant a heavy round of interviews and personal appearances and, as a reluctant interviewee at the best of times, it was an experience he was not looking forward to. Flying out to the States to promote the film there, Daniel faced days of back-to-back television and press interviews, a prospect that was enough to drive him back to smoking the cigarettes he had lately been trying hard to give up. On top of that, the film's UK release was scheduled for 11 February 1994 and the furore and controversy surrounding it, far from subsiding, was building up all the more. Thrust out into the limelight once more, it looked as if a certainly busy, and possibly even rough, time lay ahead of him.

CHAPTER ELEVEN

THE FRENCH CONNECTION

'I don't call myself subject to much at all.'

NATHANIEL POE, *THE LAST OF THE MOHICANS*

The controversy in Britain over *In the Name of the Father* was at one point so intense that certain cinema managers had given serious thought as to whether or not they were prepared to show it. It coincided with a period of increased IRA activity in Britain, which in turn had led to strenuous efforts by both governments and other parties to find a solution for peace. Indeed, the film opened the day after the announcement of the historic Downing Street Joint Declaration on Northern Ireland.

From the moment news had broken at the end of 1992 that the film was to go ahead, Jim Sheridan had been at pains to distance himself from the political quicksands of the perpetually taut Anglo-Irish relations, insisting that he had no interest in putting together anything other than a good story which would exonerate the Conlon family name. He called it a healing film and made it clear that he aimed to convince as wide a public as possible of the accuracy of the story. However, the difficulties inherent in dramatising factual events for a feature film became apparent immediately on its release.

Many voices were raised against what they considered to be blatant inaccuracies in the movie, including that of Gerry Conlon's uncle, Patrick Maguire, who strongly challenged the veracity of its portrayal of certain fundamental issues. Attention repeatedly focused on the fact that Gerry and Giuseppe were shown sharing a cell during their imprisonment, when in reality they had scarcely been in the same prison for any length of time, let alone housed in the same cell. And indeed Patrick was quoted as having cast doubt on the interpretation of the closeness of the real–life father–son relationship.

Giuseppe's series of in–depth meetings with lawyer Jean Gareth Peirce, and his being legally represented by her, was also attacked. It was claimed that Giuseppe met Peirce no more than once and in fact was not her client – he was represented by lawyer Alastair Logan along with other members of the Maguire family. Much was made of the fact that the trials which the media had dubbed 'the Maguire Seven' and 'the Guildford Four' had been in reality two entirely separate entities, and not combined together as depicted in the film, and also that Gareth Peirce, being a solicitor and not a barrister, would not have been in the position to make an impassioned speech such as the climactic scene depicts. Indeed, Alastair Logan specifically highlighted the erroneous representation of Gareth as the intrepid lone crusader, solely responsible for securing the release of the Guildford Four. While it is true that she found the damning 'Not to be shown to the Defence' note, the statement by a Charlie Burke taken in 1975 and kept from the defence – a statement which provided Gerry Conlon alone with an alibi

– was discovered by the Avon and Somerset Police in 1988 during their inquiry into the case ordered by the then Home Secretary. In the middle of all this, claims emerged that lawyers acting on behalf of members of the Maguire family had at the outset been instructed to submit a note of changes which the Maguires were requesting be made to the proposed screenplay in the interests of accuracy, but that allegedly the producers had proved unwilling to take these on board.

Needless to say, the real-life police officers involved in interrogating the Guildford Four protested that no such beatings and intimidation had ever taken place and, going one step further, they were said to be considering libel law suits against the film's makers. Conlon's uncle Patrick was by this time apparently still so upset by the film that he promptly announced that he was prepared to assist these detectives in their threatened legal action. With passions burning this brightly, the question had to be: how would the film fare in the 1993 Oscar nominations.

There was no attempt to attack the acting performances of Daniel, Pete Postlethwaite or Emma Thompson, nor the film itself as a film. It was its portrayal as a true account of a true story which was drawing all the fire. One American woman even went so far as to instigate legal proceedings against Universal Pictures for billing the film as a true story. But Jim Sheridan, undaunted, staunchly fended off all accusations that he had perhaps exercised too much artistic licence, maintaining that it was a dramatic interpretation of what really happened.

Daniel too denied that his decision to play Gerry Conlon had in any way been politically motivated and drew a fine distinction between consciously doing such a thing, as opposed to being personally drawn to a story which carried with it built-in political consequences. As to the areas of deep contention and the accusation of them being misleading, he did not believe them to be dangerously so and at the end of the day considered the furore pointless. Although, having said that, he did feel sorry that the Maguires felt as they did. He regretted, he said, that everyone had not been able to settle matters before the film went into production. Gerry Conlon himself openly defended the film's integrity and firmly stood by the portrayal of his father in it as being the real account of their relationship.

But, for every person who criticised *Father*, there were many others who held it in very high regard. Some questioned the necessity for rigid adherence to accurate detail when handling creative works based on real events. Film critic Barry Norman was one of those. He says of the film and Daniel's performance in it, 'Truly excellent. Gerry Conlon was not entirely a sympathetic character, let's face it, yet overall Daniel had the audience shouting for him, which says an awful lot for him. I personally didn't feel that all the controversy over the fact/fiction row was justified. Once cameras start rolling and you have to condense seventeen years of someone's life into a two-and-a-quarter-hour film, of course corners are cut.'

Seven years before, two radically opposite roles on display at the same time had put the spotlight firmly on Daniel and his ability to be as smooth as he could be streetwise. Now he had done it again. By the start of 1994 he had been voted runner-up for Best Actor by the Los Angeles Film Critics Association for both *The Age of Innocence* and *In the Name of the Father*, and had bagged a Golden Globe nomination for Best Actor in a Drama for *Father*, the added bonus being that these latter nominations are often considered the dry run for the Oscars.

When the award season truly got under way, the controversy, in terms of damaging the film's chances of attracting nominations, proved to have been ineffective. Two days before the film's UK release, the Academy Awards nominations were announced and this time *In the Name of the Father* featured in seven categories, including Best Film, Best Director, Best Actor, Best Supporting Actor and Best Supporting Actress. Daniel also made the 1993 nominations for the BAFTA Best Actor Award for *Father*, which film also featured in the British Academy's Best Adapted Screenplay category. As with the Oscar nominations for *The Age of Innocence*, he again missed out on being amongst BAFTA's runners for Best Actor, although the film itself attracted places in four other categories.

When the sixty-sixth annual Academy Awards ceremony came around in March, however, the man unreservedly hailed by many now as *the* major British movie star of his generation was beaten to a second Oscar by America's favourite Mr Nice Guy, Tom Hanks playing a gay lawyer dying of AIDS in *Philadelphia*.

It was an intensely moving portrayal from an actor who from the beginning had been acutely aware of the criticism surrounding his casting in the leading role – Daniel had turned down the offer to play the doomed lawyer before it was offered to Hanks – and who had gone to such lengths to research the part that in the end he has said he felt like a mercenary. But many believed it had been a mixture of politics and the sympathy card which had cost Daniel a second Oscar, which would have been a rare achievement from just two nominations.

It could be argued that the same sympathy vote had perhaps played a part in helping to secure Daniel his Oscar three years before and that that same factor was now working against him, but his friend actor Philip Jackson believes he speaks for many in his profession and beyond when he maintains, 'It was nothing to do with that. He was straight robbed of the Oscar. Hanks was good but Daniel was better and I don't think many would really disagree.'

It was not to be *Father*'s night all round. Jim Sheridan lost out to Steven Spielberg, who had for the past twenty years been shunned, recognition-wise, by the Academy, but who this time collected awards for Best Picture and Best Director for his black and white epic *Schindler's List*.

The child actress Anna Paquin from Jane Campion's *The Piano* denied Emma Thompson's bid to walk off with the Best Supporting Actress prize. While excellent as Pete Postlethwaite had been as Giuseppe Conlon, he had to make way for the actor Tommy Lee Jones who secured the Best Supporting Actor Oscar for his performance in the big-screen version of the mid-sixties television cult series *The Fugitive*.

Doubtless disappointed, though not devastated, Daniel, Jim Sheridan and the rest drowned their sorrows with a post-show party to end all bashes. Daniel and Shay had together organised what they called a simple Irish ceilidh but which, even by Hollywood's stellar standards, proved to be a legendary experience for those privileged enough to have secured an invite.

A few weeks later, the head was off the Guinness again when Daniel once more lost out at the BAFTA awards. This time he was up against just two other actors. Anthony Hopkins had been nominated twice, first for Merchant Ivory's *The Remains of the Day*, and then for Richard Attenborough's *Shadowlands*. The other contender was the Ulster-born actor Liam Neeson with whom, like Hopkins, Daniel had worked ten years before on *The Bounty*.

Liam had been nominated for his portrayal of Oskar Schindler in Spielberg's *Schindler's List*, about the wartime exploits of the Austro-German profiteer Schindler who saved over a thousand Polish Jews from Hitler's death camps. *Schindler* had mopped up seven Oscars, along with other awards across the boards, and Neeson must have been considered Daniel's toughest rival. But it was Hopkins who took the crown that night for his performance as Stevens, the butler in James Ivory's adaptation of the Kazuo Ishiguro novel *The Remains of the Day*.

While these latest awards slipped through his fingers, battles of a different kind had been preoccupying Daniel. An action over profits had been instigated, in which he was one of the claimants. This new dispute concerned the 1986 Merchant Ivory film *A Room with a View*. It was brought against Goldcrest, once considered the UK's foremost film production company, which had crashed with losses running into several million pounds, but had been rescued the year following *View*'s release by the Brent Walker group. The suit was expected to reach court in the summer of 1994.

Daniel had joined Helena Bonham Carter, Maggie Smith and Julian Sands in their various claims for a percentage of the film's profits, considered to be in the region of £8 million. *A Room with a View* had been James Ivory and Ismail Merchant's most expensive collaboration, costing £2 million to make, but its success had been such an unexpected bonanza that it had grossed ten times as much back in return. Like Julian Sands, Daniel was claiming one per cent of the profits – the £80,000 each had originally anticipated earning from the period romance. It would be pointless expecting a swift solution though, and he had to leave these financial matters in the hands of others and instead look to the future.

Regardless of losing out at the Oscars, the combination of Daniel's last three consecutive blockbuster movies substantially increased his bankability. *The Hollywood Reporter* trade newspaper regularly compiles a top twenty list, split into two categories of stars whose name in a film is considered to guarantee it worldwide success. In May 1994 Daniel was catapulted to the top of the A List, knocking on the door of the elite top-ten A+ List. That same month he featured as a new arrival in the top hundred of Hollywood's most powerful people and suddenly his name began appearing in all kinds of magazine surveys including *EMPIRE*'s July poll of the world's sexiest film stars. Daniel came sixth, sandwiched between Mel Gibson and Richard Gere.

But polls and lists were of little consequence to him. Professionally he had stepped off the treadmill to find his personal life apparently in some upheaval, at least according to the press. At the turn of 1994 reports surfaced that his relationship with Isabelle Adjani had ended, only to be almost immediately contradicted by sightings of the reclusive pair on holiday together in France. A few months later, sections of the French press alleged that Isabelle was pregnant with Daniel's child – an allegation that as at late June at least one friend close to Daniel chose to indignantly refute on his behalf.

Ignoring the tabloid speculation, his decision of the previous year to quit London and move to the Republic of Ireland had been a sound one. It was a move he had considered for years, but for various reasons resisted. On his father's death in 1972 he had taken a conscious decision to continue to regularly visit Ireland, unwilling to allow the island to become the cradle of memories past, inextricably linked to Cecil. Later, when he was in the position to consider setting up home there, he found himself aware of a nagging fear that, in a strange way, any form of permanence would shatter, or at least gnaw away at, the spiritual pleasure and sustenance he had always relied on finding within its shores. He considered it a risk, but ultimately one worth taking and so, having bought a country manor house set in acres of ground in the County Wicklow region, he had begun the long, but rewarding for a man who once considered a career in carpentry, process of refurbishment.

The past few years had been a tough slog, professionally. He had not intended embarking on a new film when Jim Sheridan snared his interest in *Father* and now what he needed most was to get away from it all. In the first two months of the year both *In the Name of the Father* and *The Age of Innocence* had opened within weeks of each other. Although he had made himself scarce in the countryside when the Oscar nominations were announced, his inclusion in these meant being catapulted into a round of personal appearances and interviews up to and including late spring. This meant that, although filming for *Father* finally wrapped in September 1993, it was around summer 1994 before he could call his time his own.

In a world not always tolerant of an actor's desire to disappear and recharge his batteries, the rumours about which role Daniel would embark on next began to circulate almost before *In the Name of the Father* was released. The first project with which he was publicly linked was that of playing the role of Sean Flynn, son of the late legendary American swashbuckling star Errol Flynn. Sean had been a photo journalist who had disappeared during the Vietnam War.

Then came reports in February 1994 that Daniel was short-listed, along with Al Pacino and John Malkovich, for the male lead in the film about to get under way called *Mary Reilly*, based around the story of a servant's love for her employer, Dr Jekyll of Jekyll and Hyde fame, and directed by Stephen Frears. The female star was Julia Roberts, with whom it had once been speculated that Daniel would work on *Shakespeare in Love*. The role in fact went to Malkovich and perhaps it was just as well that Daniel did not land the part.

Mary Reilly began in harmonious style but quickly became beleaguered with problems. Although strenuously denied by the movie's spokesmen, when shooting switched from Pinewood Studios to location in Edinburgh, stories began to emerge of ding-dong battles between a furious John Malkovich and an enraged Julia Roberts.

Another film with which Daniel's name had been linked was to prove one of the hits of 1994. This was *Pulp Fiction*, a violent but hugely successful black comedy directed by Quentin Tarantino, now universally hailed as the most innovative new director since Francis Ford Coppola and Scorsese. Winning the Palme D'Or award at The Cannes 1994 Festival and securing John Travolta a Best Actor Oscar nomination, it is credited with having single-handedly revived John's ailing career.

By the autumn of 1994, the speculation was still unremitting. Daniel was reported to have refused an offer to succeed Michael Douglas when he walked out on the film *Cutthroat Island*, a Renny Harlin-directed epic starring Harlin's wife, actress Geena Davis. The film revolves around the exploits of the fictitious female pirate Morgan Adams (Geena Davis) and her rival pirate lover.

Not only Daniel was said to have turned down the chance to play the eighteenth-century buccaneer. Fellow Brit Ralph Fiennes, fresh from his recent success as the psychotic SS commandant Amon Goeth in *Schindler's List*, is likewise said to have refused to fill the gap left by Douglas. In the end Matthew Modine of *Full Metal Jacket* and *Pacific Heights* signed up to don the cutlass and bucket-topped boots. Daniel and Fiennes found their names promptly linked again when talk emerged of those actors being considered as the new Batman, and Daniel also briefly featured as one of the favourites in the field of contenders to take over the licence to kill in the James Bond movie *Goldeneye*.

One film project, however, with which Daniel was certainly

associated was the $50 million Hollywood movie *Interview with the Vampire*, based on the 1976 novel by Anne Rice. The project had a chequered history in that, although the rights to the book – the first in Rice's gory anthology *The Vampire Chronicles* – had been sold to Paramount Pictures for $150,000 before the book was in print, the film had experienced difficulty in getting off the ground.

Eventually Paramount opted to wait for the sequel novel and along the way considered several stars to play the role of the central character, the vampire Lestat, including Richard Gere, Mel Gibson and, curiously, the sultry singer Cher. Their top choice was John Travolta, who with hit films *Saturday Night Fever* and *Grease* under his belt was the hot property in Hollywood at the end of the 1970s.

Rice's sequel did not appear until 1985, at which time Paramount chose not to pick up the rights. The original rights passed to Lorimer Telepictures, which at the end of the eighties was swallowed up by Warner Brothers. But it was not until producer David Geffen entered the picture that the project eventually managed to get up and running, at which time Geffen immediately offered the role to Daniel.

Mona Lisa and *The Crying Game* director Neil Jordan was to be at the helm and he too badly wanted Daniel on board, but after six months' deliberation Daniel disappointed David Geffen by turning him down. One reason was that he saw the film as just another costume drama, which clearly held no interest for him at that moment in time.

On the film's release, starring Tom Cruise in the role that Daniel rejected, it attracted a storm of protest over some of the bloodthirsty scenes it contained. Women fainted at the sight of debauched Lestat biting off a rat's head, while many others, repulsed, simply walked out.

Despite, or even because of, this sort of reaction, it looked set to be a major box-office hit, recouping more than half of its investment in its opening week. Cruise himself is reported to have picked up $12 million for playing Lestat. Although it had long become obvious to the Hollywood honchos and many others in the industry that fame and fortune were not automatic magnets to securingDaniel's services for a film, with talk of a sequel to *Vampire* already surfacing, one wonders if turning down this role has been a decision Daniel perhaps privately regrets.

However, while the relentless flow of speculation was taking place as to which film he was likely to surface in next, what the press and public did not know was that by January 1995 Daniel's thoughts lay a long way away from future projects. He had recently suffered the loss of a close friend which, in conjunction with a separate deeply distressing personal matter, was having serious repercussions for him.

Julian Belfrage, the theatrical agent who had represented him from practically the outset of his career, had died of cancer in December at the age of sixty and his passing had greatly shaken Daniel. Hard on the heels of this devastating blow came press reports in mid-February that he had furiously ended his stormy relationship with Isabelle Adjani. More, that the star of *La Reine Margot*, fast approaching forty years old, was, after all, pregnant despite past denials and was indeed due to have the baby in just two months' time.

The story was broken by the French magazine *Voici*, which reported that the couple had had a blazing row by telephone, at which time Isabelle had faxed Daniel to tell him that he was the father of her child, said to be a boy. The normally press-shy Adjani had also gone to the lengths of confirming publicly that Daniel had fathered her unborn child, further revealing that it had been conceived during a holiday they had spent together in St Remy de Provence.

Daniel's temper at this point by all accounts spectacularly snapped. In retaliation he used the similarly impersonal device to fax Isabelle back to inform her that this time their relationship was completely at an end. Apart from his rage at their private business being made a matter of public gossip, *Voici*'s article further claimed that Daniel was railing greatly against the very notion of becoming a parent, insisting that he was not ready for it at this point in his life.

How the story got into the hands of the French magazine in the first place, when it concerned a private telephone conversation and two presumably equally personal fax messages is bewildering, but, as soon as it broke, the British press swooped on to the tale, lambasting Daniel for dumping his seven-months-pregnant girlfriend. Condemnation seemed to be universal, especially of the fact that he had chosen to do this by electronic machine. It was perhaps not the most chivalrous of behaviour, but it could equally be argued that it had not been very sensitive of Isabelle in the first place to have landed news of their child on him by the same detached method.

This nineties way of giving partners their congé by fax had made news before, when rock star Phil Collins acrimoniously left his second wife, and former Tory Cabinet Minister David Mellor likewise opted out of his marriage. But within days headlines like 'Hypocrite of the Week' cropped up as the fickle journos and feminist columnists went lusting for Daniel's exposed jugular.

As was to be expected, Daniel himself was completely unavailable for comment and with Julian Belfrage's death, his agency must have had more to cope with than this burst of negative publicity. Isabelle it was said, had, retreated once again behind the thick barricade she normally maintained between herself and the media, and was reportedly spending most of her time, by now heavily pregnant, cooped up in her Paris Left Bank apartment, having first issued strict edicts to all around her to say absolutely nothing further to anyone.

Unused to having his dirty linen paraded in public, Daniel must surely have abhorred what had rapidly taken on the tone of scandal. Especially the determinedly heartless interpretation put on his seemingly callous ending of the affair, coming at a time when he was still trying to come to terms with yet another bereavement. However, if claims made in another French magazine, *Paris Match*, are to be believed, Daniel had already been suffering for many months before the publication of details of the fax fight with his estranged lover.

According to reports, he was said to have been suffering depression since the previous September, weighed down by both the knowledge of Isabelle's pregnancy and its future implications, as well as Julian's tragically terminal condition. It was also said that, for six months between then and January 1995, he had undergone psychiatric treatment as a day-care patient at a remote private clinic in Cour-Cheverny, near Blois. There was no official confirmation of this claim but what did soon transpire was that, whatever his business in France was, on a daily basis he was being relentlessly hounded by the press, tailed and photographed wherever he went on his powerful and distinctive canary-yellow Triumph motorbike, even while making calls from a public phone box or catching a snack in a local café.

In late February he briefly returned to London to attend a memorial service for Julian Befrage held at Piccadilly's St James's Church on 7 March. He looked drawn, with a sombreness that seemed to go beyond the sad occasion, at which he sang a moving tribute to his late mentor and friend. Judi Dench, Ian Holm and John Hurt were just a few stars who had also been on Julian's books. Seven weeks after her husband's death, his devastated young widow Tor, formerly Baroness Victoria van Moyland until their marriage little over a year before, had announced her intention to take over the reins of the agency. Daniel had been one of the first to pledge his allegiance, clearly confident that she would carry on where Julian left off in looking out for the best interests of his future career, whatever direction it might take.

Meanwhile, the course of his perpetually unpredictable relationship with Isabelle Adjani and the forthcoming birth of their child continued to attract media attention. Considering his almost lifelong preoccupation with the importance of filial duty, it seemed unlikely that Daniel would, or could, turn his back on any child of his. Indeed, by springtime any such suggestion was to be proved wrong. At the beginning of April, when Isabelle gave birth to a boy in a New York clinic, in keeping with her fierce desire for privacy, few details were released – not even the child's name. However, three weeks later, the paparazzi, always at the ready, managed to capture a private moment when Daniel was to meet his baby son, Gabriel-Kane, for the first time.

Isabelle, wrapped in a long baggy coat and wearing dark glasses, stood alone on a busy New York sidewalk. Apparently unwilling to meet Daniel herself, a nurse carried the infant into a luxury apartment block opposite for a brief union with his father. On the woman's re-emergence, mother and child disappeared into the back of a darkened limousine and were driven off into the chaotic daytime traffic. Photographed on his own later, Daniel looked preoccupied and, if anything, more drawn than during his London visit almost two months earlier.

Daniel and Isabelle had had a spirited and unconventional romance and in spring 1995, now with a child together, there were those who did not rule out their relationship re-budding. It was not to be, though, and so ended another chapter in Day-Lewis's life.

CHAPTER TWELVE

GANGS OF NEW YORK

'It's no problem for me to believe that I'm somebody else.'

DANIEL DAY-LEWIS

In 1995, not yet forty, twice Oscar-nominated and once a winner, Daniel Day-Lewis was ranked eleventh in an *Empire* magazine poll of 'The 100 Sexiest Stars in Film History'. A maverick in his profession, by this time capable of commanding in excess of $5 million a movie as one of Hollywood's hottest properties, he would not put a price on his head unlike many of his contemporaries. It remained the script, not the fee, which governed his interest in a role – he had rejected £3 million offered to him to play the lead in Jonathan Demme's *Philadelphia*, choosing instead Jim Sheridan's *In the Name of the Father* for which, speculation has it, he probably settled for a tenth of that price.

Likewise, his attraction to a role never followed the same route either. He has described the process as being similar to groping blindly around in mud, for the most part to no avail, until suddenly he grasps something gritty between his fingers. On completion of each role, he almost ritualistically vows never to lend himself out again to inhabit another person's world, but each time he breaks that vow.

After *In the Name of the Father*, he frankly confessed that he wanted to hide for a while, even though demands abounded for him to satisfy the lust among moviemakers and movie-goers alike for him to return to the screen. He managed to resist all script offers until summer 1995 when he was drawn to a new challenge.

Director Nicholas Hytner was to be at the helm of a $40 million Twentieth Century-Fox production of *The Crucible* and shooting was scheduled to begin in autumn in New England. Based on the play by the American Pulitzer Prize winner Arthur Miller, *The Crucible* deals with the seventeenth century Salem witch-hunts. It was first produced in London in 1956, three years after it was written and the same year as Miller's marriage to Marilyn Monroe. At the time it was widely thought of as an attack on McCarthy's political witch-hunts, then prevalent in the States.

Daniel's lead role was to be as John Proctor, whose wife is accused of witchery, and, in addition to reuniting him with Winona Ryder, his other co-stars would include Joan Allen, Bruce Davison, Rob Campbell and George Gaynes. The intensity of the subject matter had drawn Daniel who said, 'It perhaps represented a kind of sickness that people didn't want to touch upon. Moral clarity is the thing that makes people point the finger and say, 'That's where the danger lies.' The process of self-questioning is perhaps where some form of genuine morality can finally be born.' But the final clincher to him accepting the part came when he received what he called 'a letter of encouragement' from

Arthur Miller who was keen to see Daniel bring John Proctor to life on screen.

The Crucible would be released on 27 November 1996 to mixed reviews. The *Chicago Sun-Times* called the film, 'a drama of ideas, but they seem laid on top of the material, not organically part of it'. While the *Los Angeles Times* felt it was 'too frantic to be involving, too much an outpost of bedlam to be believable'.

Daniel's connection to *The Crucible* brought about a major change in his private life, for, during the course of working on this film, he met Arthur Miller's daughter. Born in 1962 in Roxbury, Connecticut, Rebecca Augusta Miller was an artist and sculptor before acquiring the acting bug. By the early 1990s she had appeared in movies such as *Regarding Henry*, starring Harrison Ford and Annette Bening, and the Hitchcock-style thriller *Consenting Adults* with Kevin Kline and Kevin Spacey. And in the new millennium she would move into screenwriting and directing.

She and Daniel first met at her father's house and they quickly fell in love. Two weeks prior to *The Crucible*'s release, the couple were married in Vermont on 13 November 1996. Their first child, Ronan Cal Day-Lewis, would be born in June 1998. And four years later, in May 2002, another child, Cashel Blake Day-Lewis, would enlarge their family and give Daniel, in all, three sons.

It was apparent that married life agreed with Daniel. He had a noticeably happier, more relaxed demeanour in public and professionally he opted to remain in the limelight. After filming *The Crucible*, he renewed his links with his friend director Jim Sheridan when, for their third collaboration, he agreed to take on the role of Daniel Flynn in the Irish/American-made movie *The Boxer*.

In another intense role, this time Daniel portrayed an ex-IRA prisoner who, on release from jail, returns to his old profession of boxing. He opens a gym and attempts to rebuild his life. A gritty tale of violence and redemption, it was set in Ireland still torn by religious and political strife. The film's love interest was provided by Emily Watson and it boasted strong Scottish blood in the shape of Brian Cox and Ken Stott. Daniel's preparations for this role were, as ever, meticulous and he spent a long time training with former world champion Irish boxer Barry McGuigan. *The Boxer* was released in 1997 and earned Daniel a Golden Globe nomination for Best Performance by an Actor in a Motion Picture – Drama.

After two films in succession, though, Daniel pulled a disappearing act and deliberately dropped off the film world's radar for five years. It wasn't a conscious decision to stay away so long. It was just that married life and the arrival of his children with Rebecca became his absorbing priorities.

He continued to intrigue commentators who were always interested in him. One story took legs that he had found contentment away from the madhouse of acting, working as a shoemaker in Florence, Italy. As a renowned enigma, it could very well have been an apocryphal story – literally a load of cobblers. But what the movie world waited for was concrete proof of his return to the silver screen.

It had always been possible that Daniel could walk away forever from acting without a backward glance, or could take the kind of lengthy break that would kill lesser actors' careers only to come storming back and win an Oscar. Daniel very nearly picked off the latter.

The film role which prised Daniel out of acting hibernation was that of William 'Bill the Butcher' Cutting in the violent period drama *Gangs of New York*. The man mainly credited with luring Daniel out of self-imposed semi-retirement was the film's director Martin Scorsese, with whom Daniel had worked so well on *The Age of Innocence*.

A bigger contrast between Bill the Butcher and Newland Archer is impossible to imagine. However, the actor and director met in New York and discussed the complex role of one of America's first gang leaders, a native New Yorker with an ingrained hatred of immigrants.

The film, set in the Five Points, centred on the bloody turf war between native Americans and Irish immigrants for control of the New York neighbourhood. Irish Priest Vallon is brutally slain by Bill the Butcher in front of Vallon's young son who, sixteen years later, fresh from the Hellgate House of Reform, returns to the Five Points. He is bent on cunningly inveigling himself into a position that would allow him to wreak vengeance on his father's killer. Amid this city of tribes, the portrayal of the focused yet unhinged Bill the Butcher would be central to the success of the film which also starred Leonardo DiCaprio and Cameron Diaz.

From the movie's opening minutes, Daniel would make his indelible imprint on the epic mid-nineteenth century drama, cutting an astonishingly garish figure with his stovepipe hat, plaid trousers and sporting a gigantic handlebar moustache. His preparation for the role bore a few of the Day-Lewis hallmarks.

He remained reluctant to talk about this aspect of his craft, calling what he does 'his logic' and declaring that film-making itself was 'a venture of insanity'. He maintained simply that he went about his business in a dogged way and would only confess that Method actors largely set out to 'create for yourself, by whatever means, the illusion that you're experiencing the world through a different pair of eyes'.

Stories leaked of the lengths Daniel went to get inside this particularly vivid character. Some were to be expected – for instance, that Daniel, maintaining his adopted quirkily unusual accent at all times, remained in character when off screen, and wore Bill the Butcher's threadbare coat, despite the cold conditions during filming.

But other claims were made that he listened to Eminem's music as he daily worked out to engender the volcanic rage he needed to stoke up for the part. It emerged, too, that Daniel was continually sharpening knives and took lessons from a genuine butcher on how to dismember a carcass, and that he once, carried on filming despite the fact that his nose had been accidentally injured in a fight sequence.

Martin Scorsese had been passionate for years about bringing this story to the screen and his dream was realised when *Gangs of New York* was released on 20 December 2002. The *New York Daily News* was swift to have its say on the director's latest venture calling it 'an honourable, if misguided, attempt to recreate a lost world. But it is, after all, a movie and in the end will be judged as art not history.'

While *Rolling Stone* pinned its colours firmly to the mast by singling Daniel out, praising, 'Day-Lewis is a colossus. He sets the screen ablaze. It's a performance of seductive wit and animal ferocity. Acting doesn't get better than this!'

When the time came to dish out awards, Daniel unsurprisingly walked off with a shed-load of accolades – thirteen separate Best Actor trophies from various film critics circles including the BAFTA, the Screen Actors Guild and the Golden Satellite Awards.

Daniel was also nominated for a Golden Globe and for the Academy Award for Best Actor in a Leading Role. His innate modesty at press conferences and while attending the movie's glitzy premières in America and Britain served to further endear the actor to a public starved of intrinsically great acting talent.

The plaudits for Daniel's riveting performance in *Gangs of New York* had barely died down when he threw himself into his next project; one very close to home. For years his wife, Rebecca, had worked on writing a film script centred around the story of an idealistic environmentalist who, aware that he is dying, fears for his teenage daughter whom he has raised alone on an abandoned island commune.

Almost 10 years earlier, through his agent, Rebecca had sent Daniel the script in the hope that he would be drawn to the lead role of the principled, protective but flawed widower, Jack Slavin. Daniel's interest *was* piqued – Slavin's tortured soul, the weight of regret he carries for the life choices he has made, the powerful internal conflicts the character has to grapple with and the destructive elements of a provocative story that treads on the taboo of incest, all made it a unique prospect. But Daniel had not long finished filming *The Age of Innocence*, and although he admired the writing, the timing was off. He said: 'I knew beyond any doubt that I didn't feel up to the task at that moment.' Rebecca continued to develop the script and, once married, she and Daniel often discussed the project's potential. Rebecca planned to direct the movie and for a while Daniel continued to resist the lure of the film, fearing it risky for a husband and wife to work so closely on such incendiary material. However, they finally grasped the nettle and with a $1.5 million budget in place, filming for the *The Ballad of Jack and Rose* began in summer 2003 on Prince Edward Island, off the coast of Canada.

The complex human drama also starred Camilla Belle, Catherine Keener, Paul Dano, Beau Bridges and Jason Lee and was the smallest set Daniel had worked on since *My Left Foot*.

Unusually, for him it was very much a family affair. With Rebecca at the director's helm, their two young sons, Ronan and Cashel, came too and had a great time playing on the beach every day with some of the crew's children. It was not difficult to draw the line between their personal relationship and their respective professional roles as actor and director and throughout Daniel felt at his most relaxed. The remote shooting location was a joy to him and having been involved in the pre-production process it was rewarding to see the fruits of Rebecca's labour gradually coming to life.

That said, some things did not change. Stories still leaked out that while his wife and sons stayed at a nearby hotel, in order to maintain his character's sense of isolation, during filming, Daniel billeted himself away in a hut on the beach. He also took a hands-on approach, having constructed the dining room table inside the Slavins' Celtish grass-roofed home which he had also helped to build.

Adopting a Scottish accent, Daniel turned in a typically deep and nuanced performance as Jack Slavin, walking a tricky tightrope when it came to depicting the most controversial aspect of the film – the suggestion of incest between Jack and his 16-year-old daughter, Rose. Rebecca maintained that it was her intention to script certain stages of the relationship between this fictitious father and daughter as mirroring an intense romance so as to invite the film's audience to question how an almost hermetically sealed environment, devoid of all normal precepts, could shape such a relationship.

It was challenging and the film heavily divided opinion when *The Ballad of Jack and Rose* premiered at the Sundance Film Festival on 23 January 2005. After a limited theatrical release, two months later it was shown in 74 theatres, ultimately grossing $916,051 worldwide. Daniel picked up two awards;

the Berlinale Camera Award for his contribution to world cinema at the Berlin International Film Festival and the Best Actor Award at the Marrakech International Film Festival. Meanwhile, American film critics were polarised. Kenneth Turan for the *Los Angeles Times* wrote, 'Combining an actor you can't take your eyes off with unapologetically emotional material makes *The Ballad of Jack and Rose* a model of artistic, provocative American filmmaking.' Conversely, Manohla Dargis for the *New York Times* declared, 'Rebecca Miller's attempt to elevate a small Oedipal story about two damaged souls into a grandiloquent epic misses by a significantly wide mark.'

Away from public and press reaction to the movie, Daniel was exhausted. Including post-production, the project had absorbed two years of his and his wife's life. There was, also, immense sadness at home. Rebecca's father, Arthur Miller, had been fighting a brave battle against cancer and on 10 February 2005, aged 89, one of America's greatest playwrights died of heart failure at his home in Roxbury, Connecticut. His family was at his bedside.

CHAPTER THIRTEEN

LINCOLN

'I am intrigued by a life that seems very far
removed from my own.'

Daniel Day-Lewis

With a strange wistfulness for an actor who has turned
down many film roles Daniel once said, 'You feel,
you're living in a graveyard of lost opportunities.' It is true, too,
that if a role does grab his attention, he instinctively steps back
to dissect why and to quantify just what he could bring to that
role. When writer/director Paul Thomas Anderson, however,
approached Daniel to play oil prospector Daniel Plainview in
the powerful period drama *There Will Be Blood*, Daniel had no
such hesitation. Anderson's screenplay, loosely based on Upton
Sinclair's 1927 novel, *Oil!*, had been written with Day-Lewis in
mind and almost before Daniel had finished reading the script
his bags were packed. He explained, 'When you see great
writing in a script, it's startling because it's so rare.'

Set in Southern California during the oil boom of the late
19th-century the torrid tale, soaked in corruption, greed,

religion and murder, revolves around the maniacal Plainview who will do whatever it takes in his ruthless quest to attain untold wealth. Principal photography began in June 2006 on a ranch in Marfa, Texas, and Daniel arrived on set already in character. Joining him for the summer shoot were Dillon Freasier, Kevin J O'Connor, Ciarán Hinds, Sydney McCallister, Hans Howes and Paul Dano, who had acted alongside Daniel in *The Ballad of Jack and Rose*.

Daniel continued to dislike what he sees as an obsession on the part of some people with how he prepares for a role. When asked about this by the veteran chat show host Michael Parkinson, with a degree of polite irritation, he replied, 'Even if I did cartwheels with a bunch of daffodils stuck up my jacksee, what does it matter?' Nevertheless, for *There Will Be Blood,* with rigorous dedication, Daniel applied himself to the task of understanding the make-up and the madness of those pioneering men who invested years of backbreaking, often soul-destroying, toil drilling for oil in the fervent hope of striking black gold. In studying archive letters written by prospectors which charted the incredible hardships they endured, the deaths that the endeavour often incurred and the miserable penury many were ultimately reduced to, Daniel absorbed an acute sense of desperation and of immense sacrifice. He picked over countless photographs from that era, boned up on the life of oil tycoon Edward Doheny, considered to be the inspiration for Upton Sinclair's book, and he listened repeatedly to audio recordings from the late 19th-century. Paul Thomas Anderson provided Daniel with a copy of the 1948 film *The Treasure of the Sierra Madre* to help him create the composite character of Daniel Plainview. It meant much to Daniel that the director had immersed himself in this period project to an all-consuming level, close to his own. 'With Paul I recognised that there was kin of some kind,' he later said.

The vast expanse of the Texas ranch allowed for the illusion of being back in time and as Daniel would be on screen in virtually every scene of the 158-minute movie he went to incredible lengths to preserve his embodiment of this seething, obnoxious character. Once the cameras had stopped rolling for the day he retreated to a tent, often worn out but always invigorated. Rebecca and their sons stayed at the location and while his wife supportively accommodated all that Daniel needed to do for his craft, for Ronan and Cashel it was a fascinating experience to see their father transformed into the growling, volcanic Daniel Plainview.

Other filming locations included El Mirage Dry Lake in California and Greystone Mansion in Beverly Hills, which has served as the setting for such hit films as *The Bodyguard, Indecent Proposal* and *Nixon*. Walking away at the end of a shoot has often left Daniel with a hollow feeling and his intense absorption in portraying Plainview once again made it hard for him to let go of the character once filming wrapped in the autumn, but he treasured the special symbiosis that had developed between himself and the film's director. Said Daniel, 'My working partnership with Paul is something that I will cherish for the rest of my life.'

It had taken two years to raise the $25 million budget for this movie because of industry scepticism that the gritty period drama, with such an unsympathetic lead character, would have the essential worldwide appeal, but *There Will Be Blood* was a box-office success. After a limited release in December 2007, it rolled out countrywide the following January. Globally, the movie raked in $76.1 million and with it came glory for Daniel when on 24 February 2008 at the 80th Academy Awards ceremony held at the Kodak Theatre in Hollywood his chilling, towering screen presence as Daniel Plainview beat off stiff competition from George Clooney, Johnny Depp, Tommy Lee Jones and Viggo Mortensen to earn him his second Best Actor Oscar. This win meant that Daniel joined Marlon Brando and Jack Nicholson as the only actors (at the time) to win Best Actor Oscars in two non-consecutive decades. Daniel was also the first non-American actor to win two Academy Awards for Best Actor. On the night Daniel dedicated his second Oscar to his grandfather, Michael Balcon, his father Cecil Day-Lewis and to his three sons, Gabriel, Ronan and Cashel.

While film critics around the world fell over themselves to find sufficient superlatives to hail Daniel's screen genius, a virtual shed-load of best actor trophies came his way, including the BAFTA Award, the Golden Globe Award, the Screen Actors Guild Award, the Desert Palm Achievement Award and dozens of film critics' association awards. For an actor who has confessed to experiencing moments of almost paralysing self-doubt, the annual red carpet frenzy of popping flashbulbs, clashing egos and gushing praise all seems a bit lavish. With a small smile, in the eye of that year's storm, he described it as 'complete madness'.

With universal critical acclaim ringing in his ears, Daniel dropped out of the public eye to assist Rebecca who was preparing to direct a movie, *The Private Lives Of Pippa Lee*, based on her own 2008 novel of the same name and the whole family decamped to Connecticut. If he wasn't working with the joiners building the film sets, he was helping to home-school Ronan and Cashel and had had no intention of making another movie for the foreseeable future. In mid-May, however, media reports circulated that Daniel would be starring in a film version of the opulent 1982 Broadway musical, *Nine*, to be directed by *Chicago* director, Rob Marshall. The Spanish actor

Javier Bardem, who had recently won the Best Supporting Actor Oscar for his role in *No Country for Old Men*, had withdrawn from the lead role in *Nine* due to exhaustion.

Rob Marshall considered Daniel to be possibly the finest actor of his generation but, aware that Daniel wanted to take a break after *There Will Be Blood*, initially he had not thought that Day-Lewis would be interested, especially since, to date, musicals had left Daniel decidedly underwhelmed. The vibrant exoticism, colour and sheer heart-pumping energy of box-office hits *Moulin Rouge* and *Chicago* had led Daniel to rethink but, although piqued by the prospect of starring in a big-screen musical, when the offer was first made to him he was uncertain if it was the right project for him. He bluntly told Marshall that he could not sing. The director, however, with Day-Lewis on the hook, employed considerable persuasion and circumvented every barrier Daniel erected until he gave in.

The role that had got under Daniel's skin was that of hot-blooded Guido Contini, a raffish Italian film director in 1960s Rome who, on the brink of shooting his next movie, is suffering from creative block. His marriage is in jeopardy, too, as a midlife crisis entangles him in a web of complicated relationships with seven bewitching women. Portraying those women were: Marion Cotillard as Contini's long-suffering wife, Luisa; Nicole Kidman as his sultry leading lady, Claudia; Penélope Cruz as his high-maintenance mistress, Carla; Kate Hudson as a *Vogue* journalist, Stephanie; Stacy Ferguson as a prostitute, Saraghina; Judi Dench as his costume designer and loyal confidante, Lilli, and Sophia Loren as the ghost of his doting mother; a pool of talent that included four Academy Award-winning actresses.

In the summer, Daniel wrote a note to his friend Judi Dench which stated, 'I promise not to run out on you this time,' a reference to his very public crisis of confidence 19 years earlier when during a performance of *Hamlet* at London's National Theatre, with Judi playing Hamlet's mother Gertrude, Daniel abruptly quit the stage mid-flow, leaving his understudy Jeremy Northam to step into the void.

Pre-production for *Nine* had been delayed by the 100-days writers' strike but the eight-week rehearsal began in August 2008, with the musical's songs recorded the following month. The Maury Yeston and Arthur Kopit Broadway production which starred Raul Julia, itself loosely based on Federico Fellini's acclaimed 1963 art-film *8½*, ran at New York's 46th Street Theatre for 729 performances and won five Tony awards. Filming for the $80 million movie version of the song and dance, smouldering extravaganza adapted for the screen by Michael Tolkin and the late Anthony Minghella began in October at Shepperton Studios in Middlesex and at various Italian locations, including at Cinecittà Film Studios, in Rome.

Where initially, Daniel had been uncertain about his ability to sing, it was clear from the start that he could dance with the best of them, his lanky slender frame allowing him to throw stylish shapes to great effect. Unsurprisingly, having studied Italian for months he often spoke the language in and out of character as he inhabited the role of the chain-smoking Guido Contini to the nth degree. Judi Dench described the phenomenon, 'It's as if a part gets somehow injected into him and the whole of his inside becomes that character. There's only the skin of Daniel left and so you don't call it Daniel, you call it Guido.'

Daniel thrived on working with Judi Dench, whom he deeply admired and he found a special pleasure, too, in having Sophia Loren portray Guido's mother. 'Her work is absolutely sublime,' he declared. One memorable moment for him came when he danced with Sophia. Daniel has always believed that if he plied his craft as a means of paying the bills, then he would find alternative work. As an actor, he is famously selective. Unusual projects draw him and he'd been enticed back to work by the prospect of enjoying a new experience. When filming wrapped, Daniel retreated to happy domesticity with his wife and family in his 18th-century home on his 50-acre estate in the remote Wicklow Mountains on the east coast of Ireland. It was a serene existence that continued to appeal to him, with the companionship of his wife Rebecca, whom he has described as 'my confidante, my best friend', and his family.

His feeling of well-being, however, was tragically shattered when on 18 July 2009 his mother, Jill Balcon, died of a brain tumour, aged 84. An accomplished and once beautiful woman, Jill seemed always to have been eclipsed by the famous men in her life – her film producer father Michael Balcon, her Poet Laureate husband, Cecil Day-Lewis and her double Oscar-winning highly acclaimed actor son, Daniel. Remarking on this once, she said, 'It's very chastening to be a footnote in so many people's lives.' It was doubly sad for Daniel that his mother did not live to see his new film. That Sophia Loren was playing his screen mother had delighted Jill.

Nine premiered at the Dubai International Film Festival on 9 December 2009 and was released in cinemas nine days later. Box office receipts fell substantially short of the movie's budget, and although Rob Marshall believed the musical to be 'very Sixties, very sexy', it failed to float the boat of most film critics and attracted very mixed reviews.

The Village Voice critic wrote, 'The eminently resourceful Day-Lewis hasn't appeared this rudderless in a role since the justly forgotten comedy, *Eversmile, New Jersey*, two decades ago.' While *Entertainment Weekly* weighed in with, 'Daniel spends most of *Nine* as a haunted spectator and you want to tell the guy to lighten up.' Conversely, the *Telegraph* described Daniel as, 'Cast unexpectedly and brilliantly as the crisis-plagued Guido Contini.' And *Rolling Stone* asked, 'With an indisputably gifted actor playing ringmaster to such feminine life force, what's not to like? Day-Lewis handles his two songs in high style and acts the role like the maestro he is, even if he looks as Italian as Big Ben.'

The musical received four Academy Award nominations, including one in the Best Supporting Actress category for Penélope Cruz, and attracted nominations in the best ensemble categories at the Screen Actors Guild Awards, among others. Daniel received a Golden Globe nomination for Best Performance by an Actor in a Motion Picture – Comedy or Musical, and he was especially proud to be presented on 6 December 2009 at the British Independent Film Awards (BIFA) ceremony held at The Brewery in west London with The Richard Harris Award for Outstanding Contribution to British Film by an Actor. Patently thrilled, on stage at the podium, clutching the award, Daniel spoke in his acceptance speech of having met Richard Harris on several occasions and having felt metaphorically dwarfed in the presence of the Irish screen legend who died in 2002. He cited Harris' performance in the 1963 film *The Sporting Life* as having inspired him to consider an acting career. Six months after the BIFA ceremony, Daniel took to a different stage when, gowned and capped, he was awarded an honorary doctorate in letters by the University of Bristol, in part because of his past association with the Bristol Old Vic Theatre School.

Around this time, one of Daniel's friends joked with him that, for an actor so famed for his elusive qualities, he was in distinct danger of becoming prolific and, sure enough, to the movie world's great surprise in November 2010, a Dreamworks press release announced that Day-Lewis had been cast as Abraham Lincoln in a Steven Spielberg biopic of the beloved US president, based on the book *Team of Rivals: The Political Genius of Abraham Lincoln* by Pulitzer Prize-winning historian Doris Kearns Goodwin. Spielberg had been developing a film of Lincoln when a meeting with Goodwin had resulted in his optioning the film rights to her book in 2001. The movie's first screenplay was penned by John Logan. Playwright Paul Webb undertook a rewrite and finally Pulitzer Prize-winner Tony Kushner took over the scriptwriting reins.

In 2005, the *Star Wars* and *Taken* star Liam Neeson was cast in the title role and the biopic was set to begin filming early the following year but fine tuning of the script put the project on ice again, and in July 2010 Neeson announced that he had dropped out. He spoke of his decision on Britain's *This Morning* television show, saying, 'I'm not actually playing Lincoln now. I was attached to it for a while but now I'm past my sell-by date.' Many movie watchers took that to be the kiss of death to a project that had been languishing in the to-do tray for years, so November's announcement brought a welcome wave of excitement.

For any actor, portraying the iconic, bearded 16th President of the United States is a big ask. Arguably America's most beloved president, the astute, deep-thinking Abraham Lincoln abolished slavery, guided America to end its bloody Civil War and his 1863 Gettysburg Address remains the most quoted speech in US history. Less than a week after Confederate General Robert E. Lee surrendered his army, on 15 April 1865 Abraham Lincoln became the first US President to be assassinated. The night before, along with his wife Mary, he had been attending a Laura Keene performance of English playwright, Tom Taylor's acclaimed play, *Our American Cousin*, at

Ford's Theatre in Washington D.C. when John Wilkes Booth, a famous American actor and Confederate sympathiser, slipped into the private box above the stage and shot Lincoln in the back of the head at point-blank range with a .44 calibre derringer. As bedlam erupted, Booth dramatically leapt from the balcony box onto the stage shouting the Virginia State motto, 'Sic semper tyrannis!' ('Thus always to tyrants') and fled the theatre on horseback with Union soldiers hot on his heels. Abraham Lincoln died from that single gunshot the following morning. He was 56.

Joseph Henabery, 50 years on, played Lincoln in the 1915 movie *The Birth of a Nation*, with other actors including Henry Fonda, Raymond Massey and Jason Robards over the years assuming the mantle. A biopic of an immense historical figure is a daunting prospect and so for *Lincoln*, Steven Spielberg chose to narrow the focus on to the last four months of the President's life, on the tough decisions he had to make as an emancipating president and on his intense struggle to overcome strong opposition to his dogged determination to abolish slavery from powerful men in his own cabinet. It was a story he was anxious to tell. He said, 'Lincoln had a very complicated and at the same time, extremely clear inner life. He argued both sides of every issue.'

While most movie buffs rubbed their hands at the thought of Day-Lewis stepping into such venerated shoes, some Lincoln fans believed that an American actor would have been more appropriate. At the turn of the year, Daniel was more concerned with personal matters. In late December his sister Tamasin had a lucky escape when driving in south-west England. Her car skidded on treacherous black ice and ended upside down in a wintry ditch. With one side of the car mangled, Tamasin had to kick open a door and climb out. Left bruised but not seriously injured, she was badly shaken. 'I could have died,' she said. Two weeks later, Daniel lost a dear friend when on 2 January 2011, the peerless and much-loved 64-year-old actor Pete Postlethwaite lost his battle against cancer.

In mid-February, Daniel led the addresses at a public memorial service to honour Pete held at St Leonard's Church in Shoreditch, east London. Among the hundreds of mourners who attended were actors Sean Bean, Kevin Spacey, Julie Waters and Michael Gambon. With heartfelt passion, Daniel spoke to the congregation of treasured times when he had served as Pete's understudy at the Old Vic Theatre School in Bristol, 'Pos was the one. As students it was him we wanted to be like. He had a Merlin engine inside him; refined, complex and capable of generating immense power.' Daniel sang an unaccompanied traditional Irish song to Pete's widow, Jacqui Morrish, and poignantly the Grimethorpe Colliery Band, whom Pete had conducted in his role as band leader, Danny, in the 1996 film, *Brassed Off*, played a rousing rendition of 'Danny Boy'. Oscar-nominated for his emotive role along side Daniel in *In The Name of the Father* Pete Postlethwaite had appeared in countless films, including two Steven Spielberg movies, *Amistad* and *Jurassic Park: The Lost World*, and the director had famously declared Pete to be 'the best actor in the world'. When Daniel attended the memorial service he was sporting the full beard he'd grown for his upcoming role in *Lincoln*.

Daniel's co-stars for the $50 million-budget movie included Joseph Gordon-Levitt, Tommy Lee Jones, Jared Harris, Sally Field, John Hawkes, James Spader and Hal Holbrook, who won an Emmy for playing Abraham Lincoln in the 1974 television mini-series, *Lincoln*. Sally Field was thrilled to be cast as First Lady, Mary Todd Lincoln. She told the LA press, 'To have the opportunity to work with Steven Spielberg and Daniel Day-

Lewis, and to play one of the most complicated and colourful women in American history is simply as good as it gets.'

In mid-October, the two-month shoot began in Richmond, Virginia, which with its historic connection and the beautiful period architecture made it the perfect location in which to create the Civil War setting. After wrapping up at the State Capitol, which had been turned into the White House, in December the production moved to Petersburg, Virginia, filming particularly in and around the Old Towne area. Local interest in the movie brought many people out to watch agog from the sidelines as the actors often put in 18-hour days.

Producer Kathleen Kennedy was stunned at how commanding a figure the 6'1" Daniel cut, completely inhabiting the role. More than half way through the shoot, she revealed, 'Daniel is quite remarkable. Every day, you get the chills, thinking that Lincoln is sitting there, right in front of you.' Describing it as very much a performance-driven movie, she was full of admiration for the way Daniel nailed long, stamina-draining scenes and the flawlessness with which he delivered enormous amounts of dialogue. To help maintain the sense of being in a time-warp, on set, Steven Spielberg called every actor by their character name; calling Daniel 'Mr President', throughout. It was said that Daniel's name did not even appear on the actors' call sheet and the word spread around Virginia that he had not once dropped Abraham Lincoln's accent. After filming ended in mid-December 2011, co-star Tommy Lee Jones paid tribute to Daniel, 'This is not a Lincoln that's just stepped off the dollar bill. This is not the icon. This is a real man and I don't think Lincoln has ever been portrayed as well.'

In early August 2012, Dreamworks released the first official still of Daniel as Abraham Lincoln. Seated, in profile, and looking in pensive mood his resemblance to the former President, even by his standards, was uncanny. A fortnight later the official promotional film poster followed. Striking in black and white, again it depicted a profile shot of Daniel as Lincoln looking down, his brow furrowed, his eyes thoughtful and the clamorous buzz around Daniel's dedicated performance which had been building for many months, heightened even further. *Lincoln,* now the most anticipated movie of the year, was being described as pure Oscar bait.

Lincoln premiered on 9 November 2012, a date chosen to fall after the US presidential election, and expanded nationwide a week later, followed by its UK release on 25 January around the same time as the Academy Award nominations were announced. With the 85th Academy Awards ceremony just around the corner in February, held at the Hollywood and Highland Centre (formerly the Kodak Theatre) in Los Angeles the big hope was that Daniel, if nominated, would secure his third Best Actor Oscar.

Daniel's riveting portrayal of Abraham Lincoln has further cemented his power as a true screen star and strengthened his reputation for startling versatility. An intriguing chameleon, the intense energy he brings to each diverse role never fails to impress and as a man of innate grace, his genuine humility effortlessly endears him to successive generations. 2013 is said to see Daniel reunite with *Gangs of New York* director, Martin Scorsese, to star as Father Cristóvão Ferreira in *Silence*, a film based on the novel *Chinmoku* by Shusaku Endo about 17th-century Jesuit priests. It is impossible to predict whether, going forward, Daniel will increase his workload and maintain a higher visibility or vanish from the acting scene for a long period of time, as he has done in the past. All that is certain is that Day-Lewis will continue to surprise.

CREDITS

FILM

Sunday Bloody Sunday (1971) (UK)
Director: John Schlesinger
Producer: Joseph Janni
Screenplay: Penelope Gilliatt
Studio: UA/Vectia
Running time: 110 mins (colour)
Cast: Glenda Jackson, Peter Finch, Peggy Ashcroft, Murray Head, Tony Britton, Maurice Denham
Daniel's character: Child vandal

Gandhi (1982) (UK)
Director: Richard Attenborough
Producer: Richard Attenborough
Screenplay: John Briley
Studio: Columbia
Running time: 188 mins (colour)
Cast: Ben Kingsley, Candice Bergen, Edward Fox, John Gielgud, Saeed Jaffrey, Roshan Seth
Daniel's character: Colin, racist

The Bounty (1984) (New Zealand)
Director: Roger Donaldson
Producer: Bernard Williams
Screenplay: Robert Bolt
Studio: Orion
Running time: 133 mins (colour)
Cast: Mel Gibson, Anthony Hopkins, Laurence Olivier,
Philip Martin Brown, Philip Davis, Liam Neeson
Daniel's character: John Fryer

My Beautiful Laundrette (1985) (UK)
Director: Stephen Frears
Producers: Sarah Radclyffe, Tim Bevan
Screenplay: Hanif Kureishi
Studio: Working Title Films/SAF/Channel Four TV
Running time: 97 mins (colour)
Cast: Saeed Jaffrey, Gordon Warnecke, Shirley Anne Field,
Roshan Seth, Richard Graham, Derrick Branche
Daniel's character: Johnny

A Room with a View (1985) (UK)
Director: James Ivory
Producer: Ismail Merchant
Screenplay: Ruth Prawer Jhabvala
Studio: Merchant Ivory Productions
Running time: 113 mins (colour)
Cast: Maggie Smith, Denholm Elliott, Judi Dench, Simon
Callow, Helena Bonham Carter, Julian Sands
Daniel's character: Cecil Vyse

Nanou (1986) (Anglo–French)
Director: Cornny Templeman
Producer: Andrew Mollo
Screenplay: Conny Templeman
Studio: Umbrella–Caulfield/Arion
Running time: 89 mins (colour)
Cast: Imogen Stubbs, Jean-Philippe Ecoffey
Daniel's character: Max

The Unbearable Lightness of Being (1987) (US)
Director: Philip Kaufman
Producer: Saul Zaentz
Screenplay: Jean-Claude Carrière, Philip Kaufman
Studio: Saul Zaentz Company
Running time: 165 mins (colour)
Cast: Juliette Binoche, Lena Olin, Donald Moffat, Derek de
Lint, Erland Josephson, Pavel Landovsky
Daniel's character: Tomas

Stars and Bars (1988) (US)
Director: Pat O'Connor
Producer: Sandy Lieberson
Screenplay: William Boyd
Studio: Columbia
Running time: 91 mins (colour)
Cast: Harry Dean Stanton, Joan Cusack, Laurie Metcalf,
Martha Plimpton, Keith David, Spalding Gray
Daniel's character: Henderson Dores

My Left Foot (1989) (UK)
Director: Jim Sheridan
Producer: Noel Pearson
Screenplay: Shane Connaughton, Jim Sheridan
Studio: Palace/Ferndale Films/Granada TV
International/Radio Telefis Eireann
Running time: 98 mins (colour)
Cast: Ray McAnally, Brenda Fricker, Fiona Shaw, Cyril
Cusack, Hugh O'Conor, Adrian Dunbar
Daniel's character: Christy Brown

Eversmile, New Jersey (1989) (Argentina)
Director: Carlos Sorin
Producer: Oscar Kramer
Screenplay: Jorge Goldenberg, Roberto Scheuer, Carlos Sorin
Studio: J&M Entertainment/Los Films Del Camino
Running time: 87 mins (colour)
Cast: Mirjana Jokovic
Daniel's character: Fergus O'Connell

The Last of the Mohicans (1992) (US)
Director: Michael Mann
Producer: Michael Mann, Hunt Lowry
Screenplay: Michael Mann, Christopher Crowe
Studio: Warner/Morgan Creek
Running time: 112 mins (colour)
Cast: Madeleine Stowe, Steven Waddington, Wes Studi,
Eric Schweig, Jodhi May, Russell Means
Daniel's character: Nathaniel Poe/Hawk-eye

The Age of Innocence (1993) (US)
Director: Martin Scorsese
Producer: Barbara de Fina
Screenplay: Martin Scorsese, Jay Cocks
Studio: Columbia Pictures/Cappa/De Fina
Running time: 139 mins (colour)
Cast: Michelle Pfeiffer, Winona Ryder, Richard E. Grant,
Miriam Margolyes, Siân Phillips, Stuart Wilson
Daniel's character: Newland Archer

In the Name of the Father (1993) (UK)
Director: Jim Sheridan
Producer: Jim Sheridan
Screenplay: Terry George, Jim Sheridan
Studio: Universal Pictures
Running time: 133 mins (colour)
Cast: Pete Postlethwaite, Emma Thompson, Corin Redgrave,
John Lynch, Beatie Edney, Gerard McSorley
Daniel's character: Gerry Conlon

The Crucible (1996) (US)
Director: Nicholas Hynter
Screenplay: Arthur Miller
Running Time: 124 mins (colour)
Cast: Winona Ryder, Joan Allen, Bruce Davison, Rob
Campbell, George Gaynes
Daniel's character: John Proctor

The Boxer (1997) (US/Ireland)
Director: Jim Sheridan
Screenplay: Jim Sheridan and Terry George
Running Time: 113 mins (colour)
Cast: Emily Watson, Brian Cox, Ken Stott, Gerard McSorley
Daniel's character: Daniel Flynn

Gangs of New York (2002) (US/Europe)
Director: Martin Scorsese
Screenplay: Jay Cocks
Running Time: 166 mins (colour)
Cast: Leonardo Di Caprio, Cameron Diaz, Liam Neeson,
John C Reilly, Jim Broadbent
Daniel's character: William 'Bill the Butcher' Cutting

The Ballad of Jack and Rose (2005)
Director: Rebecca Miller
Screenplay: Rebecca Miller
Running Time: 111 mins (colour)
Cast: Camilla Belle, Catherine Keener, Beau Bridges, Paul
Dano, Jason Lee, Jena Mallone, Susan Thompson
Daniel's character: Jack

There Will Be Blood (2007)
Director: Paul Thomas Anderson
Screenplay: Paul Thomas Anderson
Running Time: 158 mins (colour)
Cast: Dillon Freasier, Paul Dano, Ciarán Hinds, Sydney
McCallister, Hans Howes
Daniel's character: Daniel Plainview

Nine (2009)
Director: Rob Marshall
Screenplay: Michael Tolkin and Anthony Minghella
Running Time: 118 mins (colour)
Cast: Sophia Loren, Judi Dench, Nicole Kidman, Marion Cotillard, Penélope Cruz, Kate Hudson, Stacy Ferguson
Daniel's character: Guido Contini

Lincoln (2012)
Director: Steven Spielberg
Screenplay: Tony Kushner, John Logan, Paul Webb
Running Time: (colour)
Cast: Joseph Gordon-Levitt, Tommy Lee Jones, Jared Harris, Sally Field, John Hawkes
Daniel's character: President Abraham Lincoln

Silence (2013)
Director: Martin Scorsese
Screenplay: Jay Cocks
Running Time: (colour)
Cast: Benicio Del Toro, Gael Garcia Bernal
Daniel's character: Father Cristóvão Ferreira

TELEVISION
In order of UK transmission dates

How Many Miles to Babylon?
BBC2 Television Film Playhouse
Director: Moira Armstrong
Producer: Innes Lloyd
Running time: 109 mins
Transmission date: 26 February 1982
Daniel's character: Alexander Moore

Frost in May
BBC2 Television four-part serial
Director: Ronald Wilson
Producer: Anne Head
Running time: 90 mins each episode
Transmission dates: 19, 26 May, 2, 9 June 1982
Daniel's character: Archie Hughes-Follett

My Brother Jonathan
BBC2 Television five-part serial
Director: Anthony Garner
Producer: Joe Waters
Running time: 49 mins each episode
Transmission dates: 12, 19, 26 August, 2, 9 September 1985
Daniel's character: Jonathan Dakers

The Insurance Man
BBC2 Television Screen Two Play
Director: Richard Eyre
Producer: Innes Lloyd
Running time: 76 mins
Transmission date: 23 February 1982
Daniel's character: Kafka

THEATRE

The Recruiting Officer (Autumn 1979)
Theatre: Theatre Royal, Bristol
Director: Adrian Noble
Writer: George Farquhar
Daniel's character: Townsperson/soldier

Troilus and Cressida (Autumn 1979)
Theatre: Theatre Royal, Bristol
Director: Richard Cottrell
Writer: William Shakespeare
Daniel's character: Deiphobus

Funny Peculiar (Autumn 1979)
Theatre: Little Theatre, Bristol
Director: Pete Postlethwaite
Writer: Mike Stott
Daniel's character: Stanley Baldry

Old King Cole (Xmas 1979/New Year 1980)
Theatre: New Vic Theatre, Bristol
Director: Bob Crowley
Writer: Ken Campbell
Daniel's character: The Amazing Faz

Class Enemy (Spring 1980)
Theatre: New Vic Theatre, Bristol
Director: David Rome
Writer: Nigel Williams
Daniel's character: Iron

Edward II (Summer 1980)
Theatre: New Vic Theatre, Bristol
Director: Richard Cottrell
Writer: Christopher Marlowe
Daniel's character: Leicester

Oh, What a Lovely War! (Summer 1980)
Theatre: Theatre Royal, Bristol
Director: David Tucker
Writer: Joan Littlewood
Daniel's character: Unspecified

A Midsummer Night's Dream (Autumn 1980)
Theatre: Theatre Royal, Bristol
Director: Richard Cottrell
Writer: William Shakespeare
Daniel's character: Philostrate

CREDITS

Look Back in Anger (January 1981)
Theatre: Little Theatre, Bristol
Director: George Costigan
Writer: John Osborne
Daniel's character: Jimmy Porter

Dracula (February/March 1981)
Theatre: Little Theatre, Bristol
Director: George Costigan
Writer: Christopher Bond
Daniel's character: Count Dracula

Another Country (September 1982/May 1983)
Theatre: Queen's Theatre, Shaftesbury Avenue, London
Director: Stuart Burge
Writer: Julian Mitchell
Daniel's character: Guy Bennett

A Midsummer Night's Dream and *Romeo and Juliet* (Oct
1983/Jan 1984)
A Royal Shakespeare Company regional tour
Directors: Sheila Hancock and John Caird respectively
Writer: William Shakespeare
Daniel's character: Flute and Romeo respectively

Dracula (November/December 1984)
Theatre: Half Moon Theatre, London
Director: Christopher Bond
Writer: Christopher Bond
Daniel's character: Count Dracula

Futurists (March 1986)
Theatre: Royal National Theatre, London
Director: Richard Eyre
Writer: Dusty Hughes
Daniel's character: Volodya Mayakovsky

Hamlet (March–September 1989)
Theatre: Royal National Theatre, London
Director: Richard Eyre
Writer: William Shakespeare
Daniel's character: Hamlet, Prince of Denmark

Laura Jackson is a bestselling rock and film biographer who has interviewed many of the world's leading celebrities. For 20 years she has tracked the lives of the stars and gained access to their inner circles to produce a series of critically acclaimed biographies. To find out more, visit www.laurajacksonbooks.com.